W0006921

The Science of Proof

The Science of Proof traces the rise of forensic medicine in late eighteenth- and nineteenth-century France and examines its implications for our understanding of expert authority. Tying real-life cases to broader debates, the book analyzes how new forms of medical and scientific knowledge, many of which were pioneered in France, were contested – but ultimately accepted – and applied to legal problems and the administration of justice. The growing authority of medical experts in the French legal arena was nonetheless subject to skepticism and sharp criticism. The professional development of medicolegal expertise and its influence in criminal courts sparked debates about the extent to which it could reveal truth, furnish legal proof, and serve justice. Drawing on a wide base of archival and printed sources, Claire Cage reveals tensions between uncertainty about the reliability of forensic evidence and a new confidence in the power of scientific inquiry to establish guilt, innocence, and legal responsibility.

E. Claire Cage is Associate Professor of History at the University of South Alabama. Her first book *Unnatural Frenchmen: The Politics of Priestly Celibacy and Marriage, 1720–1815* won the Baker-Burton Prize from the European History Section of the Southern Historical Association.

See the Studies in Legal History series website at
http://studiesinlegalhistory.org/

Studies in Legal History

Other books in the series:

Alejandro de La Fuente and Ariela J. Gross, *Becoming Free, Becoming Black: Race, Freedom, and the Law in Cuba, Virginia, and Louisiana*

Elizabeth Papp Kamali, *Felony and the Guilty Mind in Medieval England*

Jessica K. Lowe, *Murder in the Shenandoah: Making Law Sovereign in Revolutionary Virginia*

Michael A. Schoeppner, *Moral Contagion: Black Atlantic Sailors, Citizenship, and Diplomacy in Antebellum America*

Sam Erman, *Almost Citizens: Puerto Rico, the U.S. Constitution, and Empire*

Martha S. Jones, *Birthright Citizens: A History of Race and Rights in Antebellum America*

Julia Moses, *The First Modern Risk: Workplace Accidents and the Origins of European Social States*

Cynthia Nicoletti, *Secession on Trial: The Treason Prosecution of Jefferson Davis*

Edward James Kolla, *Sovereignty, International Law, and the French Revolution*

Assaf Likhovski, *Tax Law and Social Norms in Mandatory Palestine and Israel*

Robert W. Gordon, *Taming the Past: Essays on Law and History and History in Law*

Paul Garfinkel, *Criminal Law in Liberal and Fascist Italy*

Michelle A. McKinley, *Fractional Freedoms: Slavery, Intimacy, and Legal Mobilization in Colonial Lima, 1600–1700*

Karen M. Tani, *States of Dependency: Welfare, Rights, and American Governance, 1935–1972*

Stefan Jurasinski, *The Old English Penitentials and Anglo-Saxon Law*

Felice Batlan, *Women and Justice for the Poor: A History of Legal Aid, 1863–1945*

Sophia Z. Lee, *The Workplace Constitution from the New Deal to the New Right*

Mitra Sharafi, *Law and Identity in Colonial South Asia: Parsi Legal Culture, 1772–1947*

Michael A. Livingston, *The Fascists and the Jews of Italy: Mussolini's Race Laws, 1938–1943*

The Science of Proof

Forensic Medicine in Modern France

E. CLAIRE CAGE

University of South Alabama

CAMBRIDGE
UNIVERSITY PRESS

University Printing House, Cambridge CB2 8BS, United Kingdom

One Liberty Plaza, 20th Floor, New York, NY 10006, USA

477 Williamstown Road, Port Melbourne, VIC 3207, Australia

314–321, 3rd Floor, Plot 3, Splendor Forum, Jasola District Centre, New Delhi – 110025, India

103 Penang Road, #05-06/07, Visioncrest Commercial, Singapore 238467

Cambridge University Press is part of the University of Cambridge.

It furthers the University's mission by disseminating knowledge in the pursuit of education, learning, and research at the highest international levels of excellence.

www.cambridge.org
Information on this title: www.cambridge.org/9781009198332
DOI: 10.1017/9781009198356

First published 2022

A catalogue record for this publication is available from the British Library.

Library of Congress Cataloging-in-Publication Data
NAMES: Cage, E. Claire, 1982– author.
TITLE: The science of proof : forensic medicine in modern France / E. Claire Cage, University of South Alabama.
DESCRIPTION: Cambridge, United Kingdom ; New York, NY : Cambridge University Press, 2022. | Series: Studies in legal history | Includes bibliographical references and index.
IDENTIFIERS: LCCN 2022012258 (print) | LCCN 2022012259 (ebook) | ISBN 9781009198332 (hardback) | ISBN 9781009198349 (paperback) | ISBN 9781009198356 (epub)
SUBJECTS: LCSH: Medical jurisprudence–France–History. | Evidence, Expert–France–History.
CLASSIFICATION: LCC KJV5390 .C34 2022 (print) | LCC KJV5390 (ebook) | DDC 614/.10944–dc23/eng/20220701
LC record available at https://lccn.loc.gov/2022012258
LC ebook record available at https://lccn.loc.gov/2022012259

ISBN 978-1-009-19833-2 Hardback

Contents

Figures

Acknowledgments

It is a pleasure to acknowledge the many people and institutions who helped and supported me during the process of researching and writing this book.

This project has benefited from generous financial support from a number of sources. Research for this book was made possible by funding from the American Philosophical Society, the Huntington Library, and the Boston Medical Library Fellowship in the History of Medicine at the Francis A. Countway Library of Medicine. Additionally, the National Endowment for the Humanities provided crucial support for both the research and completion of this book through a summer stipend award and a NEH Fellowship. Any views, findings, conclusions, or recommendations expressed in this book do not necessarily reflect those of the National Endowment for the Humanities.

I have also received financial and institutional support from the University of South Alabama. The following faculty research grants funded my research: the Seed Grant Program to Support the Arts and Humanities, Faculty Research Productivity Grant, Support and Development Award, Faculty Development Council Award, and Mahan-Brandon Grant for Research in Gender Studies and Women's History. I thank Lynne Chronister, Angela Jordan, Kim Littlefield, Dave Messenger, the late Clarence Mohr, and Andrzej Wierzbicki for their support. I am deeply grateful to the University of South Alabama Department of History and my terrific colleagues. I also thank the librarians at the University of South Alabama Marx Library.

In addition, I benefited greatly from the opportunities that I had to present material in this book at various colloquiums, conferences, and workshops. I thank Mary Fissell for inviting me to the Johns Hopkins Colloquium in the History of Science, Technology, and Medicine. Her invaluable suggestions as well as the questions and constructive criticism from other participants in the colloquium have improved this book immensely. I am also grateful to Binyamin Blum and Mitra Sharafi for organizing the Global Forensic Histories Workshop. This project benefited from discussions with them and the other participants, including Susanna Blumenthal, Ian Burney, Catherine Evans, Khaled Fahmy, Christopher Hamlin, Mina Khalil, Projit Mukharji, and Keren Weitzberg.

I appreciate the other colleagues, mentors, and friends who read drafts of portions of the manuscript or discussed its ideas with me. They include Elinor Accampo, Maria do Sameiro Barroso, David Bell, Rafe Blaufarb, Will Brown, Hannah Calloway, Lisa Cody, Manuel Covo, Venita Daas, Shane Dillingham, Jeffrey Freedman, Julie Hardwick, David Head, Jennifer Heuer, Jessie Hewett, Catherine Hinchcliff, Katie Jarvis, Eddie Kolla, Khalid Kurji, Seth Lejacq, Tim Lombardo, Cathy McClive, Kenny Moss, Robert Nye, Meghan Roberts, Alex Ruble, Kelly Urban, Erika Vause, Laurie Wood, and Nic Wood. I extend special thanks to David Bell, who has been a constant and generous source of support, encouragement, guidance, and insight.

I owe a tremendous debt to Michael Lobban who read the entire draft of my manuscript. His excellent suggestions and astute questions have immeasurably improved the book. I am beyond grateful for his support of my work and his editorial guidance. It is an honor to be included in Cambridge University Press's *Studies in Legal History* series. I thank him, the other book series editors, and the American Society for Legal History for sponsoring the series. My thanks to Cecelia Cancellaro, Victoria Phillips, Natasha Whelan, and other Cambridge University Press editorial staff who made the publication of this book possible.

Lastly, I thank my family, especially my parents, Roy and Sharon Cage, for their love and support. My mother is a tireless and devoted reader of my work, and her close reading of this book has spared me from a number of errors. I thank the Cages, McCallons, and Monks for their encouragement, especially my grandfather, the late Dr. Earl McCallon, for being my most enthusiastic champion.

Introduction

Could the eyes of a murder victim hold the secret to the identity of their killer? The question of whether a photograph of a victim's retina could provide an image of the murderer at the time of the killing fascinated forensic doctors and laypersons alike in late nineteenth-century France. Those who were hopeful about this possibility posited that practitioners of forensic medicine could capitalize upon the advent of photography in order to solve crimes. A periodical in 1863 speculated that if forensic doctors operated on and photographed the retina of a murder victim within twenty-four hours of death, the image examined under a microscope could reveal the last object or person the deceased saw before their death.[1] The courts soon thereafter explored the possibility. During a criminal investigation of a rape and murder in Châtellerault near Poitiers in 1866, the investigating magistrate (*juge d'instruction*) called upon a medical expert to photograph the victim's retina. The doctor complied by removing her eyeballs but refused to proceed further, deeming the experimental technique beyond his capacities and only suitable for leading forensic doctors in Paris.[2] In 1869 the Society of Legal Medicine took up the issue when a doctor sent a photograph of the retina of a woman who was murdered along with her child and dog in 1868. The society enlisted its member Doctor Maxime Vernois to study the case. Vernois concluded that the photograph merely reproduced the superficial anatomical state of the retina. He discounted the notion that the image of a murderer could be found on a victim's eyes.[3] However, interest in the theory persisted, particularly in reference to high-profile murder cases. For example, a concerned citizen wrote to judicial authorities to call for this procedure during the 1887 criminal investigation of Enrico Pranzini, an Egyptian migrant, for the murders of a high-end prostitute, her daughter, and her servant in Paris.[4] A periodical had earlier issued a similar appeal during the investigation of Sébastien Billoir for a grisly murder in Paris in 1877, but the prominent forensic doctor Georges Bergeron whom the court summoned in this case rejected the proposed technique.[5]

The controversial theory of the tell-tale eye was part of broader debates about the possibilities and limits of forensic medicine, also known as legal medicine. Moreover, it revealed the enormous public interest in the field. Both lay persons and forensic doctors grappled with the question of the extent to which legal medicine could reveal truth, furnish legal proof, and serve justice. This question was particularly salient in the context of new legal changes ushered in by the French Revolution and the rapidly changing state of medical knowledge. This book examines how new forms of medical and scientific knowledge, many of which were pioneered in France, were applied to legal problems and the administration of justice from the Revolution to the end of the nineteenth century.

During this period, France was at the forefront of the field of forensic medicine. While it did not emerge as a distinct specialty until the nineteenth century, its origins can be traced to antiquity. What would eventually become known as forensic medicine began to take shape in the sixteenth and seventeenth centuries. Important early works included those of Ambroise Paré, the sixteenth-century French surgeon, and Paulo Zacchia, the seventeenth-century Italian physician to Pope Innocent X and medical expert for the Rota Romana, the highest court of canon law. In Old Regime France, the position of a court-appointed medical expert was usually a venal office; in other words, these offices were a form of property, sold by the state in order to raise money for the crown. Revolutionaries abolished venal office holding and the *médecins jurés*, the sworn physicians or surgeons holding these offices. In Revolutionary and post-Revolutionary criminal and judicial proceedings, the courts called upon medical practitioners whom they designated as medical experts as needed. These *médecins légistes* replaced the office-holding *médecins jurés* of the

Old Regime.[6] Additionally, Revolutionaries dissolved and then reestablished French medical schools. In 1794 the Revolutionary legislature created newly appointed chairs in legal medicine at the medical schools in Paris, Montpellier, and Strasbourg.[7] Revolutionaries also reformed and centralized hospitals, which became the primary place of medical teaching and learning with an emphasis on hands-on instruction. Paris became the epicenter of a new form of "hospital medicine" that emerged during the Revolution and subsequently spread across the rest of Europe and beyond. Physical examinations and autopsies became principal techniques of hospital or clinical medicine and the nascent "clinic."[8] This period also saw the rise of medical specialization, and legal medicine became a distinct specialty.

Revolutionaries also made sweeping legal and judicial changes, including introducing trial by jury for felony offenses and making legal representation available to the accused in criminal cases. The introduction of juries for these crimes marked a shift from the strictly inquisitorial procedures of the Old Regime to the introduction of some accusatorial procedures – within a largely inquisitorial system – that allowed for defense counsel and privileged oral testimony and debates during jury trials. Subsequent Napoleonic law codes dictated that jury trials were limited to the assize courts, the trial courts for the most serious offenses or felonies (*crimes*). Every *département* in France had its own assize court, which held quarterly sessions headed by a presiding judge (*président*), whom associate judges assisted. Twelve jurors decided guilt by answering a series of specific questions posed by the presiding judge. Seven jurors were needed for convictions. Medical experts needed to present their findings in a clear and persuasive manner to jurors. Revolutionary and post-Revolutionary lawmakers operated under the principle that well-educated and well-trained medical experts could establish scientific proof and enlighten jurors, who would then deliver just verdicts.

Despite the succession of different political regimes between 1789 and 1900, there was considerable continuity in the basic structure of France's legal system. The Napoleonic Code of 1804 (still in force) and the Penal Code of 1810 (in force until 1994) laid the foundations of French civil and criminal law. Napoleon's codification of French law created a unified modern judicial system. The highest court, or the supreme court, was and remains the Court of Cassation (*cour de cassation*), the highest court of appeal that has jurisdiction over all civil and criminal matters in France. The court determines whether lower courts have properly applied the law. French appellate courts (*cours d'appel*) hear appeals on matters of fact for cases judged by the courts of first instance. Civil courts of first instance include regional courts (*tribunaux de grande instance*) and district courts (*tribunaux d'instance*). Criminal courts of first instance include the assize courts; the correctional courts (*tribunaux correctionnel*), composed of three professional judges in each *arrondissement* or district that try misdemeanor offenses or lesser felonies (*délits*); police or local courts that try petty offenses (*contraventions*); and specialized criminal courts, including military tribunals.

French legislators envisioned an important role for medical experts in forging justice by providing evidence during preliminary investigations as well as trials. Nineteenth-century criminal proceedings generally began with an investigation by a pretrial judge or investigating magistrate who composed the dossier of the case, including the depositions of witnesses, the testimony of the accused, and medicolegal reports if applicable. The examining magistrate weighed whether there was enough evidence to warrant bringing the case to trial. He would then either drop the inquiry by issuing an *ordonnance de non-lieu* or send the dossier to the correctional court for misdemeanors or the *chambre des mises en accusation*, an indictment court composed of judges, for felonies. Examining magistrates increasingly relied upon the written reports of the medical practitioners whom they summoned to gather forensic evidence. These reports were often decisive in judges' and juries' verdicts, but many factors influenced how heavily they weighed these reports in any given case. Medicolegal experts became a growing presence in the courts through their written reports as well as their oral testimony in assize court trials, where their authority depended on their ability to present evidence clearly and convincingly to juries.

The period from the late eighteenth century to 1900 was a crucial one in the rise of expertise and professionalization in general, particularly with regard to jurisprudence and medicine. The status of the legal and medical professions rose in the nineteenth century, yet doctors' status was below that of lawyers.[9] In 1803 the French state passed a law reorganizing the medical profession and setting the conditions under which medicine could be legally practiced.[10] The law established the first uniform licensing system for medical practitioners in France. It distinguished between "doctors of medicine or surgery," lesser-trained *officiers de santé* (health officers), and certified midwives. Doctors and surgeons sought to emphasize the boundary between them and less credentialed practitioners as well as those with no formal training who engaged in unofficial, illegal medical practice, including empirics, folk healers, and charlatans. The practice of legal medicine presented doctors, surgeons, and *officiers de santé* with the opportunity to advance their professionalization agenda and to try to demonstrate their superiority over their unlicensed rivals. It also carried risks of diminishing public confidence in learned medical knowledge and authority. While elite doctors teaching legal medicine at the medical faculties in large cities eagerly carved out a greater role for themselves and their colleagues in the legal arena, the attitudes of other medical practitioners varied more widely. Some practitioners, particularly those in rural areas with a dearth of physicians and surgeons, were reluctant recruits whom the state compelled to perform medicolegal duties. Other medical men practiced legal medicine as an avenue of professional advancement to build their reputation or clientele and earn a modest income. Although the practice of legal medicine was central to the professional identities of a cadre of doctors, it was merely incidental and a state-imposed obligation for many medical practitioners. Considerable social diversity within the medical profession, including wide disparities in income and specialized training, shaped these varied attitudes.

Much of the work of historians studying the intersection of law and medicine concerns the Anglo-American context.[11] One of the most significant themes in Anglo-American scholarship is the controversial role of the coroner, an appointed or elected public official in England and North America who did not necessarily have any background or training in medicine or death investigation.[12] Historian James Mohr has traced the declining importance of medicolegal education in medical schools and the increasingly strained relationship between medicine and the law in America over the course of the nineteenth century.[13] Moreover, Tal Golan has argued that the more English and American courtrooms featured scientific expert testimony during the nineteenth century, the less common law courts and the public respected it.[14]

However, a different story emerges from the model of legal medicine in France, where forensic expertise was met not with constantly diminishing respect but with varied responses and mostly critical acceptance. France developed a fully fledged, formal academic discipline of forensic medicine earlier than England and America, where its development lagged behind that of continental Europe. France's pre-eminence in forensic medicine in the early nineteenth century only became rivaled or eclipsed by Germany in the mid to late nineteenth century. While the circulation of scientific knowledge crossed national boundaries, the practice of forensic medicine operated in distinctive ways within particular legal, political, social, and cultural contexts. This study is a social and cultural history of legal medicine in modern France, which takes the French Revolution as its point of departure and focuses on nineteenth-century developments. Its endpoint is the turn of the century, when the nascent field of forensic science, much of which focused more broadly on crime-scene investigation and laboratory analysis of trace evidence, eclipsed forensic medicine. I use the terms forensic medicine and legal medicine synonymously to refer to the application of medical and scientific knowledge and expertise to the enforcement of laws and to legal problems.

Legal medicine was a vast field encompassing several disciplines and specialties, including, but not limited to, psychiatry, toxicology, chemistry, pathology, and anatomy. Psychiatry emerged as a fully distinct clinical profession and discipline in nineteenth-century France, and its contested uses in the legal arena have inspired a substantial body of scholarship. French psychiatrists advanced new understandings and controversial theories of insanity that sparked medical and legal debates about the scope of criminal insanity.[15] While this study primarily focuses on the forensics of the body rather than the mind, it deals with psychiatry to a certain extent to illuminate other aspects of forensic medicine under examination. Clashes between medical and legal professionals were generally more pronounced in forensic psychiatry than legal medicine as a whole. Medical practitioners' efforts to persuade judges, juries, and the public were often more effective when dealing with visible material matters rather than states of mind.

This book homes in on several kinds of medicolegal interventions and builds upon Frédéric Chauvaud's work on the history of medicolegal expertise in modern France.[16] It considers not only autopsies and toxicological expertise but also less studied medicolegal interventions, such as those involving sexual offenses against children and efforts to detect malingering, the practice of feigning medical conditions for a specific purpose. This study focuses on forensic evidence in criminal investigations and trials, particularly for felony crimes including murder, poisoning, infanticide, and sexual assault. The rise of forensic medicine also shaped civil legal proceedings, which increasingly featured forensic evidence in cases involving personal-injury litigation, contracts, marriages, wills, and divorces. Although these medicolegal matters in civil law are beyond the scope of this work, the book nonetheless ventures beyond the strictly criminal context when discussing death verification and malingering in relation to the administration of the law.

This book demonstrates the centrality of gender in legal medicine. Women, particularly midwives, had played a significant role before the courts under the Old Regime as experts on women's bodies, but women were largely excluded from the practice of forensic medicine in nineteenth-century France.[17] Practitioners of forensic medicine, which included physicians, surgeons, chemists, pharmacists, and *officiers de santé*, were almost exclusively male during this period. Furthermore, medical men called into question women's status as authorities on their own bodies and those of their children. In their efforts to establish their authority, practitioners of legal medicine reinforced patriarchal norms, particularly in relation to debates and cases involving sexual assault, infanticide, the murder of intimate partners and family members, and gendered notions of criminality and duplicity.

This study illustrates how the practice of legal medicine was bound to the interests of the French state, the professional aspirations of male medical practitioners, and to the lives and bodies of ordinary French men, women, and children. Medicolegal authority and state power were inextricably linked in modern France. Medical practitioners whom judicial or state authorities summoned served in many respects as agents of the state. These medical men also sought to advance their own agenda and ambitions. The practice of forensic medicine offered doctors an avenue to elevate the status of their profession as a whole and to demonstrate their own professional standing and competence. However, serving as a medical expert in criminal investigations and trials carried inherent risks, including those that could result in judicial errors and wrongful convictions as well as the loss of professional credibility. The risks were most pronounced in areas of medicolegal expertise that were in great flux, such as toxicology, and for medical practitioners who lacked knowledge and experience in forensic medicine. Additionally, some criminal trials involved public battles among medical experts. These contests often pitted lesser-trained provincial medical practitioners against elite forensic doctors in Paris or other cities and raised questions about the role of forensic expertise in the pursuit of justice.

This book argues that the growing authority of medical experts in the legal arena was nonetheless subject to skepticism and sharp criticism. It reveals the tensions between a new confidence in the power of scientific inquiry to establish guilt, innocence, and legal responsibility and uncertainty about the reliability of forensic evidence, particularly when assessed by poorly trained practitioners. Issues of uncertainty, error, competence, and confidence were at the heart of forensic medicine. Practitioners of forensic medicine had to navigate the uncertainty inherent in their field. Medical men faced considerable challenges in investigating death and performing autopsies, combatting malingering, detecting poison, providing evidence in criminal inquiries involving reproductive matters, and evaluating the signs of sexual assault. Nevertheless, in their efforts to establish authority and to raise the profile of their profession, many forensic doctors articulated great confidence in their abilities and findings. This confidence was not always well founded, particularly in the context of rapidly changing medical knowledge and practitioners' limited training and experience in certain medicolegal matters. Medical men's involvement in criminal proceedings influenced the course of justice in ways that elicited both praise and criticism from public prosecutors, defense attorneys, judicial magistrates, fellow doctors, and the press.

The legitimacy of medical and scientific expertise depended upon the public's acceptance of it. Additionally, the practice of forensic medicine involved the interplay of different kinds of knowledge. Expert testimony in the courtroom aimed in part to bridge the gap between learned and lay medical knowledge for jurors. In turn, the popular press, particularly its coverage of highly publicized trials, spread public awareness of medicolegal issues. On the one hand, growing awareness of doctors' investigative methods and the popularization of forensic pathology and toxicology possibly discouraged some potential criminals. On the other hand, as laypersons became more familiar with legal medicine, some sought to use this knowledge to their advantage to evade the law. Many forensic doctors expressed confidence that doctors and justice would prevail, but others were less sure. The importance that the public and the courts placed on scientific or medical proofs depended on the confidence or skepticism with which they received expert testimony in addition to other considerations. Moreover, juries weighed forensic proofs against another model of proof in the French legal system: "moral proofs."[18] The boundaries between so-called scientific and moral proofs were often blurred. While forensic doctors presented their findings and claims as objective scientific realities, the practice of forensic medicine was steeped in the moral judgements and social assumptions of its practitioners. Moreover, medical knowledge was constructed and received in tandem with shifting political configurations, new social dynamics, and cultural changes.

This study draws upon a wide range of sources, including archival records of criminal investigations and proceedings, published and unpublished forensic medical reports, newspapers, periodicals, forensic treatises, textbooks, and manuals. The most extensive body of archival sources for this book consists of records from criminal cases at the assize courts, where serious crimes were tried before all-male juries during the nineteenth century. These records include commentary on the proceedings and trial outcomes by the president or other magistrate of each assize court and *dossiers de procédure*, which contain interrogations, depositions, and forensic medical reports. Some doctors also published the forensic reports that they submitted to judicial authorities as books or articles. The early nineteenth century saw an explosion of medicolegal publications, and these publications proliferated over the course of the century. The *Annales d'hygiène publique et de médecine légale*, the first journal on legal medicine, founded in 1829, became the leading venue for forensic doctors to publish their research, findings, and case studies. The work of medicolegal experts reached a larger audience through press coverage of their roles in trials. The *Gazette des tribunaux*, a popular legal periodical established in 1825, published accounts of court cases across

France, and many of these accounts featured trial transcripts of the testimony of medical experts. Moreover, this daily periodical offers the most complete records of courtroom testimony and arguments, since French courts did not create their own jury trial transcripts.[19]

The following chapters of this book are organized thematically around different kinds of medicolegal interventions, bodies, and legal problems. The book begins by examining doctors' efforts to diagnose death and their role in investigations of sudden or suspicious deaths. Chapter 1 also explores the growing public fascination with dead bodies, particularly those on display at the Paris morgue. It analyzes the tensions between doctors' confidence in their abilities and the field of forensic medicine, on the one hand, and anxiety about insufficiently trained and incompetent practitioners who performed medicolegal duties that exceeded the limits of their knowledge and skills, on the other. Chapter 2 examines the construction and contestation of expert authority in cases of suspected poisoning. In tracing the rise of forensic toxicology, this chapter highlights conflicts among experts, uncertainty about a rapidly changing state of knowledge, and disagreements about standards of proof and the risks of judicial errors. Turning our attention from dead to living bodies, Chapter 3 analyzes medical men's methods of distinguishing between real and faked conditions in order to unmask malingerers and establish their professional authority. Malingering became a pressing concern for many practitioners of legal medicine, largely in response to the introduction of conscription during the Revolutionary and Napoleonic Wars. Some doctors went to great lengths to detect and expose malingerers by using deceit, coercion, painful procedures, and altered states of consciousness as diagnostic tools.

The last two chapters consider medicolegal expertise in relation to gender and sex, revealing the entanglements between moral judgments and medical evidence that determined judicial verdicts. Chapter 4 examines the challenges that medical men faced in reproductive matters and crimes, particularly infanticide. It argues that medical experts played central roles in infanticide investigations and prosecutions, yet jurors often privileged their sympathies for the women on trial over damning forensic findings. Social attitudes toward infanticide and the women accused of these crimes shaped jurors' consideration of forensic evidence and trial outcomes. The final chapter analyzes the role of doctors in the prosecution of sexual crimes against children. In some cases, doctors provided forensic evidence that was critical to prosecuting these crimes. In other cases, doctors dismissed accusations of sexual assault and maintained that children, particularly girls and working-class children, were not as innocent as they seemed. Lastly, the conclusion and epilogue consider the shift from legal medicine to forensic science at the end of the nineteenth century and explore the enduring public interest in forensics and changing attitudes toward expertise in the twentieth and twenty-first centuries. Forensic medicine was a crucial arena in which the legitimacy and authority of scientific expertise was established for society at large, even as it was also contested.

The Science of Death

In a small town in the *département* of the Tarn in September 1839, the body of Mathieu Dauzats was discovered hanging in the stable of his home in an apparent suicide. Due to rumors of foul play, the local justice of the peace summoned two doctors to perform an autopsy. They determined that the corpse did not display signs consistent with a hanging. They also found that Dauzats's genitals were wounded and bloody, but his clothing was free of blood stains. The medical experts' report suggested that his hanging was staged postmortem, presumably in order to conceal a murder. The investigation revealed familial strife stemming from Mathieu's reluctance to hire a substitute for his twenty-two-year-old son so that Joseph could avoid military service and conscription. The Tarn assize court tried Joseph and Mathieu's wife Catherine Beauté for murder. The jury found both guilty. The day after they were condemned and sentenced to death, they confessed to attacking and killing Mathieu. They had squeezed his genitals until he fainted and then suffocated him until he died. Catherine and Joseph later revealed that they were in an incestuous relationship – the underlying reason for their crime. In 1840, Mathieu Orfila, the eminent professor of legal medicine, published a study on hanging that centered on the Dauzats affair, but the significance for Orfila was the science of the hanging – not the oedipal drama surrounding the murder.[1] Ambroise Tardieu, professor of legal medicine at the medical faculty in Paris, observed that doctors' ability to distinguish between suicide by hanging and homicide could prevent the kinds of miscarriages of justice that had been seen under the Old Regime, such as the conviction and execution of Jean Calas for the murder of his son who had actually committed suicide.[2]

Revolutionary and post-Revolutionary leaders sought to rely upon medical experts to help uphold laws and bring transgressors of the law to justice, while safeguarding the innocent. The introduction of trials by jury shifted the balance of power in the courtroom from magistrates to ordinary citizens and expanded the role of medicolegal practitioners who presented their findings to both investigating magistrates and jurors. Revolutionaries transformed the field of legal medicine by abolishing venal office holding in 1789 and reestablishing a system of medical and university training with newly appointed chairs in legal medicine at the medical schools in Paris, Strasbourg, and Montpellier in 1794. A subsequent 1803 law specified that medical experts summoned by judges to intervene in legal investigations and trials needed to have the requisite formal educational training in medicine or surgery.[3] French law effectively excluded women from the ranks of court summoned medical experts in the nineteenth century. Male practitioners of legal medicine in Revolutionary and nineteenth-century France presented themselves as guardians of justice who applied their scientific and medical knowledge for the good of society and the state. They also had an expansive view of the scope and functions of legal medicine and commonly defined the field as the application of all knowledge pertaining to medicine and auxiliary sciences to matters pertaining to law, justice, governance, and public administration.

Death investigation was a central aspect of forensic medicine. However, doctors struggled with uncertainty in defining and evaluating signs of death at the same time as popular fears of premature burial and being buried alive abounded. Many doctors shared and stoked these fears. They debated the problem of "apparent death," or persons seemingly dead but actually alive. Concerns about doctors' abilities to diagnose death gave rise to debates about the necessity of establishing waiting mortuaries to house bodies until the onset of putrefaction and other measures to prevent persons from being buried prematurely and alive. Verifying death was the first step for doctors conducting autopsies, including those performed at the Paris morgue, where death was on display for public view and entertainment. Medical practitioners performing autopsies often faced considerable difficulties in distinguishing between homicides, suicides, and natural or accidental deaths and in determining the cause of death. As forensic knowledge became popularized, some criminal offenders attempted with varying degrees of sophistication and success to evade detection by staging homicides as suicides and mutilating, dismembering, or incinerating bodies. Criminal dismemberment and grisly murders captured the cultural imagination. Many causes célèbres and lesser-known trials highlighted the strengths and shortcomings of forensic expertise. As the field gained prominence, it attracted greater scrutiny and calls for reform. Nonetheless, over the course of the nineteenth century, practitioners of forensic medicine projected greater confidence in their abilities to evaluate suspicious or violent deaths, as they sought to increase the visibility and status of their profession.

Diagnosing Death

Dead bodies, or those seemingly dead, generated anxiety and interest among the French public. A preoccupation with the problem of "apparent death" and premature burial initially emerged in the mid-eighteenth century. Some scholars suggest that nineteenth-century physicians did not share their Old Regime predecessors' uncertainty over the signs of death.[4] However, uncertainty persisted, and popular anxieties about apparent death and premature burial actually intensified in the nineteenth century. This period saw an explosion of medical literature on uncertain signs of death and premature burial. By discounting lay persons' abilities to interpret uncertain signs of death, doctors sought to expand their roles in verifying death and to advance their profession.[5]

Medical practitioners promoted various means of resuscitation to combat the problem of "apparent death." In 1790 Jean-Baptiste Desgranges, a physician and surgeon in Lyon, wrote about the uncertainty of signs of death, particularly among drowned persons. He called for more resources and establishments dedicated to the treatment and resuscitation of drowned persons and those presumed dead, including the use of tobacco smoke enemas.[6] This method of treating apparent death typically involved using a tube and bellows to inject tobacco smoke into the rectum. By the late eighteenth century, these devices were supplied in resuscitation kits for drowning victims at various points along major rivers in Western Europe, including the Thames, Seine, and Rhône. Tobacco smoke enemas remained a common method of resuscitating persons presumed dead in the decades that followed.[7] Medical practitioners advised their use for testing life and apparent death and stimulating respiration through the 1880s, although by that point they had been eclipsed by other means of resuscitation, including chest compressions and mouth to mouth resuscitation.[8]

Revolutionary writers concerned about the problem of apparent death demanded government action. In 1790 the renowned *salonnière* and writer Suzanne Necker published *Premature Burials*, in which she lamented that there were no laws or regulations in France addressing the problem. Necker urged the French state to enlist medical practitioners throughout the country to perform tests in the presence of witnesses to verify that death was "absolute" and then provide a death certificate. Necker also called for the construction of well-ventilated buildings to serve as waiting mortuaries, where a surgeon would perform a variety of tests, including applying friction and a hot iron, on those presumed dead in order to confirm that they were truly deceased. Necker also recommended that the government pay a reward to anyone brought back to life.[9]

The Revolutionary and Napoleonic governments implemented legal reforms concerning the verification of deaths and burials. Revolutionary legislators passed a decree on September 20, 1792 that created the *état civil*, or civil registry, to register the births, marriages, and deaths of all French citizens. It required all deaths, including stillbirths, to be registered by public officials in the civil registry. Corpses that displayed signs of violent death could not be buried until authorities filed an official report; however, this law did not prescribe a role for medical practitioners. This omission was a crucial problem in the minds of those concerned about the problem of apparent death. On October 13, 1800, the Prefect of the Seine declared a simple declaration of death by relatives or neighbors was not sufficient, since uncertain signs of death could mislead them. The Prefect decreed that mayors and municipal officials would appoint *officiers de santé* to verify deaths. In 1806 physicians with more formal medical education replaced *officiers de santé*, and the number of medical practitioners

appointed to verify deaths in Paris grew over the course of the nineteenth century.[10] These measures were restricted to Paris and its
environs, but the promulgation of the Civil Code in 1804 brought
nationwide change. Article 77 of the Napoleonic Code prohibited the
burial of bodies prior to twenty-four hours after the official declaration
of death but did not obligate medical practitioners to verify death.
However, Article 81 required the involvement of doctors in cases of
suspicious or violent deaths and prohibited the burial of the body until
authorities drew up a formal report on the state of the corpse. This
latter measure implicitly recognized the importance of medical expertise in detecting crime.

    Some doctors suggested that the greatest danger surrounding pre-
mature burial was not people being buried alive but murders going
undetected. In 1818 the physician Jean-Baptiste Monfalcon insisted
that doctors must perform an attentive medical examination not only
to verify death but also to ensure that a suspicious death resulted in an
autopsy. Moreover, he claimed that some inattentive doctors performing autopsies had not first verified death and plunged their scalpels into
living persons whom they presumed dead. He noted that doctors could
perform a wide variety of tests for life, including placing a candle flame
or mirror in front of the mouth or nostrils to check for breathing; using
tobacco smoke enemas; applying boiling oil or water, an actual cautery, or blistering agents to the flesh; or resorting to painful surgical
procedures. Nonetheless, Monfalcon observed that these tests were
not infallible, and some extreme ones, such as a surgeon making an
incision into the heart and using his finger to verify that the heart was
motionless, were "a great way to kill a man who was still living."[11]
Monfalcon and other medical practitioners agreed that the most certain sign of death was putrefaction.

    Beyond this consensus about putrefaction, doctors disagreed about
the fallibility of signs of death and the solution to the problem of
apparent death. In the early nineteenth century, doctors cast doubt
on the diagnostic value of cadaveric rigidity as a certain sign of death,
in part due to the anatomist Marie-François-Xavier Bichat's research
on the physiology of death. Some claimed that all signs of death were
fallible except putrefaction yet warned that the answer was not for
people to keep corpses in their homes until decomposition, which
posed a danger to health. They rather demanded the establishment of

waiting mortuaries, modeled after the *Leichenhäuser* constructed in Germany in the early nineteenth century, in cemeteries throughout France to house bodies until the onset of putrefaction. In 1818 Orfila's book on the distinction between real and apparent death identified putrefaction as the surest sign of death but warned of the dangers of waiting until a body was clearly putrefying before burying it. Orfila also rejected the commonly held view that lay persons could easily assess the onset of putrefaction and insisted that only medical practitioners could.[12] Those sharing Orfila's views dismissed the establishment of waiting mortuaries without a full staff of doctors as futile and unnecessary. In 1829 the physician Charles-Chrétien-Henri Marc articulated his own objections to waiting mortuaries, concerning their costs and the problem of personnel who lack medical education and the ability to remain hypervigilant day in, day out after surveilling thousands of corpses. Marc deemed the utility of waiting mortuaries "illusory." He considered other measures adopted or proposed by Germans to prevent premature burial, such as attaching to a corpse's toe a cord leading to a bell that would ring with the slightest movement, misguided as well. Marc and other like-minded physicians insisted that the answer was relying upon doctors to verify death, primarily based on either putrefaction or the use of a "Voltaic pile," the first electric battery, to test muscle spasms or twitches. Marc also lamented that French law did not require doctors or surgeons to verify death and to determine cause of death and that only the city of Paris had adopted a sufficient system of death verification.[13]

During the 1830s, proliferating publications on the subject of apparent death called for a greater role for medical experts in verifying death. C. F. Tacheron, a physician charged with verifying deaths in Paris, expressed grave concerns about crimes going undetected. In 1830, after ten years of service in his position, Tacheron insisted that the Parisian system should be extended throughout France and that the legal verification of death should be confined to physicians who had studied legal medicine and who carefully crafted clear and intelligible reports for magistrates. In French communes where there were no such doctors, he recommended that either *officiers de santé* or midwives perform this function.[14] Prosper Touchard, an *officier de santé*, similarly argued that it was completely unacceptable that mayors instead of medical practitioners verified death in the French countryside.

He demanded immediate change in the name of justice. He declared, "This state of affairs cannot last. It is contrary to common sense, to justice. It is hostile to the preservation of society. It favors murders and poisonings in the countryside by giving hope of impunity, which the inability of those chosen to examine cadavers promises."[15] The pharmacist and chemist Jean-Sébastien-Eugène Julia de Fontenelle's 1834 book on uncertain signs of death and the dangers of hasty burials also insisted that France's system, in which mayors or other civil servants without any medical training verified death, was "absurd," especially given the difficulties that even the most knowledgeable and well trained medical practitioners had in interpreting uncertain signs of death.[16] In 1834 doctor Alphonse Devergie, who copublished the journal *Annales d'hygiène publique et de médecine légale*, founded in 1829, observed that while medical practitioners could verify death through an external bodily examination, they must open up the cadaver in cases of suspicious deaths in order to identify cause of death and manner of death, whether a homicide, suicide, or accident, or else risk crimes going unpunished.[17]

During this period of keen interest in the subject of apparent death, the Italian physician Pietro Manni donated 1,500 francs to the Academy of Science to award a prize for the best work on the question of apparent death. The Academy held competitions in 1839, 1842, and 1846. On the third occasion, the Academy found a recipient they deemed worthy: the physician Eugène Bouchut. He proposed using the stethoscope, invented by René Laënnec in 1816, to determine death by verifying the absence of a heartbeat. Bouchut later published his findings in a lengthy treatise on the signs of death in 1849. He rejected waiting mortuaries as useless and costly. Rather he proposed extending the system of doctors verifying death in Paris and certain other French cities to the countryside.[18] In 1848 the Academy of Science's Manni Prize committee published a report praising Bouchut's work. It also identified the following signs of death as "certain": the cessation of heartbeat, cadaveric rigidity (rigor mortis), the absence of muscular contractility under the influence of electricity, and general decomposition. The report declared that only doctors could assess these signs, with the exception of putrefaction, and that doctors alone must verify deaths in both cities and the countryside. The committee also concluded that doctors' assessment of the signs of death rendered waiting mortuaries useless.[19] However, the committee's report was not the final word on the subject, and debates within and beyond the medical community continued.

Physicians offered novel solutions to the problem of uncertainty in diagnosing death. Some physicians proposed pinching nipples with a tenaculum, a surgical clamp with sharp hooks, or with a special instrument designed expressly for the purpose of verifying death or rousing a person from a state of apparent death.[20] In 1861 Dr. Plouviez proposed acupuncture of the heart with a steel needle as a means of distinguishing real from apparent death, and the Society of Practical Medicine in Paris deemed Plouviez's method an improvement upon Bouchut's.[21] In 1862 Dr. Léon Collongues published a book on a new model of auscultation. He recommended sticking the patient's finger into the doctor's ear in order to detect a buzzing sound if the person were still live.[22] Nevertheless, the prospect of presumably dead bodies not being seen by any doctor or subjected to any of these competing methods distressed those concerned about the problem of apparent death.

Consequently, physicians, social commentators, and some politicians continued to demand legal and policy change. In 1863 doctor Antoine Barrangeard insisted that each city, town, village, and commune needed a system of death verification and certification that involved doctors or death inspectors who were salaried by the French state or the local commune, able to distinguish between real and apparent death, and vigilant about suspicious deaths. Barrangeard warned about cases of greedy heirs, treacherous spouses, or other hateful persons committing horrible murders that were "covered by a thick veil by the lack of the regular inspection of the deceased."[23] Other authors expressed similar warnings, and citizens who were concerned about apparent death wrote to their legislators. As a result, the issues of apparent death, undiscovered murders, and premature burial reached the Senate floor in 1865, 1866, and 1869. During Senate debates in 1866, Cardinal Ferdinand-François-Auguste Donnet, Archbishop of Bordeaux, declared that he was nearly buried alive after a doctor had declared him dead forty years earlier.[24] Political pressure spurred the Ministry of Interior to publish, on December 24, 1866, a circular outlining measures to combat the problem of hasty burials. The circular stipulated that the mayor of every commune should appoint one or more doctors or surgeons, or *officiers de santé* in their absence, as official death verifiers who would alert authorities about signs of violent death. The Minister of the Interior also identified two signs of death, putrefaction and cadaveric rigidity, as "infallible."[25]

However, the certainty or fallibility of various signs of death remained highly contested. Wealthy benefactors incentivized prolonged controversy. In 1867 the Marquis d'Ourches donated 20,000 francs to the Academy of Medicine to be awarded for a work identifying an unequivocal sign of death that lay persons could recognize and another 5,000 francs for a reliable method of diagnosing death that required a doctor's intervention. Another donation in 1874 to the Paris Academy of Sciences established a similar prize, the Prix Dusgate.[26] Many leading figures in legal medicine insisted that interpreting the complexities of the numerous, varied signs of death required medical expertise and should not be left to laypersons. Reporting on behalf of the Health Department of the Seine, Devergie proclaimed in 1867, "Declaration of death can only be entrusted to a doctor. Medical science alone has sure means of recognizing the state of real death and distinguishing it from the state of apparent death."[27] In 1875 Gabriel Tourdes, professor of legal medicine in Strasbourg, dismissed the public's preoccupation with identifying a single sign of death as misguided and dangerous:

The public demands a single, infallible sign that everyone can perceive as the surest guarantee against the danger of being buried alive. But this guarantee is illusory if the appreciation of the sign is left to a person who is a stranger to the art of medicine. The surest sign may be poorly ascertained. Error is more likely and more serious when the observation concerns only one point.[28]

Tourdes suggested that the medical community was partly to blame for this preoccupation with premature burial by irresponsibly responding to and stoking public fears through circulating often apocryphal stories about apparent death and persons being buried alive. He claimed that the issue of apparent death generated so much medical commentary that "no aspect of medical literature is richer." Tourdes deemed this body of literature extremely problematic, "since the science is cluttered with uncritically accumulated facts and tales inspired by imagination or by fear."[29]

The science of apparent death was also gendered, as medical men viewed women as particularly prone to medical conditions that could be mistaken for death. Marc claimed that doctors' verification of death was especially important for women, whose nervous systems were more "excitable" than men's and who were more susceptible to conditions that could simulate death, such as hysteria, hypochondria, catalepsy, syncope or loss of consciousness, lethargy, and heavy blood loss.[30] Doctors maintained that menstrual bleeding could produce loss of consciousness and a state of apparent death. They also observed that pregnancy and childbirth presented even graver dangers and risks. Noting that verifying the absolute loss of life in pregnant women could be quite difficult, Marc cautioned fellow doctors to avoid hastily declaring their death, since a premature or erroneous declaration could result in the death of both the mother and fetus. However, doctors had a short window of time to save the life of the fetus after a woman's death. Marc observed that uncertainty about the signs of death was the only reason for doctors not to extract a fetus immediately. At a time when cesarean sections rarely resulted in preserving the life of both mother and child, doctors widely advocated only performing a cesarean operation after the death of the mother in order to try to save the life of the child. But, these doctors observed that if a woman was in a state of apparent death, the procedure would kill her. Consequently, Marc and others advocated extracting the fetus from a deceased or apparently dead woman without making incisions into her abdomen.[31] Additionally the problem of apparent death at the time of childbirth could afflict not only mothers but also their newborns. Published works on apparent death among newborns proliferated, particularly during the second half of the nineteenth century.[32] Meanwhile, medical men continued to return to the problem of apparent death among women in all stages of the lifecycle and stressed the prevalence of hysteria among women. In 1875, Tourdes claimed that "hysterical syncope" was the most common form of apparent death.[33]

The final years of the nineteenth century saw no shortage of works proposing solutions to the problem of apparent death. Debates about the utility of waiting mortuaries were ongoing. In 1890 Doctor Manni won the Prix Dusgate for his simple assertion that the only reliable sign of death was putrefaction. He advocated for the establishment of mortuaries in cemeteries where the presumably deceased could remain until the onset of putrefaction, which had been a rallying cry among those concerned about apparent death for most of the nineteenth century.[34] The city of Paris established France's first waiting mortuary in Montmartre cemetery in 1890 and its second in Père Lachaise cemetery in 1892. Despite the numerous appeals for these establishments, they ultimately proved to be unpopular and unsuccessful. Some commentators even deemed them a spectacular failure. As Jules Rochard of the Paris Academy of Medicine observed, the Montmartre mortuary received only five bodies over the course of eighteen months, and the Père Lachaise mortuary received only one.[35] Meanwhile physicians continued to propose inventive methods of determining death and resuscitating the "apparently dead." For example, Jean-Baptiste-Vincent Laborde, professor of medicine in Paris, proposed rhythmically pulling the tongue of the presumably deceased for up to three hours, a method which either would resuscitate those in a state of apparent death or would serve as a "sure sign of real death." Laborde developed a tongue-pulling device precisely for this purpose.[36]

While Laborde and other physicians developed novel methods of diagnosing death, other medical practitioners expressed dissatisfaction with the system of verification of death within France. A number of physicians observed that most of France, particularly rural areas, lacked well-established systems of death verification, with the exception of Paris and other major cities. Even large cities lacked enough officially appointed doctors to verify death, particularly in certain neighborhoods. Many communes altogether lacked any doctor appointed for this purpose. Moreover, some medical practitioners issued death certificates without seeing the body. Medical practitioners concerned with deficiencies in the system of death verification warned of the dangers of both premature burial and undetected murders.[37]

Throughout the nineteenth century, physicians discounted lay knowledge and claimed that only skilled medical practitioners could accurately interpret a host of signs, to which they attributed varying degrees of importance and certainty, in order to diagnose death reliably. Physicians advanced this narrative to an anxious public who were hungry for assurances against premature burial. In doing so, medical experts sought to increase the public's faith and confidence in doctors' capacity to assess the signs of death. There was considerable disagreement over the extent to which fears of premature burial and the problem of "apparent death" were well founded. Many physicians and others who dismissed alarmist claims about the frequency with which persons were buried alive nevertheless insisted that doctors should examine dead bodies prior to burial in order to determine whether foul-play or a murder occurred. Medical experts positioned themselves as indispensable to the administrative and judicial functions of the state and to the public seeking reassurance about the uncertainties surrounding death.

Autopsies and the Afterlives of Corpses

Doctors played essential roles in criminal investigations involving dead bodies. These roles included identifying unknown dead bodies, performing autopsies to determine whether a death was a homicide, and establishing the corpus delicti, the body of the crime or the material evidence of the crime. In Paris, the morgue provided a physical space for these activities, and it became a locus of forensic medical practice and teaching. Moreover, as Vanessa Schwartz and Bruno Bertherat's works have shown, the Paris morgue was also a wildly popular public attraction.[38] The popularity of the Paris morgue was tied to the rising public profile of forensic medicine and the popularization of forensic knowledge. Some men and women sought to put this knowledge to use to cover up their crimes. Doctors faced sometimes formidable challenges in death investigations, particularly in cases in which perpetrators sought to destroy forensic evidence and the bodies of their victims. Nonetheless, leading forensic doctors frequently expressed confidence in their own abilities and in the profession, even in the face of scientifically informed criminal ingenuity.

Conducting postmortem examinations and autopsies were among the most essential tasks of practitioners of forensic medicine. Orfila outlined in his publications and teachings the steps that doctors should take when judicial authorities summoned them in cases of suspicious death. The first step was ensuring that the person was truly dead. If the doctor had any doubt, he should use all means at his disposal to bring the person back to life. Orfila advised doctors, when possible, to go to where the body was located in order to evaluate the conditions there that could shed light on a possible crime and to avoid altering it in transportation. He also advised doctors to proceed swiftly to the postmortem examination. The examination entailed taking note of external marks on the corpse and the conditions surrounding its discovery before then dissecting the body and conducting the internal examination.[39] Thorough autopsies generally took between one and a half and three hours.[40] Upon the completion of the autopsy, the medical expert composed an official written report responding to the questions posed by the investigating magistrate. Outside of Paris, doctors performed autopsies most often at the site of the body's discovery, as Orfila advised, for example in the woods, in gardens, at inns, along a body of water, or in a home. Domestic settings were the most common site of autopsies in the provinces. Doctors also carried out autopsies in judicial or administrative spaces, workplaces, or medical establishments.[41] Over the course of the nineteenth century in Paris, medical experts performed a rising number of autopsies at the morgue.[42]

The institution of the morgue originated in Paris. The Prefect of Police in Paris founded the morgue in 1804, when it opened its doors to the public so that they may identify the anonymous dead. By the early eighteenth century, the term morgue had come to describe the place in the Grand Châtelet prison, or *basse-geôle*, where dead bodies were displayed for the purposes of identification. The Châtelet prison was demolished in the early nineteenth century, and the morgue opened shortly thereafter in the center of Paris in a new building at the place du Marché-Neuf on the Ile de la Cité. Decades later, Baron Georges Haussmann's transformation and modernization of Paris entailed the demolition of the morgue at the place du Marché-Neuf. In February 1864 the new morgue, four times the size of old, opened behind Notre-Dame Cathedral on the quai de l'Archevêché at the eastern tip of the Ile de la Cité.[43]

The autopsy room was the center of forensic activity at the morgue and was closed to the public. The number of bodies that the morgue received annually more than tripled from the mid-1830s to the mid-1880s, and doctors autopsied a portion of these bodies.[44] In the year 1887, for example, the morgue received 928 human remains and conducted 340 autopsies.[45] Forensic doctors determined that the most common manner of death among adults at the morgue was suicide and the most common cause was drowning.[46] The medical directors, or

FIGURE I.I Visitors viewing corpses through the glass in the exhibition room of the Paris morgue. Louis Courtin, "Vue intérieure de la morgue," lithograph, Musée Carnavalet, Histoire de Paris

médecins-inspecteurs, of the morgue used its forensic activities as learning opportunities for medical students. In the 1830s Devergie, the first *médecin-inspecteur* of the morgue, offered "practical lectures" in forensic medicine to medical students twice a week at the morgue. Paul Brouardel, who became the second *médecin-inspecteur* and professor of legal medicine in Paris, began teaching at the morgue in 1877.[47] Late nineteenth-century commentators on the morgue described the institution as a school for legal medicine.[48]

The morgue's exhibit room, or *salle d'exposition*, was designed to allow large crowds to view through glass windows the bodies displayed on marble slabs (Figure 1.1). Unidentified corpses that arrived at the Paris morgue were displayed nude, with a cloth covering their genitals, for three days in the exhibit room. Their clothes were washed and placed above the body to aid in identification. In 1877 the morgue ended the display of nude bodies and began displaying corpses in the clothes that they had been wearing when found. Cold water dripped on the corpses to slow decay, until the installation of an extensive refrigeration system in 1882 (Figure 1.2). The morgue was open to the

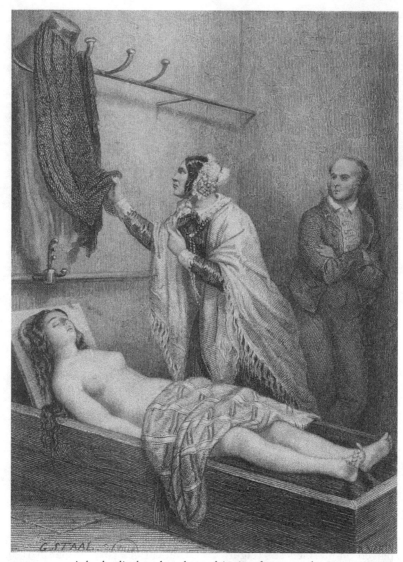

FIGURE 1.2 A body displayed under a dripping faucet at the Paris morgue. Adolphe Varin and Pierre-Gustave Staal, "La Morgue," engraving, Musée Carnavalet, Histoire de Paris

public seven days a week, year-round, from the morning until the evening. From 1836 to 1871, its hours were 6 am until 8 pm during summer and 7 am until nightfall the rest of the year.[49] In the early nineteenth century about two-thirds of the unidentified corpses at the

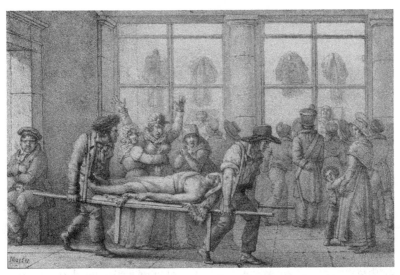

FIGURE 1.3 Visitors at the Paris morgue witnessing the intake of a corpse and viewing bodies displayed on marble slabs. Jean Henri Marlet, "La Morgue," lithograph, Musée Carnavalet, Histoire de Paris

morgue were eventually identified. Beginning in the 1830s, the proportion increased to roughly three-fourths.[50] However, contemporary descriptions of the morgue and its crowds suggested that the public fascination with the morgue went far beyond concerned persons hoping to identify a body.

The morgue was not only an important site of forensic instruction and death investigation but also a popular public attraction. The prominent forensic doctor Tardieu contributed a description of the morgue for *Paris Guide*, published for visitors to the International Exposition of 1867. Tardieu wrote in the guidebook that every day a "multitude of curious" men, women, and children of all ages viewed the bodies at the morgue, and their varied reactions included "terror and disgust" (Figure 1.3). Tardieu also noted that the throngs of visitors to the morgue not only were interested in viewing victims of crime but also hoped to spot a murderer. Tardieu, other forensic doctors, and social commentators maintained that criminals went to the morgue to view their victims or to overhear what the crowds were saying about their crimes.[51] The morgue attracted Parisians, people from across France, and international visitors. Discussions of the morgue commonly appeared in nineteenth-century Paris guidebooks.

A guidebook for British visitors disdainfully described the morgue's popularity:

A perpetual stream of men, women, and children is running in and out of this horrible exhibition, and there they stand gazing at the hideous objects before them, sometimes uttering exclamations of horror, but usually with great indifference. The lower orders in Paris are fond of theatrical horrors and effects, but still it is not easy to understand how so disgusting and revolting an exhibition can be tolerated in a civilised country.

The guidebook denounced the spectacle of the morgue as "cruel to the dead and destructive of the morals of the living."[52]

Periodicals and the sensationalist press fueled keen public interest in the morgue and violent deaths. Changes associated with industrialization, urbanization, social unrest, and mass culture heightened anxieties about and fascination with the "dangerous classes," the underworld, and crime, particularly violent crime. The sensationalist mass press satisfied popular demand for stories about crime and the criminal underworld.[53] In 1878 Devergie maintained that press coverage of crimes directly contributed to the large crowds at the morgue, where violent deaths were frequently on display. Devergie observed, "We see a large number of curious people flocking to the morgue when the newspapers announce the commission of some crime." He noted that 1,000–1,500 people often waited in line outside of the morgue the day after newspapers reported a violent death.[54]

In November 1876 the discovery of a woman's body cut into pieces floating in the Seine just north of Paris attracted massive crowds to the morgue. Thousands of men, women, and children of all social classes came to view the mutilated body each day during its display. Police estimated that in one hour alone over 5,000 filed through the morgue. Newspapers at the time estimated that the crowd was between 20,000 and 68,000 people each day.[55] The French mass press extensively covered the "affair of the woman cut into pieces," which captured the popular imagination and became alternately known as the Billoir affair, once the woman's lover Sébastien Billoir was charged with murder. On November 8, authorities recovered from the Seine River the woman's head, legs, abdomen, arms, and chest. Later that month she was identified as Jeanne-Marie Le Manach. In December, authorities searched Billoir's home and found her hair and entrails in the cesspit there. Billoir later confessed to murder but insisted that it was not premeditated. However, his account of events contradicted the findings of the court-appointed medical expert, Georges Bergeron. Billoir claimed that he killed Le Manach by violently kicking her in the stomach one evening; he cut up her body the next day. In contrast, Bergeron reported that she was strangled, lost consciousness, and then was cut while alive; she died due to hemorrhaging. The assize court of the Seine convicted Billoir of murder on March 15, 1877, and he was subsequently executed.[56]

The Billoir affair was part of a string of crimes across France involving murderers who dismembered the bodies of their victims. Several years earlier, workers on the banks of the Seine spotted the body of a man without a head and limbs in March 1867. Three months later another torso was discovered, and the arms, legs, and head of the corpse were also found a few days later. The former butcher Jean-Charles-Alphonse Avinain confessed to the murders and was executed.[57] A decade after the Billoir affair, the dismembered body of Marie Salat was found in Marseille. The Bouches-du-Rhône assize court charged her teenage daughter and her older boyfriend with Salat's murder in July 1877. The president of the court remarked that Billoir's trial undoubtedly inspired the accused to dismember Salat and to mutilate her face with the apparent aim of making her identification more difficult.[58] The following year in 1878, a newspaper reported, "We are in the presence of a new Billoir affair," when human thighs and arms were discovered in a room in the rue Poliveau in Paris and later a trunk containing a woman's head and other body parts was found in Le Mans. Some speculated that the human remains found on the rue Poliveau were the remains from a body dissected in an anatomical amphitheater. The court summoned a chemist to test these remains and this hypothesis. He ruled out this possibility, since the remains did not contain arsenic, the substance used at the time to slow down decomposition in bodies used for dissection. The court also summoned three physicians to examine the body parts found in the trunk at Le Mans. They concluded that the woman had been stabbed in the heart. Authorities determined that Paul Lebiez, a medical student, and his friend Aimé Barré, a notary, had rented the room on the rue Poliveau. The assize court of the Seine tried them for murder. Lebiez and Barré were convicted and executed.[59] The press also linked the Billoir affair to the 1879 trial of Victor Prévost, tried for murdering a man three years earlier and cutting up his body into over seventy pieces.[60] The presumed intention behind these dismemberments was to make it more difficult to identify the victim, the perpetrator, and the manner and cause of death.

In 1880 Louis Menesclou's efforts to destroy forensic evidence of a presumed sexual assault led the public prosecutor to observe that he "was following the method of Lebiez, Billoir, and Prévost, which seems to be becoming odiously classic in Paris."[61] Authorities arrested Menesclou the day after four-year-old Louise Deu went missing from her parent's home in Paris. Menesclou lived in same building and was found with Louise's forearms in his pockets. Authorities later concluded that Menesclou had sexually assaulted and strangled Louise and then tried to dispose of her body. He had initially hidden her body under his mattress. The next day he began to cut the cadaver into small pieces to burn in his stove. Louise's head was discovered there, and over forty pieces of her body were found elsewhere in Menesclou's room. The public prosecutor's office noted that Menesclou carefully disposed of her genital organs, since these could have provided material proof of a sexual crime. The forensic doctor Brouardel was able to reconstitute nearly all of the cadaver, but her genitals were never recovered.[62] Doctors Brouardel, Lasègue, and Motet conducted a psychiatric examination of Menesclou. They observed that he became extremely animated and indignant when they raised the question of rape. Brouardel acknowledged that it was natural to assume that "so monstrous" a crime could only be the work of an insane person, but the doctors concluded that Menesclou was sane. The assize court of the Seine convicted him and sentenced him to death.[63]

Contemporary commentary on these and other causes célèbres advanced a narrative of medical experts triumphing over criminals' efforts to destroy bodily evidence and elude detection. In 1888 the eminent Lyonnais forensic doctor Alexandre Lacassagne and his student Louis Ravoux both published forensic studies on the practice of murderers cutting up the bodies of their victims. Lacassagne and Ravoux observed that it was not uncommon in infanticide cases for a mother to kill her newborn, cut the body into pieces, and then throw the pieces in a cesspit or more rarely into a furnace or boiling liquid in order to dispose of the body. Lacassagne also maintained that forensic postmortem examinations of bodies cut into pieces took longer but

were not necessarily more burdensome or difficult than forensic examinations of intact bodies. These examinations frequently resulted in the
identification of the victim, even those whose heads had been removed
or mutilated. However, Lacassagne noted that no one ever correctly
identified "the woman of Île-Barbe," whose remains were found on the
bank of the Saône in 1881 and displayed at the morgue of Lyon, which
had been established in 1853 on a barge floating on the banks of the
Rhône.[64] In contrast, the identification of a woman's severed head
publicly displayed at the Lyon morgue in January 1900 led to the
arrest of Luigi Richetto and the identification of four persons whom
authorities believed Richetto killed and dismembered between
1893 and 1899 in Lyon.[65] Lacassagne described "a sort of rivalry"
and escalating contest between forensic doctors who refined their
scientific techniques and criminals who adopted increasingly complicated methods to evade detection. Lacassagne viewed forensic medicine as the victor: "In this struggle, truth and science often have had
the upper hand."[66]

Medical experts sometimes evaluated cases in which perpetrators
employed multiple methods of concealing a murder by destroying the
body and its evidence. Lacassagne maintained that attempts to inciner-
ate a body after mutilating and cutting it into pieces were relatively
rare, but medical experts concluded that the murder of a mother and
her four-year-old daughter in Chaumont in April 1893 was one such
case. Their bodies had been mutilated, partially dismembered, and
burned. Authorities observed that the murderer had removed the
victims' genitals and surmised that a rape of the thirty-eight-year-old
woman preceded the murders.[67] Judicial authorities summoned a
pharmacist to conduct chemical analyses and three doctors to answer
a number of forensic questions, including what were the causes of
death and how were the bodies dismembered and burned. The doctors
received authorization to conduct experiments on human combustion
using three corpses from the Paris morgue of persons who had committed suicide. While the medical experts were unable to identify the
substance used to burn the bodies, possibly kerosene, oil, alcohol, or
other combustible substance, they determined that the burning lasted
at least four hours. After investigating authorities uncovered evidence
implicating Eugène-Ernest Durand, the Haute-Marne assize court tried
him for the murder of his wife and daughter in December 1893.[68]

Authorities at times asked forensic doctors to determine whether a body had been intentionally set on fire to disguise a murder as an accident, and a contingent of doctors worried that their colleagues would wrongfully conclude murder in cases of spontaneous human combustion. The medical discourse on this theory had originated in 1725, when the court in Rheims acquitted Jean Millet of his wife's murder on the basis of the surgeon Claude-Nicolas Le Cat's insistence that spontaneous combustion was her cause of death.[69] In the early nineteenth century, most doctors who supported the notion, including Orfila, maintained that victims of spontaneous human combustion generally consumed considerable amounts of alcohol and were disproportionately fat, older women. Some doctors claimed that excessive alcohol consumption rendered certain parts of the body flammable and fire more easily consumed fat bodies or body parts where fat accumulated. They also contended that spontaneous combustion generally consumed most of the human body and all organs, but often spared the extremities, such as hands and feet, and did not spread to nearby flammable objects, thus leaving surrounding furniture intact.[70] One adherent of the theory lamented in 1827 that some doctors were not convinced of the existence of spontaneous human combustion. He warned of the harms of "such a skepticism," which could result in doctors mistaking spontaneous combustion for murder.[71] Later polemics over the death of the German Countess of Görlitz in 1847 led to the decline of the theory of spontaneous human combustion. The court in Darmstadt eventually tried the countess's servant Johann Stauff for her murder in 1850, although the medical examiner had attributed the countess's death to spontaneous human combustion. Convincing expert testimony during the trial challenged the theory of spontaneous combustion. The jury convicted Stauff, who later confessed to killing and burning the countess to hide his crime. Many French forensic doctors closely followed the trial, and Tardieu became embroiled in the controversy. While Tardieu contested the theory of spontaneous human combustion, other forensic doctors, such as Devergie, were reluctant to abandon it entirely. Nevertheless, the theory had fallen out of favor among medical men in France and throughout Europe around this time.[72]

In the late nineteenth century, forensic doctors generally expressed confidence in their abilities to answer medicolegal questions in death investigations, including those involving burned bodies.[73] Despite the eventual medical and scientific consensus that human bodies did not burn without an external source of ignition, Tourdes noted in 1876 that some judicial authorities still asked medical experts in investigations involving burned bodies whether there were indications of spontaneous combustion. More common questions included whether the person was burned while alive or post-mortem, whether the fire caused the person's death, whether the fire was designed to destroy the body of a murder victim, and whether doctors could establish the identity of the cadaver based on remaining anatomical characteristics.[74] Additionally, dentists began to join doctors in assisting authorities' efforts to identify recovered human remains. The field of forensic odontology emerged in the wake of the fire at the Bazar de la Charité in Paris on May 4, 1897, which killed more than 120 persons. Dentists identified many of the severely burned and disfigured victims by their teeth. The following year, Oscar Amoëdo, a Cuban-born dental surgeon and professor of dentistry in Paris, published the first comprehensive treatise on forensic odontology.[75] Forensic specialties proliferated at the turn of the century, and death investigations increasingly relied upon specialized knowledge and training in multiple areas.

Although the scope of the field of forensics expanded over the course of the nineteenth century, corpses remained the central objects of inquiry for practitioners of legal medicine. Dead bodies were the subject of extensive forensic medical research and the focus of investigations of suspicious deaths. While doctors often performed autopsies at the site of the body's discovery, the morgue in Paris became not only the site of an increasing number of autopsies and practical forensic instruction but also a public spectacle and tourist attraction. A periodical in 1892 estimated that one million people visited the morgue annually.[76] Moral concerns surrounding this popularity resulted in the morgue closing its doors to the public in 1907. As forensic medicine gained greater cultural traction, some criminal offenders in Paris and elsewhere sought to mutilate or destroy the bodies of their victims, presumably to avoid detection. Forensic doctors published their findings to celebrate their triumphs over perpetrators, to disseminate expert knowledge, and to establish their authority. As the state increasingly relied on their expert knowledge, this reliance carried the risk of errors and injustice, which forensic doctors themselves readily acknowledged.

Forensics on Trial

The rising prominence of legal medicine in both French courts and culture during the nineteenth century also attracted scrutiny and calls for reform. Leading figures in the field were among the most vocal proponents of reform. Their critiques crystallized around a number of key issues concerning systemic shortcomings as well as the incompetence of individual medical practitioners. Proposed medicolegal reforms included disqualifying less-credentialed *officers de santé* from serving as medical experts in the courts, increasing the honorariums for medical experts, creating a special diploma in legal medicine, and adopting official lists of medical experts. As medicolegal expertise played a more and more decisive role in criminal investigations and prosecutions of murder, flawed forensic expertise became an increasingly salient problem.

Some of the problems surrounding the practice of legal medicine stemmed from issues of education and training. In 1824 the doctor and anatomist François Chaussier reflected on how his medical studies under the Old Regime did not impart him with the skills necessary to offer medical expertise in cases of suspected infanticide, murder, and other crimes. He observed, "Despite all my studies, my diligence in taking the most famous professors' courses, and the clinical visits of the great masters, I still had a lot of work to do to in order to fulfill the new functions entrusted to me."[77] Around the time that the French Revolution began, Chaussier began studying and conducting research in legal medicine. In 1790 he began teaching legal medicine to medical students studying in Paris. In 1794 the Revolutionary government called upon Chaussier and the chemist Antoine-François Fourcroy to reestablish and reorganize medical education in France, and Chaussier identified the need for a special course in legal medicine to be offered to medical students.[78] Although French medical students thereafter received instruction in legal medicine, they did not necessarily receive practical training. Devergie lamented that forensic medical instruction generally offered "nothing practical."[79] He had sought to remedy this problem by offering "practical" instruction for medical students at the

Paris morgue. Nonetheless, hands-on experience in forensic medicine, particularly for certain aspects of the field, was often lacking for medical students, whom the courts could summon to serve as medical experts upon the completion of their studies.

There were two tiers of medical education completed by the practitioners who served as medical experts, and the gap between the education and experience of doctors and *officiers de santé* was a source of concern. Doctors acquired the right to practice medicine and surgery throughout France after attending medical school and completing four years of study, five public exams, and a thesis. *Officiers de santé* received training for either three years in medical school, five years in a civil or military hospital, or six years in a sort of apprenticeship under a doctor. They could then practice medicine only in the *département* where they completed their medical training. But, many lacked training in legal medicine specifically. French law did not distinguish between *officiers de santé* and doctors in terms of medical expertise in the courts. Article 44 of the 1808 Code of Criminal Instruction simply required the magistrate conducting the investigative hearing that preceded a criminal trial to summon either one or two doctors or *officiers de santé* in cases of violent or suspicious death to examine the cadaver and produce a written report that answered a number of the magistrate's questions, including those concerning the cause of death. Leading forensic doctors and jurists commonly complained that the inferior qualifications of *officiers de santé* left them ill-equipped to grapple with complex forensic medical matters. For example, in 1817 doctor Charles-Alexandre-Hippolyte-Amable Bertrand criticized the courts for relying upon *officiers de santé* for "even the most complex" forms of forensic expertise, such as challenging poisoning cases.[80] In 1829 Marc complained, "A swarm of ignoramuses, who having practiced the most routine operations of minor surgery, believe themselves equally entitled, under the banal title of *officiers de santé*, to practice courtroom medicine."[81] Some *officiers de santé* themselves expressed concerns about being out of their depth. For example, in 1822 an *officier de santé* whom a justice of the peace called upon to examine the body of a newborn in an advanced state of decomposition refused to conduct the autopsy alone without a doctor present.[82] Nevertheless, the title and status of doctor offered no guarantee of effective forensic medical expertise.

Rising expectations about forensic expertise accentuated the problem of incompetent medical experts. In 1822 Orfila decried the deficiencies in French law, which did not ensure that the doctors or *officiers de santé* whom magistrates summoned were competent. Orfila complained of "the serious disadvantages that result from the latitude left by the law that allows any man exercising the art of healing, however well or badly, to be called to enlighten justice."[83] In 1835 another doctor lamented that magistrates often called "the first doctor who [was] available or closest to the site of the event," rather than doctors with more experience and knowledge of forensic medicine.[84] In 1852 Devergie similarly criticized magistrates' and police commissioners' choice of medical experts. Sometimes they selected their personal physician or a medical practitioner who was ill-equipped to serve the courts as a medicolegal expert. Devergie complained that many medical practitioners called by the courts had little interest in legal medicine; they neither published their findings nor advanced the field and state of knowledge.[85] Some medical practitioners readily admitted their lack of experience and limited knowledge of forensic medicine. A doctor testifying before the assize court of the Seine-Inférieure in 1855 about the inconsistencies in his autopsy reports explained that he had studied legal medicine only briefly twenty years earlier and was "very ignorant" about its practices.[86] What is more, some medical practitioners were grossly negligent and falsified reports in rare cases. For example, in 1856 two *officiers de santé* who documented an engorged brain in an autopsy report had fabricated the results and never opened the body.[87]

Commentators on forensic medicine stressed the importance of practitioners having both broad and highly specialized knowledge as well as awareness of the limits of their competence and judicial role. During the July Monarchy in 1842, doctor Emile Pereyra declared that practicing forensic medicine required comprehensive medical knowledge and skill: "To be a good forensic doctor today, one must be a good anatomist, a good physiologist, and a good practitioner."[88] The physician Charles Vibert later observed, "The most extensive scientific erudition is not all it takes to be a good expert." He continued, "One must know how to apply one's general medical knowledge to this quite special form of medicine." Vibert also acknowledged that even highly regarded and skilled forensic doctors were not masters of all domains, but they were aware of this fact. Vibert stated, "The foremost virtue of a forensic doctor is to know the lacunae in his education and to dare to confess them."[89] Marc observed that another virtue of a medical expert was impartiality. Marc maintained that medical experts must not take the part of either the prosecution or the defense and must refuse to work with any defense attorneys who wish to misconstrue the forensic evidence. Marc declared, "The forensic doctor is an expert not a lawyer."[90] Lawyers resoundingly agreed with Marc's stance. In 1849 Adolphe-Victor Paillard de Vielleneuve, the lawyer and chief editor of the *Gazette des tribunaux*, similarly declared, "The doctor is an expert. He is not a judge."[91] The medical expert's role was not to determine whether the accused was guilty or innocent but to establish the medical and scientific facts of the case. Paillard de Vielleneuve complained that experts often exceeded their mandate. The medical expert was neither a lawyer, judge, nor juror, but he needed to clearly convey his findings to these persons who lacked medical knowledge and training. As Paillard de Vielleneuve observed, forensic reports needed to be not only scientifically precise but also clear and "perfectly comprehensible" to lay persons.[92]

Judicial authorities in some *départements* had difficulty securing qualified medical experts, given the sacrifices it often entailed for these practitioners. The difficulties were most pronounced in *départements* with geographically dispersed populations and a shortage of well-trained medical practitioners. Devergie noted that many doctors in such areas were reluctant to travel to examine a dead body when there were people whom they could treat at home.[93] Furthermore, treating their own patients was more remunerative than serving as a medical expert for the courts. The president of the Finistère assize court observed in 1841 that the burdens of practicing legal medicine were greatest for doctors living outside of a departmental capital, since they would have to leave their practice to travel to the court and send their patients to doctors elsewhere. Furthermore, the amount the courts paid for their service was often not even enough to cover their travel costs. The magistrate also maintained that doctors with many patients often managed to avoid serving as medical experts, while young, inexperienced medical practitioners served instead.[94] Some doctors observed that the sacrifices they made to serve as experts also included the continual efforts that they made to stay current in the field.

A doctor in 1840 observed that the maintenance of his personal library alone cost him more than what he earned for his medicolegal expertise. Complaining about his "pecuniary sacrifices," he asked, "What would it be if I added now the loss of my time, relative to my clientele, and my traveling expenses?"[95] Some reluctant doctors indeed refused to serve as experts and could be subjected to fines.[96]

In some trials, rival medical experts offered contradictory evidence, which offered the promise of serving as a corrective to flawed medicolegal reports but also risked sowing confusion and undermining public confidence in medical experts. Rival doctors' contradictory evidence could take the form of a medicolegal consultation requested by either magistrates or defense lawyers. These doctors whom magistrates or defense lawyers approached for medicolegal consultations would review the original autopsy or other medicolegal report and offer their own evaluation, either based exclusively on their analysis of the written autopsy report or supplanted by additional experiments or tests that they conducted in order to judge the validity of the findings. Professor of legal medicine François-Emmanuel Fodéré highlighted the limits and risks of these medicolegal consultations, in which doctors did not examine the body in question but merely reviewed a written report. A defense lawyer could call upon a prominent forensic doctor to challenge a sound autopsy report, and this challenge could be scientifically suspect yet successful. Fodéré observed, "The authority of a great name, specious reasoning, and the magic of eloquence" often had a much greater effect on the courts than the factual narration of findings in a report written by someone of lesser stature.[97] Doctors worried about the effects of contradictory medical evidence on impressionable juries. In 1835 a doctor in Poitiers declared that it was "unseemly to have two doctors argue against each other and thus challenge science before judges, jurors, and the public." These conflicts threatened to reverse the progress of medicolegal expertise in trial courts. Highlighting the influence of medical expertise on judicial verdicts, he observed, "When the doctor gives clear, positive and well-motivated conclusions, they generally serve as the basis for the jury's declaration."[98] Contradictory medical evidence risked diminishing jurors' confidence medicolegal expertise, which was still fragile.

Nonetheless, forensic expertise played a greater role in the courts during the second half of the nineteenth century, and defense lawyers increasingly called upon their own medical experts to contest the findings of those summoned by investigating magistrates. In 1864 a public prosecutor in the Alpes-Maritimes complained about defense lawyers employing this strategy in every trial involving forensic expertise. He deemed the practice perfectly legitimate if used to uncover the truth but lamented the irresponsible use of unqualified experts. The prosecutor declared, "Nothing is more saddening for justice than to hear the risky opinions of people without ability who are in search of clients and whose often-impudent words result in a disturbance in the courtroom debate and in the jury." He warned of the "serious dangers" of this practice, which undermined justice and only served the guilty.[99] Other magistrates and forensic doctors shared these concerns about defense lawyers indiscriminately summoning doctors to challenge sound and carefully conducted forensic expertise.

Throughout the nineteenth century, magistrates and forensic doctors worried about the role of incompetent medicolegal experts in death investigations and demanded reform. One of the most common proposals for reforming forensic expertise called for specially designated and appointed medical experts. For example, in 1832 a magistrate in Brittany proposed that such doctors serve as appointed medical experts for fixed terms and be the only persons authorized to perform autopsies. He believed that this reform would remedy the problem of untrained and incompetent medical experts carrying out this important task.[100] In 1842 a presiding judge in Saint-Brieuc also called for reforms due to the frequency with which "incapable men" produced forensic reports that undermined the pursuit of justice. The jurist implored the Minister of Justice to name in each *arrondissement* certain doctors who would exclusively issue forensic reports and receive a modest annual salary.[101] Complaining about an autopsy report of an inexperienced country surgeon in an 1860 infanticide case, the president of the Finistère assize court called for a special physician dedicated to medicolegal affairs in each *arrondissement*.[102] Some forensic doctors proposed the convocation of a special jury comprised of doctors, pharmacists, and chemists to establish the corpus delicti, in other words to establish whether or not a crime had occurred, prior to bringing a case before a grand jury who would then determine whether the evidence against the accused was strong enough for an indictment.[103] Concerned doctors and magistrates advocated these various structural changes to the judiciary to improve the function of medicolegal expertise in the courts.

Doctors and magistrates proposed additional reforms to remedy problems associated with medicolegal expertise, particularly those stemming from the insufficient education of medical practitioners, legal professionals, and lay persons. Prominent professors of legal medicine insisted upon more practical instruction and training in legal medicine at medical schools. Some forensic doctors and jurists called for legal medicine to be taught in law schools as well so that lawyers and magistrates would have a basic foundational knowledge. By the late nineteenth century, the law faculty in Lyon offered instruction in legal medicine. However, the magistrate Joseph Drioux, who proposed a special diploma in legal medicine, observed that the high degree of uncertainty that characterized the field of forensic medicine made teaching the subject matter challenging.[104] The difficulties in under- standing forensic medical knowledge were even greater beyond med- ical and law schools. A major area of concern was jurors' inability to analyze medicolegal expertise. Accordingly, some forensic physicians published works designed to educate lay audiences and sought to communicate their findings in written medicolegal reports and oral testimony as clearly as possible.

Appeals for medicolegal reform peaked during the 1880s and 1890s. In 1884 Brouardel lamented that doctors often performed autopsies alone and had difficulties writing up their forensic reports during the procedure, which soiled their hands with bodily fluids and was physically exhausting. He complained that most medical practi- tioners hastily composed their reports afterwards, sometimes days or even a week later, just from memory without notes. He maintained that the majority of autopsy reports from provincial practitioners that he had reviewed revealed that they had never opened the skull. Brouardel insisted that two medical experts should serve in all criminal cases involving forensic expertise. Furthermore, in response to the problem of contradictory findings among medical experts, Brouardel proposed convoking a commission of medical and scientific authorities to settle the issues.[105] Additionally, doctors and jurists insistently called for an increase in the honorariums for medical experts, which had not increased since 1811.[106] Legislators finally raised them in November 1893. As a result, doctors performing a standard autopsy received twenty-five francs, whereas they had previously received between five and nine francs, depending on whether they were working in a large or small city, a town, or the countryside.[107]

Other reform measures addressed the question of who should serve as medical experts in death investigations and other criminal proceedings. Some jurists and forensic doctors called for summoning specialists according to the nature of the expertise, whether on an ad hoc basis or as fixed-term appointees. During the second half of the nineteenth century, several forensic doctors and magistrates proposed that the courts rely upon lists of doctors competent in legal medicine. During the early Third Republic in the 1870s, the tribunal of the Seine and the appeals court in Paris established semiofficial lists of accredited doctors who could offer medicolegal expertise. Some magistrates and forensic doctors called for the nationwide adoption of official lists of medical experts for *juges d'instruction* and defense lawyers to use exclusively. However, others considered such a system best, or only, suited to large cities.[108]

In November 1893 French legislators passed a law establishing official lists of medicolegal experts for the courts. It restricted these lists to French doctors who had been practicing medicine for at least five years and required all French doctors to obey judicial requests for medicolegal expertise.[109] The prominent forensic doctor Lacassagne complained that this reform did not remedy the problem of doctors serving as medical experts who were unprepared or ill-equipped for the task. Moreover, it excluded potentially knowledgeable doctors, and Lacassagne challenged the decision to exclude doctors who had finished their medical studies more recently. Practicing general medicine for at least five years did not ensure competence in legal medicine, and Lacassagne maintained that some doctors would forget the medicolegal methods and procedures that they learned in medical school by the time that the courts summoned them years later. Furthermore, the uneven geographical distribution of doctors meant that a sole doctor, typically disinterested in the field of legal medicine, had to serve in all medicolegal investigations in some areas in the countryside. Many doctors serving as medical experts, whether in cities or the countryside, lacked sufficient education, experience, or competence and failed to complete all of the steps in a thorough autopsy or erroneously interpreted lesions and cause of death.[110]

Commentators also observed that deficiencies in forensic expertise were responsible for wrongful convictions and for undermining the field of legal medicine. The trial and retrial of Pauline Druaux put this problem in relief. In 1887 the assize court of the Seine-Inférieure tried Druaux for poisoning her husband and brother in Malaunay, outside of Rouen. The two doctors in Rouen who performed the autopsies observed lesions in the men's stomachs and intestines, which they attributed to poisoning. The doctors also found what they suspected to be tiny pieces of cantharides, also known as blister beetles or Spanish flies, in samples of vomit that they examined under a microscope. They theorized that both men had been poisoned with Spanish fly. A professor of chemistry in Rouen analyzed samples of the men's stomachs, kidneys, livers, and intestines but found no trace of any poison. He used the vomit and organ samples in physiological experiments on rats and other animals, which did not demonstrate any signs of poisoning. Nonetheless, the medicolegal report concluded that the men had been poisoned, probably by cantharides. The jury convicted Druaux on the basis of the experts' suspicions of poisoning and the "moral proofs" against her. Prosecutors portrayed her a "dissolute," "perverse," drunken, and adulterous woman whose husband caught her in flagrante delicto with another man a few days before his death. While Druaux was serving her sentence of a life of hard labor, new occupants in her former residence became ill with the same symptoms as her late husband and brother, including vertigo and loss of consciousness. One woman died. People began speculating that emissions of carbon monoxide from the neighboring lime kiln were responsible. Once it was shut down, these afflictions stopped. The public and the press thus concluded that Druaux was innocent. Consequently, the assize court of Amiens retried Druaux in 1896. During this trial, reports from an engineer and architect from Rouen and three medical experts from Paris all supported this theory. Lamenting that the doctors from Rouen had never analyzed the victims' blood or lungs, Brouardel maintained that a simple ten-minute blood analysis could have prevented the ordeals that followed. The court acquitted Druaux and provided her with an indemnity of forty thousand francs.[111] This case and other fin-de-siècle causes célèbres involving problematic forensics provoked public outcry and outrage among leading forensic doctors about the manner in which some medical practitioners conducted autopsies.

Nonetheless, many appeals for medicolegal reform went unheeded. These calls for reform included the creation of a permanent commission of prominent forensic doctors, chemists, magistrates, and lawyers to examine forensic reports in all criminal cases and the prohibition of any unapproved medicolegal reports. Some commentators expressed concerns that this system would cause the wheels of justice to grind to a halt. They instead advocated other reforms, such as further increasing the honorariums for medical experts and creating a special diploma in legal medicine.[112] In 1898 the lawyer and politician Jean Cruppi raised the issue of medicolegal reform in the Chamber of Deputies. He proposed establishing a system in which each appeals court in France would annually compile a list of medical experts, based partly on the recommendations of faculty at the medical schools. The investigating magistrate would select one or more experts, and the accused would be entitled to select the same number of medical experts from this list. The state would pay all of these experts to work and draft a report together. Cruppi proposed that an additional medical expert arbitrate cases in which the medical experts had opposing viewpoints. The Society of Legal Medicine of France, which had been founded in 1868, extensively debated and critiqued the proposed law, which many forensic doctors predicted would generate constant disputes among medical experts and be costly for the state.[113] Cruppi's proposal proved divisive, and the question of reform remained unresolved.

Throughout the nineteenth century, frustrated doctors, lawyers, magistrates, and lawmakers cried out about flaws in the practice of legal medicine in France. While a chorus of voices demanded reforms, a consensus never coalesced around which reforms, aside from increased honorariums, should be implemented to remedy these problems. Demands for reforming medicolegal expertise were in some respects a testament to the gains that medical men had made in the legal arena. While more and more doctors examined dead bodies and carried out various medicolegal duties, their presence in the courts and public discourse grew. Their greater influence heightened the problem of flawed forensic evidence, an issue affecting not just death investigation and autopsy reports but all facets of legal medicine.

In sum, medical men capitalized upon public fear and fascination with dead bodies to stake out greater professional territory in the late eighteenth and nineteenth centuries. Many doctors sought to expand their roles in verifying death, ascertaining its cause, and performing autopsies in cases of suspicious deaths whether on site or at the Paris morgue, where corpses were on public display. A far greater proportion of doctors had basic knowledge and training in legal medicine by the end of the nineteenth century than at its beginning, although many medical practitioners' hands-on experience and practical training in the field remained limited. Some doctors displayed discomfort or a lack of confidence in diagnosing death, distinguishing between various manners and causes of death, or performing medicolegal duties that exceeded the limits of their knowledge or training. Flawed autopsy reports were a lightning rod for criticism; at the same time, the forensic autopsy had become indispensable to the state's investigations of suspicious deaths. Doctors and magistrates worried about medical incompetence in death investigations and the dangers of contradictory forensic evidence. They expressed serious concerns that medical experts' erroneous findings could result in miscarriages of justice. The growing influence of forensic medicine in the courts lent a sense of urgency to demands for medicolegal reform. The most insistent calls for reform came from within the medical and legal professions; these calls intensified in the late nineteenth century.

But, many of the most ardent proponents for medicolegal reform were also the staunchest champions of legal medicine. In 1880 the lawyer and magistrate Charles Desmaze expressed his utmost confidence in legal medicine. Extolling the "utility and necessity of legal medicine," Desmaze claimed that it reduced crime: "As forensic medicine progresses, criminals are fewer." Considering forensic medicine indispensable to the pursuit of justice, Desmaze declared that forensic medical expertise saved the innocent and revealed the guilty.[114] Many other forensic doctors also emphasized the triumph of science and justice, while at the same time acknowledging the difficulties that practitioners of forensic medicine confronted in death investigations during this period. While doctors often advanced a similar triumphant narrative concerning poisoning cases, poison presented unique and vexing challenges.

2

Poisoning and the Problem of Proof

In 1840 a young aristocratic Frenchwoman went on trial for poisoning her husband, Charles Lafarge. Lafarge had presented himself as a wealthy manufacturer and owner of a large chateau. Shortly after their marriage, Marie Lafarge found that her husband was bankrupt and that their residence was dilapidated and rat infested. She obtained arsenic purportedly to exterminate the rats. Not long afterwards, her husband fell violently ill and died. Doctors who conducted the autopsy and chemical analyses found that arsenic was present in Charles's stomach and in the remains of the milk that Marie served him. But subsequent tests that chemists from Limoges performed using the newly developed Marsh apparatus found no trace of arsenic in the exhumed corpse.[1] As a result of the disagreements among medical experts during Marie's trial at the assize court in Tulle, the court called upon the renowned toxicologist Orfila to settle the dispute. To the defense's dismay, Orfila found traces of arsenic in the samples taken from the cadaver. The jury convicted Marie of murder, and the court sentenced her to life imprisonment. The well-known chemist and socialist politician François-Vincent Raspail challenged Orfila's findings – but arrived in Tulle eight hours too late to testify. The trial generated prolonged public controversy, and questions about Marie Lafarge's guilt divided French society. The Lafarge case was the first highly publicized criminal trial whose verdict seemed to hinge upon the Marsh test and toxicological evidence.[2]

At the heart of forensic medicine in nineteenth-century France was the problem of proof and determining what constituted reliable evidence, particularly in the nascent field of forensic toxicology. Changing understandings of the absorption of poisons in the body and the advent of new techniques, including the Marsh test, not only presented possibilities for demonstrative evidence of poisoning but also revealed the dangers of flawed forensic expertise. The Marsh apparatus could detect as little as 0.02 mg of arsenic by placing a sample in a flask with zinc and sulfuric acid. If the sample contained arsenic, arsine gas would form and pass into a narrow, horizontal tube. A flame beneath the tube heated the gas, and elemental arsenic would condense as a dark metallic film or 'mirror' beyond the heated area on a cold surface. Some scientists, jurists, and commentators issued warnings about the high sensitivity of the Marsh test, the possibility of numerous sources of contamination, and the problem of incompetent practitioners operating beyond the bounds of their knowledge and training. Cases such as the Lafarge trial led the public to ask whether forensic medicine would prevent miscarriages of justice, or lead to them.

Expert authority was both constructed and challenged in suspected poisoning cases in nineteenth-century France, amidst varying degrees of skepticism about and confidence in scientific and medical evidence. Poisoning investigations and trials often revealed a great deal of uncertainty surrounding the changing and contested state of toxicological knowledge.[3] Medicolegal experts frequently struggled to discern whether a death was caused by poisoning or natural causes, particularly during cholera epidemics, and had difficulty detecting traces of poison in cadavers. Their role in poisoning trials was often indecisive during the early nineteenth century, but their influence grew during the 1830s and 1840s. As doctors and chemists became more adept at detecting arsenic, poisoners resorted to poisons that were harder to detect, and the prosecution of poisoning declined during the second half of the nineteenth century. Throughout the century, controversies arose that pitted prominent Parisian experts against lesser-trained provincial practitioners and raised questions about the nature of toxicological knowledge and forensic expertise. Medicolegal experts sought to expose errors that could compromise the pursuit of justice and harm the dignity and reputation of their profession. However, their public battles over the state of scientific and medical knowledge in poisoning cases raised concerns that the very means by which they sought to establish their authority might undermine it.

The Rise of Forensic Toxicology

In most criminal investigations of suspected cases of poisoning, doctors performed an autopsy to determine whether the corpse displayed lesions that were characteristically produced by poisoning; then they or other experts, often pharmacists or chemists, subjected a portion of the stomach and intestines removed during the autopsy to chemical analyses. The findings of the doctors conducting the autopsy sometimes conflicted with those of the chemists performing chemical analyses. Practitioners of legal medicine, jurists, and jurors considered whether chemical evidence was necessary or whether medical and circumstance evidence were sufficient. The reports and testimonies of medicolegal experts, who sometimes engaged in courtroom and public battles, played an increasingly prominent, but not always decisive, role in poisoning trials. It was, of course, juries – neither doctors nor chemists – who made the ultimate determinations of guilt. During the early nineteenth century, medicolegal experts sought to refine their methods and communicate their findings to juries, judges, peers, and broader audiences, at the same time as they debated the shifting limits of forensic knowledge.

Poisoning was widely seen as a pervasive and pernicious crime. In 1803 Leclerc, a Strasbourg physician, declared in his forensic treatise on poisoning that the crime had never been more common in France and constituted a "horrible moral epidemic." He was troubled both by the secret nature of the crime and the close relationships between most victims and perpetrators. These perpetrators included monstrous fathers and husbands who poisoned their wives and children; "libertine" wives who, at the urging of their secret lovers, poisoned their husbands; and "unnatural" sons who poisoned their parents.[4] Poisoning inspired so much fear and interest because it was a crime shrouded in secrecy that could easily go undetected.

Practitioners of forensic medicine in Revolutionary and Napoleonic France insisted upon the importance and the difficulties of detecting poisoning. They commonly observed that detecting traces of poison in a cadaver or living person was one of the "most important" and "most difficult" aspects of legal medicine.[5] Leclerc stressed the problem of uncertainty among doctors trying to distinguish between a natural death and murder by poisoning. He observed, "Nothing is more equivocal than the signs of poisoning and nothing is more difficult to acquire than the certainty of his proofs." Leclerc lamented that the errors of incompetent practitioners led to the executions of innocent persons. Leclerc and other commentators observed that medicolegal experts and the courts needed to strike a delicate balance between preventing wrongful convictions and ensuring that poisoning crimes did not go unpunished.[6] In 1811 the physician François Chaussier similarly noted that medicolegal practitioners often struggled to detect material proof of poisoning and produced flawed forensic reports. He also observed that while the detection of poison was "so important for the social order and public security," forensic treatises offered little or limited instruction on the subject.[7] Fodéré maintained that there were strategic reasons behind the lack of instructive forensic publications on poisoning. He warned of "the danger of involving the public in some forms of knowledge that should only be in the hands of a small number of wise men." Reluctant to reveal certain scientific matters to the general public, Fodéré expressly omitted a discussion of "a large number of newly discovered poisonous substances" from his 1813 forensic treatise.[8] Other doctors bemoaned the paucity of medicolegal works on the subject of poisoning, although the body of literature rapidly expanded during the decades that followed.[9]

Some practitioners sought to expose the flawed methods and findings of their colleagues, and a battle among experts occurred when a twenty-two-year-old woman died suddenly in June 1814 in Montargis in the *département* of the Loiret. The doctors who conducted the autopsy, Dufour and Raige, observed a dark lesion in her stomach and concluded that the cause of death was arsenic poisoning. Another doctor, Elie Calabre de Breuze, later examined the stomach and refuted Dufour and Raige's findings. He declared, "The most novice doctors would easily recognize here an upset stomach that ended with cholera morbus. No wise and reflective doctor could find in any of these symptoms the slightest indication of a poisoning."[10] He criticized Dufour for signing off on Raige's "incoherent" and "most inept report" and Raige for soliciting the signatures of four military surgeons who had been in Montargis by chance and had never seen the cadaver. Calabre de Breuze insisted that none of these individuals had the appropriate forensic training or knowledge to weigh in on this affair.[11] When the deceased's husband went on trial before the assize court in Orléans for murder, seven professors at the medical faculty in Paris intervened, declaring that Raige and Dufour's forensic report was deeply flawed in every respect. They described it as "absurd, contradictory, and reprehensible" as well as "a monument...of ignorance." The following month, five other members of the Paris faculty of medicine intervened on behalf of the accused and issued a similar assessment. The *Journal of General Medicine* urged Raige and Dufour not to contest these findings for their own good and that of the profession: "Why would forensic doctors, before magistrates and before all citizens, dare to dampen confidence [in forensics] and expose themselves to ridicule?"[12] Nonetheless, Dufour and Raige published a defense of their report. They accused Calabre de Breuze of libel and insisted that they were right to dismiss cholera as a cause of death on account of the lack of vomiting.[13]

This conflict sparked debates about whether the chemical detection of poisons was necessary for cases in which doctors identified distinctive lesions indicative of poisoning. Jacques Raige-Delorme argued in defense of his father that it was not necessary. In his 1819 work on poisoning by corrosive substances, Raige-Delorme argued that doctors too frequently erroneously attributed deaths by poisoning to natural causes, due to their flawed ideas about the burden of proof. Raige-Delorme warned of the dangers of the precept, widely held by jurists and doctors, that it was better for ten guilty people to go free than one innocent person be convicted. He insisted that this laudable precept, indebted to Enlightenment-era critiques of miscarriages of justice, had become harmful when followed too rigorously and had allowed too many poisoners to escape justice. What is more, he argued that absolute certainty was an illusion in the natural sciences and an impossible criterion for forensic evaluations of poisoning. Raige-Delorme maintained that certain distinctive lesions on cadavers, specifically those produced by corrosive poisons, could constitute proof of poisoning. He observed that chemical analysis could be difficult or impossible when dealing with small quantities of poisons or poisons that had been evacuated through vomiting. He argued that an autopsy alone,

without a chemical analysis, could provide proof of poisoning in a
number of cases – the material discovery of poison was not necessary.[14] But, a growing number of medical practitioners and the first
scientists to refer to themselves as toxicologists insisted, on the contrary, that chemical evidence was the most decisive and necessary form
of proof of poisoning.

The state of toxicological knowledge was rapidly changing at that
time, and Orfila emerged as the leading figure in the field of forensic
toxicology. In 1812 Orfila began offering courses in chemistry, legal
medicine, anatomy, and botany in Paris. Orfila later recounted his
failed attempt to demonstrate to his students that standard liquid tests
could be used to detect arsenic. These liquid tests used various chemical reagents that would react in the presence of arsenic and other
poisons to produce characteristically colored precipitates. Orfila told
his students the tests would yield the same results regardless of the
organic substances mixed with the poison. However, the precipitate
that formed when Orfila added limewater to a solution of arsenic and
coffee was not the white color that he expected but instead violet-grey.
In dismay, he purportedly exclaimed, "Toxicology does not exist."[15]
He subsequently performed many experiments involving liquid tests
and found that most were unreliable, particularly for biological
samples. He also conducted postmortem autopsies and hundreds of
experiments on live animals, primarily dogs, to study the effects of
poisoning. He published his findings in his influential *Treatise on
Poisons* (1814–15), which examined the chemical properties of various poisons, their physiological effects on the living body, the treatment of poisoned persons, signs of poisoning in cadavers, and methods
of identifying poisons. The work also systematically classified poisons,
identified toxicology as a branch of medicine, and was a groundbreak-
ing study at the time.[16]

As Orfila's renown grew, he became the subject of praise, criticism,
and controversy. After Orfila published a book on poisoning for
medical men and laypersons alike in 1818, doctor Hector Chaussier
accused Orfila of copying his work, even its errors.[17] Orfila also drew
criticism for his animal experiments. The nature of this controversy in
France was not primarily ethical in nature. French physicians' experiments on live animals provoked far more outrage in Britain, where
strong antivivisection movements took shape.[18] In France, much of the

debates over Orfila and other physicians' animal experiments concerned the validity of extrapolating the findings of studies on poisons' effects on dogs and other animals to humans. At the same time that Orfila was conducting extensive animal experiments on poisons, drugs, and antidotes, François Magendie, the foremost figure in experimental physiology, was doing the same. Orfila's and Magendie's experimental techniques faced objections. The most controversial technique in their experimental toxicological research on live animals involved tying the esophagus in order to prevent animals from vomiting after introducing poison into their stomach. Critics argued that the ligature of the esophagus rendered their results inconclusive, since the surgical procedure and the animal's pain might produce inflammation and other effects that the researchers would mistakenly attribute to poison. Moreover, the prominent physician and anatomist Antoine Portal criticized Orfila for basing his work solely on experiments involving animals or chemical tests rather than clinical observations on poisoned persons.[19]

On the basis of their animal experiments, Magendie and Orfila independently came to similar conclusions regarding the absorption of poisons. Both physicians came to reject the received view that the effects of poisons on the body were localized in the digestive tract. They concluded that poisons were absorbed in the body and had harmful effects on the circulatory and nervous systems. Orfila also noted that poisons could be ingested or introduced into the body through other means, such as cutaneous absorption through the skin or insertion into the vagina or rectum, either during life or after death. He claimed that no crime "inspired as much horror" as introducing a poisonous substance in the rectum of a cadaver in order to frame an innocent person for poisoning. Orfila conducted animal experiments in which he hanged dogs and introduced various poisonous substances into their rectums after death. Based on these experiments and his understanding of absorption as a process only occurring in living bodies, Orfila maintained that medical experts could distinguish between poisons introduced before and after death based on whether the poison was absorbed in the internal organs.[20]

However, doctors and chemists faced considerable difficulties in detecting poison, particularly plant-based poisons, in human bodies, and the sensational murder trial of the physician Edme Castaing in

1823 put this problem into relief. In 1821 Castaing completed his medical studies in Paris, where he developed an interest in poisons, especially plant-based poisons that played an important role in Magendie's experimental research. He befriended two brothers, Hippolyte and Auguste Ballet, who were wealthy lawyers. In October 1822, Hippolyte, who was under Castaing's care, became suddenly ill and died. Hippolyte's will was not found. Castaing told Auguste that he had found it and destroyed it, after learning that their sister was the primary beneficiary. Castaing claimed that there was another copy of the will filed with a notary, and Auguste agreed to pay him 100,000 francs to arrange for its destruction. In December Auguste made a will naming Castaing the sole legatee and filed it on May 29, 1823. Two days later, Auguste became ill, and he died on June 1. Authorities investigating Castaing found that he had purchased 10 grains of morphine acetate seventeen days before Hippolyte's death and purchased 36 grains one day before Auguste's death. Although the doctors who conducted Auguste's autopsy did not find evidence of poisoning, authorities arrested Castaing and tried him for the murder of both Hippolyte and Auguste and for the destruction of Hippolyte's will.[21]

Castaing might have been the first person to use morphine to commit murder, and his trial, which was packed with spectators, fueled debates about the limits of chemical tests for poisons. Prominent Parisian physicians, including René Laënnec, Louis-Nicolas Vauquelin, Magendie, and Orfila, intervened in the trial. Orfila reviewed Auguste Ballet's autopsy report and could not determine whether Ballet had been poisoned, since the doctors could not detect traces of poison in the cadaver. Orfila explained that the challenge was a lack of remains from Auguste's vomit to chemically analyze. Orfila expressed confidence that if a sample of vomit contained morphine, he could furnish proof. He declared, "I could easily discover a single half grain of morphine acetate in a pint of liquid." He also praised the progress of forensic toxicology: "Until two or three years ago, it was a common error to suppose that certain vegetable poisons left no trace exclusive of any other symptom of disease; it was even an axiom of legal medicine. Today chemistry has made progress, and it is almost as easy to discover the vestiges of vegetable poisons as mineral poisons."[22] Other physicians testifying in the trial observed that certain plant poisons could cause death and yet leave no detectable trace.[23] The prosecutor Jacques Nicolas de Broë insisted that while the limits of forensic knowledge prevented doctors from furnishing forensic proof of poisoning against Castaing, the circumstantial proof of his guilt was overwhelming. Broë warned jurors that acquitting Castaing would give license to and encourage criminals to poison with impunity. Broë maintained that all citizens should fear the prospect of a doctor, a figure of authority in whom people put their trust and confidence, abusing scientific and medical knowledge by using it to harm and kill rather than to preserve life, while also evading justice.[24] The jury convicted Castaing for the murder of Auguste Ballet and sentenced him to death. After his conviction, he tried unsuccessfully to commit suicide by poison and was executed.[25] As a result of his trial, some judicial authorities appealed to the government to regulate poisonous substances more closely and to place medical practitioners under surveillance.[26]

Other trials revealed conflicts between prominent Parisian medical faculty who lambasted the medicolegal reports of medical practitioners in the provinces. This dynamic played out during the 1824 trial in the Aube involving a woman accused of poisoning her husband ten days after their wedding. The provincial doctors and *officiers de santé* who performed the autopsy determined that arsenic poisoning was the cause of death. However, authorities subsequently ordered the exhumation of the body and a new series of tests to be conducted by two doctors and a pharmacist. They did not find proof of poisoning. They also sent the suspected substance seized from the home of the accused and samples taken from the stomach of the deceased husband to Paris for analysis. Orfila, Vauquelin, and Barruel concluded that the substance was not poison. Orfila, who testified before the assize court in Troyes and later published his findings, denounced the initial forensic report as incomplete, insufficient, flawed. He maintained that its authors were unequipped to determine whether poisoning was the cause of death. He insisted that magistrates must only allow medical practitioners who were well trained in legal medicine to produce medicolegal reports for the courts.[27] Orfila and other practitioners continued to articulate growing concerns about inadequate forensic reports in poisoning cases in the provinces.

In doing so, these metropolitan practitioners sought to shore up their authority and combat the medical and scientific practices, particularly the garlic smell test, that they dismissed as outdated and antithetical to the pursuit of justice. In the aforementioned trial, the original provincial practitioners tested the stomach matter by placing the extract on hot coals. They concluded that the substance was arsenic oxide, since it exploded, burned, and gave off a garlic odor. Orfila dismissed their conclusion and declared that arsenic oxide neither explodes nor burns. He insisted that a garlic smell was not sufficient proof of arsenic, since other substances in the stomach could also emit the smell. Orfila also dismissed the notion that the death of thirteen leeches applied to the ailing man before his death could be seen as a proof of poisoning. Orfila insisted that carefully conducted liquid tests that could produce colored precipitates were necessary to prove the presence of poison.[28] Doctor J.-B. Seurre-Bousquet's 1829 treatise on arsenic echoed Orfila's condemnation of practitioners who concluded that a garlic odor was proof of arsenic in suspecting poisoning investigations. Their flawed conclusions put the lives of innocent persons at risk. Seurre-Bousquet also insisted that medical experts must not affirm poisoning unless the substance yielded the characteristic precipitates in rigorous chemical analyses.[29] Liquid tests involving chemical assays were the preferred method of establishing proof during this period, despite the difficulties associated with these tests and the subjective nature of evaluating the color of precipitates.

Magistrates questioned the effectiveness of such tests when bodies had been buried for weeks, months, or even years. During the 1820s, Orfila and other practitioners insisted that putrefaction was not an insurmountable obstacle in detecting poisoning.[30] During the 1829 trial of Joséphine Bouvier, the investigating magistrate asked the medicolegal experts whether they could detect poison in a long-buried corpse. Authorities had suspected Bouvier of poisoning her wealthy father seven years earlier, when she feared that he might disinherit her. Joséphine purchased arsenic nine days before a dinner party she hosted. After that dinner, her father became violently ill and died shortly thereafter. The cook, Marie Michel, was suspicious about the circumstances surrounding his death and was convinced of Joséphine's role in it. Joséphine offered Michel large sums to be paid out years later if she remained silent. When the payments never materialized, Michel alerted the authorities. Medicolegal practitioners performed precipitate tests on a sample extracted from Joseph

Bouvier's exhumed body and determined that he had ingested a large amount of arsenic. In November 1829 the Ain assize court tried Joséphine for poisoning her father, and her defense counsel claimed that the original forensic report was erroneous. Despite this challenge to the forensic evidence, Joséphine was found guilty. In 1832 she faced a new hearing, in which her defense not only cast further doubt on the forensic evidence but also depicted Joseph Bouvier as licentious and alleged that Marie Michel had been having an affair with him. The jury acquitted Joséphine.[31] Although medicolegal practitioners and magistrates became convinced that poison could be detected long after death, jurors might have viewed these cases with skepticism.

Doctors and scientists tended to have the greatest difficulties in detecting poison in human tissues; they more commonly detected poison in samples of vomit and suspected substances, such as white powder, seized from the residence of the accused. This was the case in the 1829 trial of twenty-four-year-old Françoise Trenque before the Gers assize court. Trenque purportedly slowly poisoned her family members over the course of six months in 1828 and 1829. Her father, mother, and two brothers died. Two other family members became gravely ill. Two doctors and one *officier de santé* performed autopsies on the four deceased family members. They observed physical symptoms of poisoning but could not detect traces of poison in the bodies. Investigators attributed this absence to prolonged vomiting prior to death. A professor of medicine in Paris and a pharmacist performed chemical analyses on samples of vomit and a white powder found in Trenque's armoire and detected arsenic. The jury convicted Trenque, and she was executed.[32] But in this and other trials during the period, the role of forensic evidence in shaping juries' verdicts was unclear.

Doctors' inability to detect poison in the bodies of presumably poisoned persons did not necessarily deter juries from convicting accused poisoners on the basis of other evidence. For example, jurors serving at the Pas-de-Calais assize court convicted Séraphine Pruvost of poisoning her son-in-law in 1829. Pruvost had served him soup, which he said had a strange taste and burned his throat. She urged him to continue eating it. He gave a little to the dog, and it became ill for two days. The son-in-law became sick with vomiting and died two days later. Doctors were unable to detect any inflammation or other signs of poisoning in his body but surmised that prolonged vomiting might have eliminated the traces of poison. Despite the absence of forensic evidence, jurors convicted Pruvost on the basis of "overwhelming moral proofs," and she was executed.[33] Jurors in the *département* of the Somme in 1830 similarly convicted a man accused of poisoning his wife with arsenic even though prominent medical experts, including Orfila and Barruel, did not find proof of poisoning.[34] These jurors weighed the circumstantial evidence against the absence of forensic evidence and found the circumstantial evidence or "moral proofs" sufficient.

There was considerable uncertainty among jurors, magistrates, doctors, and the public about the nature of toxicological knowledge in the early nineteenth century. Forensic doctors debated whether physiological symptoms of poisoning and physiological evidence constituted proof of poisoning and which methods for detecting poison were reliable. Many forensic doctors, who recognized their inability to distinguish between the signs of poisoning and those of diseases such as cholera, insisted that discovering the corpus delicti, the poison itself, was crucial. However, jurists often observed that physicians and scientists were unable to establish the corpus delicti in many cases in which the guilt of the accused seemed evident. Proliferating works on poisons and toxicology often questioned what constituted proof of poison and sought to expose errors in the detection of poisoning.

Poison in the Time of Cholera

In the 1830s, medicolegal experts' influence in poisoning trials greatly increased, and the prosecutions of poisoning peaked. Poisoners hoped that poisonings would be mistaken for deaths by natural causes and diseases, such as cholera, yet the poisoners also feared medicolegal experts' findings. These fears led a man accused of murdering his goddaughter by poisoning her soup with arsenic in 1832 to approach one of the two surgeons conducting the autopsy and beg him to convince his colleague that the cause of death was not poisoning.[35] Growing confidence in medicolegal experts' abilities to detect poison in long-buried bodies led judicial authorities to order the exhumation of the bodies of persons whose deaths had been attributed to cholera or other natural causes and to ramp up efforts to bring poisoners to justice. However, public battles over the state of toxicology during the

1830s and early 1840s raised questions about whether justice would be served and expert authority preserved.

The cholera epidemic of 1832 heightened fears of innocent people being falsely convicted of poisoning and guilty persons going free, with their crimes mistaken for natural deaths. There were concerns that poisoning was on the rise, as some saw a moment of opportunity in cholera epidemics to poison those whom they wished dead. Moreover, the epidemic sparked fears that those presumed to be suffering from cholera were actually victims of poisoning. During the cholera epidemic of 1832, the *Gazette médicale de Paris* printed a report from Brest declaring, "Everywhere that cholera has broken out, rumors of poisoning have spread." The journal urged doctors conducting autopsies to be careful not to mistake a murder by poisoning for cholera.[36] Additionally, some Parisians who feared that the state was ordering physicians to secretly poison persons afflicted with cholera attacked and murdered several medical practitioners in April 1832.[37]

Most poisonings were tied to marital or familial conflicts, matters of inheritance, or both. Some doctors and social commentators attributed the prevalence of poisoning to the inability of couples to divorce. After the July Revolution of 1830, legislators in 1831 attempted to reestablish divorce (which had been legalized during the Revolution but abolished in 1816), by introducing a bill that passed the Chamber of Deputies but was later rejected by the Chamber of Peers. In January 1833 the Parisian doctor Chabaneau appeared before the Chamber of Deputies and argued poisonings would decline if divorce were legalized. He observed that French courts did not prosecute any murder or poisoning of spouses after the Chamber of Deputies approved the divorce bill in 1831 but that the number of these prosecutions rose dramatically after the Chamber of Peers rejected the legislation in March 1832.[38] Others viewed greed and the desire to secure an inheritance as a more important motivation for poisoning than marital discord.

Both matters of marriage and inheritance shaped the 1834 trial of Rose Quesney. The forty-four-year-old domestic servant appeared before the Eure assize court on charges of poisoning her unmarried master, Jacques Deshayes. The two had been in a sexual relationship, and Deshayes's will named her an heir. When Quesney took another lover whom she wished to marry, Deshayes disapproved, and Quesney worried that he would disinherit her. Once Deshayes became ill after eating a soup that Quesney served him, he suspected poisoning. Deshayes promptly tore his will into pieces, which Quesney snatched up, and then died. Quesney presented the will to the courts, and suspicions led to Deshaye's exhumation and autopsy. Medicolegal experts determined that he had died from poisoning. They detected a considerable amount of arsenic in his intestines in repeated tests and determined that he had been poisoned with a large dose. The jury sentenced Quesney to death.[39]

The chemist Alphonse Chevallier and physician Jules Louis Charles Boys de Loury analyzed patterns and motives in poisoning trials and suggested possible means of curbing these crimes. In 1834 Chevallier and Boys de Loury published a study based on ninety-four poisoning trials involving sixty men and thirty-four women, among the 273 persons charged with the crime between 1825 and 1831. They determined that financial interests motivated the greatest number of poisonings. They also identified "libertinism," vengeance, and jealousy as other common motives. The accused often procured poisonous substances under the pretense of killing pests or nuisance animals or using the substance in their line of work. They administered poison most frequently in soup but also in milk, flour, wine, bread, chocolate, or medications. The authors observed that death in some cases was averted due to a suspicious taste or color, such as greenish food or drink when poisoners used verdigris, which consisted of poisonous copper compounds. They recommended adding pigment to white arsenic and other poisons, especially when the taste of a poisoned substance was not distinctive, so that the color of the poison would serve as a warning and prevent accidental deaths as well as murders.[40] Nevertheless, the assumption underlying most medicolegal literature of the period was that reliable detection of poisoning was the most effective means of preventing the crime and deterring would-be poisoners.

However, chemical evidence of poison often remained elusive. For example, medicolegal experts struggled to provide chemical proof of poisoning in the trial of Marie-Adélaïde Hébert in Calvados in 1834. Hébert was accused of poisoning her wealthy seventy-four-year-old mother in order to secure her 500 francs inheritance more quickly. Hébert had purchased a large quantity of arsenic, purportedly to exterminate rats, and discussed the effects of arsenic with a neighbor. Hébert served her mother curdled milk, which she observed tasted strange. She then experienced vomiting, vertigo, and cramps. The dog that ate the rest of the milk died. Medicolegal experts performed chemical analyses of its intestines, but none of the tests detected poison. Nonetheless, the doctor who examined the animal's organs was convinced that it had died from poisoning and maintained that violent vomiting preceding its death had eliminated the traces of poison in its body. Despite the negative results of the chemical analysis, the court sentenced Hébert to death.[41] Jurors convicted the accused despite the lack of chemical evidence in this and other trials when medical evidence – in this case, the lesions and inflammation in the dog's digestive organs – was consistent with the circumstantial evidence.

Some judicial authorities questioned whether deficiencies in forensic evidence were a product of the limitations of certain practitioners or the limitations of the science itself. In a report to the Minister of Interior in 1838, the president of the assize court of Riom denounced the incompetence of the medicolegal experts involved in the investigation of Anne Betoin, a wet nurse tried for poisoning her employer. The doctors and chemists in Montluçon who conducted the autopsy and chemical analyses could not detect the presence of arsenic. The jurist attributed the medicolegal experts' inability to do so to their incompetence or their faulty instruments and laboratory – possibly both. These experts were aware of their own limitations and reported that they only used part of the samples provided to them and conserved the remainder to be analyzed by more knowledgeable experts or those with better laboratories. The court ordered more distinguished scientists to perform new experiments. The president of the court was eager for the jury to hear the testimony of the new experts who could better articulate and elucidate their findings in clear terms to the jurors.[42] Additionally, the president of the Gard assize court remarked that a case tried before the court in December 1838 hinged upon the scientific, medical, and chemical evidence or lack thereof, on the one hand, and the circumstantial and testimonial evidence, on the other. The trial featured long scientific debates involving experts, some of whom initially detected morphine in the stomach contents, while three chemists later found no trace of morphine or opium. The president of the court remarked, "The science is too uncertain and too conjectural to offer sufficient facts for conviction in criminal matters."[43] The forensic detection of poisoning was challenging for scientists and medical practitioners who needed to persuade juries of their findings, and the rapidly changing state of the field of toxicology heightened these challenges.

One of the significant changes in toxicology during this period involved new understandings of the absorption of poisons and the means of their detection in human tissues. Earlier in the nineteenth century, Orfila had maintained that poisons were absorbed from the gastrointestinal tract and then accumulated in certain tissues. Nonetheless, medicolegal experts typically searched for traces of poisons only in the digestive tract and samples of vomit. When doctors performing an autopsy did not detect the presence of arsenic in the stomach or intestines, they declared in their forensic reports that they found no trace of poison. In 1839 Orfila first extracted arsenic from human organs outside the gastrointestinal tract in the body of Soufflard, a convicted murderer who committed suicide in the Conciergerie prison by taking a large quantity of arsenic. With the enhanced sensitivity of the Marsh test that the British chemist James Marsh first developed in 1836 (see Figure 2.1), Orfila detected arsenic in Soufflard's liver, kidney, and lungs.[44] Orfila later applied these same procedures when he served as a medicolegal expert in the trial of Louis Mercier, accused of poisoning his son in December 1838 following his remarriage to a woman who abhorred her new stepson. The doctors conducting the autopsy suspected poisoning. However, three chemists in Dijon who tested liquid from the son's intestines, first with hydrogen sulfide and then with the Marsh apparatus, were unable to find any arsenic, even when they repeated these tests on pieces of his stomach and intestines that they boiled in nitric acid. Continued suspicions led the court to send the body in a barrel to Paris for examination by Orfila, Devergie, Le Sueur, and Ollivier. It had been buried five months earlier and at that point was in an advanced stage of decomposition, but Orfila and his colleagues detected arsenic in Mercier's liver and the putrid fluid surrounding his body in the barrel. They also analyzed the soil where the body had been buried and found no arsenic, thus concluding that the arsenic present in the body had not been absorbed from the ground surrounding it. During the trial, the defense

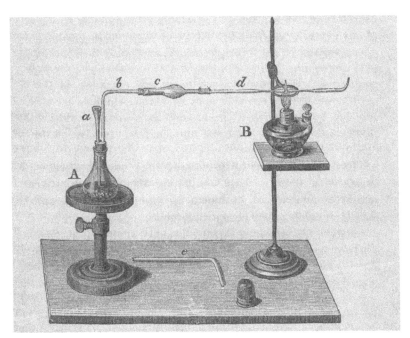

FIGURE 2.1 An engraving of the Marsh apparatus. Theodore G. Wormley, *Microchemistry of Poisons,* 1867, National Library of Medicine

summoned the rival expert Raspail to challenge Orfila and Devergie's methods and findings. The judge ordered Orfila, Devergie, and three other colleagues to conduct more testing in Raspail's presence, and their results confirmed the presence of arsenic. The trial culminated in Mercier's conviction.[45]

Raspail emerged as Orfila's most dogged critic, insisting that his flawed forensic reports resulted in the wrongful conviction of innocent men and women. The republican Raspail and royalist Orfila clashed on both ideological and scientific grounds. Raspail was convinced that Orfila and other forensic experts were committing tragic errors, which future advances in toxicology would someday bring to light, but medicolegal errors could not be truly corrected once the sword of justice had swung to convict and execute a person. Raspail declared, "A mistake may be corrected in chemistry, but in legal medicine it is irreparable."[46] Raspail was particularly concerned about provincial trials in which the prosecution called upon Orfila and other Parisian professors who wielded great authority and inspired fear among provincial practitioners, who were reluctant to mount a strong challenge against them. Moreover, jurors and judges were too deferential toward medical experts, especially elite practitioners, in Raspail's estimation. Raspail complained, "In the eyes of the court, to doubt the supremacy of the expert is to utter a blasphemy against forensic medicine."[47] Raspail embraced the role of defense expert to contest purportedly flawed forensic evidence. He proclaimed, "Since 1828, I have not stopped seizing any opportunities that present themselves to rebuke the temerity with which medicolegal opinions are generally given before the law."[48] When combatting Orfila in the Mercier trial of 1839, Raspail declared, "Gentlemen, you must doubt the omnipotence of forensic chemistry because it refutes itself every six months."[49] The unreliable doctrines of forensic chemistry, constantly changing from month to month, resulted in wrongful convictions. Raspail maintained that there were probably more innocent than guilty people among those convicted on the basis of medicolegal expertise.[50] He argued that Orfila was personally responsible for a number of wrongful convictions and accused Orfila of operating under the principle that it was better for one innocent to perish than for one guilty person to escape justice. In contrast, Raspail espoused the doctrine that it was better for twenty guilty persons to escape justice than to compromise the life or liberty of one innocent person.[51]

Moreover, Raspail was alarmed about the high sensitivity of the Marsh test and the possibility of numerous sources of contamination, for example, impurities in the reagents used to create chemical reactions in the Marsh apparatus, in the vessels used for transporting cadavers, and on the painted green surfaces upon which cadavers might rest. Raspail argued that arsenic was nearly everywhere in nature and in France's industrial economy and society. Indeed, it was sold by pharmacists as rat poison and as medication (Fowler's solution), inhaled by workers in certain factories, and present in soil.[52] Raspail's warnings about the risks of testing for arsenic with the Marsh apparatus and his attacks on Orfila's overconfidence led Orfila to defend himself vigorously and to spread public awareness of the Marsh apparatus. Moreover, the clashes between Orfila and Raspail engendered broader debates within and beyond the medical community, and the Lafarge trial thrust these debates into the national limelight.[53]

Orfila's methods, particularly his animal experiments, attracted more scrutiny and criticism beyond the medical community as his celebrity grew. Some French commentators objected to the scope and methods of Orfila's thousands of fatal animal experiments.[54] An 1840 article in a social science journal distinguished between legitimate animal experiments, which could lead to developments in the treatment for various conditions, and "cruel experiments" involving the unnecessary poisoning and torturing of dogs. The article also complained that the preoccupation with forensic medicine and detecting poison led to the relative neglect of the social dimensions of the crime and means of prevention. It maintained that those who detected an atom of arsenic in the body of a poisoned person were met with "celebrity and honors," while "disdain and taunts" greeted those who sought to eliminate the underlying causes of the crime of poisoning.[55] Scientific celebrity and debates over the futility, utility, and validity of toxicological research and forensic findings found visual expression in Honoré Daumier's *The Friendship of a Great Chemist Is Not Always a Godsend.* The 1841 satirical lithograph was captioned: "I am so sure of my findings that now, if you wish, I will poison my close friend...and I will find arsenic in the lens of his glasses." Two dogs, presumably also poisoned by the "great chemist," lie dead in the corner of image (Figure 2.2).

Medical practitioners and laypeople questioned the reliability and effectiveness of medicolegal expertise. In the wake of the Lafarge trial, one doctor writing about the challenges of forensic expertise recommended the creation of a committee of forensic doctors to be consulted as needed by the assize courts.[56] The following year in 1841, Léonard Borie, a doctor in Tulle, discussed the problem of the courts summoning medical practitioners who lacked the experience and means to evaluate poisoning and produced flawed reports as a result. He noted that some doctors had been calling for the assize courts to summon only specially designated doctors and pharmacists as experts and to provide these men with all of the instruments and chemical reagents necessary for their work. Maintaining that forensic expertise hinged upon jurors' understanding of it, Borie announced that the purpose of his *Toxicological Catechism* was to present complex forensic knowledge in terms that lay persons could readily understand. Nevertheless, he acknowledged that this state of knowledge,

FIGURE 2.2 A satirical lithograph of a toxicologist, presumably a caricature of
Orfila, presenting his friend as an experimental subject to prove his ability to
detect arsenic. Two dead dogs are hidden from the onlookers' view. Honoré
Victorin Daumier, *L'Amitié d'un grand chimiste...* 1841, National Gallery
of Art, Washington, D.C.

particularly concerning the Marsh test, was rapidly changing and in
flux: "There is not a week that goes by when the [Marsh apparatus] is
not modified, which obviously proves that it still has serious draw-
backs."[57] Other doctors, such as Tardieu, observed that the recent
advancements in toxicology "introduced doubt about the value of the
tools."[58] The writer George Sand, for one, doubted the reliability of

toxicological expertise. In a letter to the painter Eugène Delacroix in 1840, Sand wrote, "Maybe Orfila will discover in the next six months that arsenic does exist in the liver or in the brain of all corpses." Sand's remarks were somewhat prescient, as some doctors soon insisted that while arsenic may not be in the liver and brain of all corpses, it could be found in trace amounts in certain parts of all human bodies.[59]

Shortly after the introduction of the Marsh test in France, controversy erupted over the so-called discovery of "normal arsenic" and its subsequent rejection. In 1838 the physician and chemist Jean-Pierre Couerbe introduced this concept that arsenic was found in healthy human bodies. After finding arsenic in the bones and flesh of the decomposing bodies of persons who had not been poisoned, Couerbe wondered whether the process of putrefaction produced arsenic or whether arsenic was a natural component of a healthy human body. He worked alongside Orfila to resolve the question, and Orfila became convinced that arsenic could be found in very small quantities in the bones of unpoisoned animals and corpses. Nonetheless, he considered the existence of "normal arsenic" a dangerous principle for forensic medicine because attorneys and judges could cast doubt on the discovery of arsenic in a corpse in a poisoning case by suggesting it was "normal arsenic." He sought to resolve these troubling medicolegal implications. He believed that normal arsenic was located in bones and not dissolved in boiling water, thus it could be distinguished from ingested arsenic. Consequently, Orfila advised boiling the corpses of suspected poisoning victims and only examining their internal organs. In 1840 pharmacist Charles Flandin and glass-blower Ferdinand Danger refuted the notion of normal arsenic on the basis of their experiments with the Marsh apparatus. France's Academy of Science and its Academy of Medicine created special committees tasked with reassessing the Marsh test and examining the issue of normal arsenic. The committee of the Academy of Science requested that Orfila repeat his experiments in their presence, but he was unable to obtain any trace of normal arsenic when he did so. A report by the committee in 1841 concluded that normal arsenic did not exist, but the issue of normal arsenic continued to sow confusion in the courts during the years that followed.[60]

Many poisoning trials and investigations in the early 1840s, such as those of Auguste Michel and Jules Phalipon, involved conflicting toxicological reports, contested forensic findings, and marital infidelity. In 1838 Michel impregnated his mistress and purchased arsenic with the declared intention of poisoning rats. Shortly thereafter, Michel's wife became ill and subsequently died. Doctors at the time did not attribute her illness or subsequent death to poisoning. But, in 1839 authorities exhumed her body after receiving an anonymous letter declaring that she had been poisoned. Three professors of medicine at the faculty of Montpellier found arsenic in her corpse and attributed her death to chronic poisoning. Two years later in 1841 Francesco Rognetta, an Italian physician and critic of Orfila, intervened to refute the findings of these physicians and argued that the "recent progress of science" nullified their report. He denounced their work as flawed in many respects and protested that they did not ensure the purity of the reagents in their chemical analyses. After four hours of deliberation, the jury acquitted Michel.[61] Phalipon, accused of poisoning her husband Jean-Antoine Gautier in 1839 in order to marry her lover, met a different fate. Experts in Villefranche conducted chemical analyses using the Marsh apparatus but did not detect arsenic in Gautier's body. Phalipon was released on the basis of the report. She then gave birth eight months after her husband's death, and the paternity was attributed to Gautier. The child lived only twelve days, and upon the child's death, Phalipon gained inheritance rights to her husband's estate. She married four months later in May. Lafarge's trial in 1840 inspired authorities to reopen the case. In June 1841 they sent samples of Gautier's stomach and intestines, which had been hermetically sealed and preserved, to Montpellier to be newly examined, since medicolegal experts had refined their methods of detecting arsenic since the initial examination. Three professors at the faculty of medicine and pharmacy in Montpellier detected arsenic in Gautier's remains. Phalipon went on trial before the Aveyron assize court in 1842, and the experts who had performed the initial analyses admitted that Gautier's death could only be attributed to poisoning. The court sentenced Phalipon to death.[62]

The Marsh test and other toxicological developments presented possibilities and perils for medical experts in poisoning cases. During trials, attorneys and medical experts, particularly those summoned by the defense, often highlighted the risks of error due to the Marsh apparatus's high sensitivity and the element of uncertainty. A defense lawyer in an 1843 arsenic poisoning trial asked, "But what is science, if not a continuous succession of incomplete and relative truths and uncertain probabilities? What is science, which denies tomorrow the axioms of today and walks hesitantly and without a guide through the maze of doubtful progress?" He insisted that "deplorable controversies" over poisoning and toxicology within the medical and scientific communities had called the very notion of scientific certainty into question. He asked, "Do you know whether new discoveries will soon shatter your present-day certainty and your scientific pride like glass?"[63] Judges and jurists also expressed frustrations over forensic expertise, particularly when it was inconclusive or hesitant. During an 1843 trial in Riom involving possible lead poisoning, a jurist objected to the medicolegal experts' hesitant formulations, such as poisoning being "probable," "extremely probable," or "excessively probable." He ordered Orfila to give definitive conclusions: "Toxicology cannot admit any doubt...There either is or is not a poisoning."[64] Pharmacist Jules Barse declared that chemists and magistrates should proceed with "extreme delicateness" due to the nature of the Marsh test. Barse wrote, "Arsenic was found everywhere. This new method, this shining light, will soon only illuminate a state of chaos."[65] He observed that scientific developments following the adoption of the Marsh apparatus and debates over normal arsenic had created a state of confusion.

Forensic expertise in a number of poisoning trials left jurors and judges perplexed. Through highly publicized press coverage of poisoning trials, the public gained increasing awareness of the dissidence of opinions of experts summoned by the courts and the contested state of toxicological knowledge. In some cases, doctors performed an autopsy and found medical indications of poisoning, but chemical analyses only produced negative results. Nonetheless, juries would sometimes convict on the basis of other evidence and "moral proofs." In other cases, the high sensitivity of the Marsh test and impurities in the reagents yielded false positives and raised concerns about judicial errors and wrongful convictions. Moreover, fear of poisoning was widespread. Commentators observed that poisoning was a hidden crime with often subtle effects, which could elude scientific detection and sow doubt among jurors. Doctor Cormenin described poisoning as "a crime that hides in the shadows, creeps into the family household, and terrifies society." Like more and more

doctors, jurists, and concerned citizens, Cormenin called for more
regulations and restrictions on the sale of arsenic.[66] However, some
commentators articulated concerns that poisonings by other substances were more difficult to detect, and they saw no easy answers
to the problem of poisoning and its detection.

The Chemistry of Crime

Arsenic poisonings continued to concern forensic experts, the courts,
and the public throughout the rest of the nineteenth century. However,
as medical experts became more adept at detecting arsenic and metallic
poisons, toxicologists' attention shifted to plant-derived alkaloid
poisons, a class of toxic, naturally occurring organic compounds.
These newly studied alkaloid poisons, including strychnine,
morphine, and nicotine, seemed to become the preferred weapon of
murderers who were knowledgeable about poisons and toxicology.
Medicolegal experts grappled with challenges in developing chemical
tests for alkaloid and other poisons and in conducting physiological
animal experiments. Forensic expertise inspired both skepticism and
confidence, while continuing to generate controversies within and
beyond the medical and scientific communities and the judicial arena.

Practitioners of legal medicine expressed concerns about criminals
using toxicological knowledge to their advantage as well as lay persons dismissing the medicolegal findings of elite outsiders. In his 1845
Assize Court Manual for Questions of Poisoning, Barse observed that
criminals could learn the limits of forensic toxicology and discern
which poisons were the most difficult to detect by reading forensic
treatises, like his own, and studying poisons and toxicology. Barse
noted that some of his peers called for a ban on the sale of arsenic but
warned that such a ban would lead to criminals using poisons that
were less familiar to medicolegal experts and thus harder to detect. He
insisted that scientists needed to continue to study all poisons and that
only highly trained experts should conduct chemical analyses and
toxicological tests. Barse complained about the problem of overzeal-
ous authorities, such as a mayor, justice of the peace, or police com-
missioner, enlisting a herbalist, grocer, or empiric to examine a portion
of a suspect substance. Barse lamented that many villagers respected
their flawed findings more than the scientific expertise of renowned

physicians and scientists from Paris.[67] However, most judicial verdicts revealed that jurors gave the findings of Parisian experts greater weight than provincial practitioners' findings.

Medical experts' expanding abilities to detect poisoning led some poisoners to go to great lengths to destroy bodily evidence. For example, in 1845 the body of Jean-Georges Gloeckler was found in a cesspit with several organs removed. The Bas-Rhin assize court charged Gloeckler's wife, Salomé Riehl, with poisoning him as well as murdering her five-year-old step-daughter who died from falling – or being pushed – from the window of their fifth-floor home five years earlier. Authorities maintained that Riehl had slowly poisoned her husband with arsenic and then cut up his body. She removed his intestines, stomach, kidneys, liver, pancreas, spleen, and heart, which were later recovered from the cesspit. The assize court summoned Gabriel Tourdes, professor of legal medicine in Strasbourg, and his colleague to analyze Gloeckler's remains. They attributed his death to typhoid fever, and chemists in Strasbourg who tested samples of his organs found no trace of arsenic or other poison. The court later summoned experts in Paris who used a different protocol and detected arsenic in Gloeckler's organ samples. The court convicted Riehl and sentenced her to life of hard labor.[68] Forensic expertise also resulted in the conviction of Joseph Boyard in 1846, despite his efforts to evade justice. Boyard purportedly poisoned his mother-in-law with arsenic so that his wife would more rapidly secure her inheritance. The investigation revealed that Boyard had approached a doctor to inquire about exhumations and autopsies. He asked whether a poisoned person's vomiting would effectively eliminate the traces of the poison. The doctor told him that it would not. Boyard then waited until night to dig up the body of his mother-in-law and switched it with that of a woman of a similar age who had recently died. Authorities discovered the switch, and the doctors who examined his wife's actual body found arsenic in all of her digestive organs. The Isère assize court sentenced Boyard to death.[69]

Other poisonings went undetected for years until a troubling pattern came into relief, such as with the serial killer Hélène Jégado. Her spree probably began in 1833 when she was working as a domestic servant for a priest in Brittany. Within the span of three months, seven people in his household became violently sick and then died, including the priest and Jégado's sister. Hélène then assumed her late sister's former position working at the rectory of a parish priest. Three people died there in the span of three months, including Jégado's aunt and relatives of the priest. The pattern continued in the subsequent households where Jégado was employed as a cook or servant for nearly two decades in various towns across Brittany. In 1850 Jégado entered into the service of Théophile Bidard de la Noë, a law professor in Rennes. Two weeks after Jégado's arrival, the domestic servant Rose Texier became ill and died. Her replacement became ill and promptly quit her position. A doctor later determined that she had been given poison in small doses. Then another servant, Rosalie Sarrazin, died. Bidard and local doctors suspected foul play. The autopsies of Texier and Sarrazin documented signs of arsenic poisoning. Malagutti, professor of chemistry in Rennes, conducted the chemical analysis of the samples extracted from their corpses and that of a third victim. He detected arsenic in all three. In December 1851 Jégado went on trial in the Ille-et-Vilaine assize court for three murders by poisoning, three attempted poisonings, and eleven thefts. Many other poisonings, attempted poisonings, and thefts were not tried, owing to the statute of limitations. The estimated number of poisoning victims was over thirty; some, like Raspail, considered it to be over forty.[70] Jégado's mental state was an issue in the trial, but she was deemed sane, convicted, and executed. Raspail and others lamented that Jégado's killings had gone on for so long without doctors calling for criminal investigations or identifying poisoning as the cause of death for Jégado's numerous victims prior to 1851.[71]

Raspail complained of a broader pattern of doctors mistaking poisonings for natural diseases. Raspail claimed that on average only one out of every twenty murders by poisoning was investigated, in part due to medical men's incompetence. Furthermore, he argued that people were hesitant to throw suspicion on the truly guilty as a result of previous flawed forensic expertise that victimized innocent persons. Meanwhile, flawed forensic expertise continued to lead to wrongful convictions.[72] It is, of course, impossible to quantify how many people were wrongly convicted or got off scot-free. Some forensic experts struggled to balance the need to proceed cautiously amidst scientific uncertainty in order to protect and safeguard the innocent and the risk that too much circumspection would result in poisoning crimes continuing unabated and without justice.

Poisoners' study of chemistry and poisons became a stimulus for further toxicological research and new techniques. During the 1851 murder trial of the Belgian nobleman Count Hippolyte Visart de Bocarmé for poisoning his brother-in-law Gustave Fougnies, Bocarmé's wife revealed that her husband sought lessons in chemistry to learn how to extract nicotine from tobacco. Bocarmé admitted that he studied this process and consulted Orfila's work and other writings on nicotine. He confessed to burning Orfila and Chevallier's books so that investigators would not discover his study of chemistry. However, at the same time as Bocarmé's poisoning of Fougnies in 1850, the Belgian chemist Jean Servais Stas pioneered a method for extracting alkaloids from biological specimens for toxicological purposes, which he employed in Bocarmé's trial. Stas, a former student of Orfila, extracted nicotine from Fougnies's stomach and other tissues with an acidic alcohol solution.[73] The defense called upon Orfila to respond to several forensic questions pertaining to the trial. However, Orfila's testimony and his own animal experiments involving nicotine did not undermine Stas's damning findings. Bocarmé was convicted and executed.[74] But, academic controversy ensued, as Orfila was accused of claiming credit or scientific priority for Stas's discovery.[75] During the years that followed, the Stas's method became widely taught and adopted as the standard means of extracting alkaloids.

Over the course of the nineteenth century, the prevalence and nature of poisoning shifted, as the state of scientific knowledge evolved. Arsenic had been the preferred poison, since it was readily available and also odorless and tasteless. However, as forensic experts refined methods of arsenic detection with the Marsh test, poisoning by other mineral poisons and plant-based alkaloids became more common. By 1860, trials involving poisoning by phosphorus, most commonly extracted from matches, became more common than those involving arsenic.[76] Doctors and scientists attributed this shift to the ease with which medical experts could detect arsenic and their difficulties in detecting phosphorus poisoning.[77] Some doctors called for a ban on white phosphorus, the highly toxic and most common allotropic form of phosphorus. They advocated substituting red phosphorus, a nontoxic type of phosphorus discovered in the mid-nineteenth century, in the manufacturing of matches. They intended this reform to protect the health of workers in matchstick factories and to prevent criminal poisonings by white phosphorus.[78] However, phosphorus and arsenic remained the most commonly used poisons, followed by copper sulfate, verdigris, sulfuric acid, and cantharides.[79] French forensic doctors also studied less common forms of poisoning, such as strychnine poisoning, which gained notoriety through the 1856 trial of the English doctor William Palmer.[80] During the 1850s and 1860s, medicolegal and toxicological research largely moved away from the study of arsenic to other poisons.

When unable to detect poison through chemical analyses, medical experts often conducted physiological animal experiments, such as in the Pommerais affair. Following the death of Julie de Pauw in 1863, authorities began investigating her lover, the homeopathic doctor Edmond-Désiré Couty de la Pommerais, whom they suspected of murder and insurance fraud. Pommerais had instructed de Pauw to take out eight life insurance policies naming him as beneficiary. The couple subsequently falsely claimed that de Pauw had fallen down the stairs.[81] Weeks later de Pauw became suddenly ill and died. Immediately after her death, Pommerais submitted claims to the insurance companies. Suspicions of Pommerais led to the exhumation of her body. Tardieu's autopsy found that de Pauw was pregnant but did not find conclusive proof of poisoning. Tardieu and Roussin then chemically analyzed her viscera and the vomit residue scraped from the floor of de Pauw's bedroom, but they did not detect poison. They injected the sample of extracts of de Pauw's stomach and intestines into a dog's thigh. The dog vomited twice and appeared to be in pain but eventually recovered. A rabbit that was fed the extracts died. Tardieu and Roussin conducted the same experiments with the vomit residue, resulting in the deaths of a dog and a rabbit. Tardieu and Roussin surmised that the vomit contained a higher concentration of poison than de Pauw's organs. Based on their animal experiments, they inferred that de Pauw had been poisoned with a vegetable poison, probably digitalin extracted from the leaves and seeds of foxglove plants, which could not be chemically detected.[82] In May 1864 Pommerais went on trial for poisoning de Pauw as well as his mother-in-law, having attempted suicide three times while awaiting trial. The defense, which included an attorney who had previously represented Lafarge, stridently attacked the medical evidence against Pommerais. The attorney enlisted the doctor Louis Hébert to examine Tardieu and Roussin's reports and to conduct his own analysis, experimenting on frogs, dogs, and rabbits with the samples extracted from de Pauw's organs. Hébert's experiments did not yield any animal deaths. He maintained that Tardieu and Roussin's experiments were flawed and that de Pauw had not been poisoned.[83] Weighing the circumstantial and conflicting forensic evidence, jurors convicted Pommerais, resulting in his execution.

Most practitioners of legal medicine considered physiological animal experiments crucial for forensic expertise involving poisons whose known chemical characteristics were not well understood and clearly defined; however, these physiological animal experiments generated new controversy. In his 1866 treatise on animal experimentation in forensic medicine, Devergie objected to Tardieu's experimental methods and his and Roussin's "excess of experimentation" in the Pommerais affair of 1864. According to Devergie, Roussin and Tardieu misleadingly presented their experiments as definitive proof that de Pauw was poisoned. Devergie maintained that animal experiments only offered incomplete or insufficient proof of poisoning. He expressed alarm over colleagues who considered evidence from physiological experiments to be definitive proof, even more valuable than chemical proof.[84]

Moreover, some forensic doctors expressed anxiety about highly skilled poisoners and advised new directions in toxicological research. Devergie observed, "The practice of poisoning has proceeded much faster than the science." He lamented that forensic chemistry was "in a period of powerlessness." He maintained that criminals would continue to outpace forensic chemistry and find unknown alkaloid poisons. Nonetheless, he suggested that chemists and forensic doctors should not focus on new alkaloids but study known poisons, particularly the chemical properties of digitalis and mushrooms, in order to devise methods of detection.[85] The *Weekly Gazette of Medicine and Surgery* in 1867 urged doctors and chemists to look not only at the past but also to the future and conduct studies in anticipation of new criminal machinations. The journal observed that before the trials of Castaing in 1823, Bocarmé in 1850, Palmer in 1855, and La

Pommerais in 1863, no one spoke of poisoning by morphine, nicotine, strychnine, or digitalis, respectively. It declared that science should not remain reactionary and "so poorly equipped against crimes that catch experts off guard and give judicial magistrates and the audience of the assize courts the sad spectacle of their uncertainties and their dissent." The publication called for medicolegal expertise, which was "sure enough of itself and powerful enough not to leave any shadow of a doubt on the accuracy of its results in order to shelter its judgments from any criticism, to foil all of the culprit's tricks, to unmask the smallest indications of the attack, and to make its evidence clear in the eyes of the most incredulous." The journal insisted that knowledge of the most common poisons – "the poisons of the *past*" – was "certainly indispensable," but not enough. Studying the least known poisons and "the poisons of the *future*" was equally, if not more, important, and the journal advocated further physiological experimentation on animals.[86]

Medicolegal experts' animal experiments could either bring criminal poisonings to light or undermine the state's case for poisoning, such as in the Lerondeau affair. In January 1878 the assize court of Versailles convicted Mélanie Lerondeau of poisoning her husband, who had been ill for eighteen months including three months of violent stomach pains. The medical experts who conducted the autopsy maintained that his stomach had lesions consistent with poisoning. They concluded that he had been poisoned with oxalic acid. The assize court of the Seine later retried her case in June 1878. Three medical experts from the faculty of Paris intervened and performed experiments in which they poisoned dogs with oxalic acid in various doses over varying periods of time. They found that the symptoms Lerondeau's husband displayed prior to his death were inconsistent with the brief period of suffering experienced by the poisoned dogs prior to their deaths. They ruled out possibilities of either a slow, progressive poisoning or an acute poisoning by oxalic acid. Ultimately, the Parisian experts determined that his death was not caused by poisoning, and the jury acquitted Lerondeau.[87]

Fear of medicolegal experts' abilities to detect poisons, particularly arsenic, led the watchmaker Albert Pel to take extreme measures to destroy evidence of his crimes. In 1879 Pel's domestic servant, Marie Mahoin, became seriously ill. His lover Eugénie Mayer began to suffer

from the same symptoms as Mahoin – severe nausea, vomiting, and
diarrhea. Mahoin recovered, but Mayer disappeared under mysterious
conditions. No one saw or heard from her again. Rumors spread that
Pel had poisoned both women. On August 26, 1880, Pel married
Eugénie Buffereau. She became sick with violent vomiting a month
later and died in October. Her doctor attributed her death to acute
gastroenteritis, and no autopsy followed. Nine months later in 1881,
Pel remarried. Shortly thereafter, his wife and his mother-in-law
became ill with the same symptoms as Mahoin, Mayer, and
Buffereau. During this time, Pel obtained authorization from the
Paris Prefecture of Police to sell poisonous substances and chemicals,
and he filled his home with poisons. In 1884 his lover Elise Boehmer
became violently ill with vomiting, and then disappeared like Mahoin.
Despite Pel's efforts to mask his windows with black fabrics and
carpets, witnesses testified that they saw flames and fire in his home.
They complained of terrible smells emanating from his kitchen. The
prosecutor's office suspected Pel of incinerating Boehmer's corpse and
ordered his arrest. Investigators accused Pel of committing seven poisonings over ten years but only pursued charges on two counts: the
murders of Buffereau and Boehmer. Following the exhumation of
Buffereau's corpse, Brouardel and Désiré L'Hôte examined her
remains and a sample of the soil surrounding her grave. Using the
Marsh apparatus, they found a significant quantity of arsenic in her
liver and intestines. When they went to Pel's home, they noticed a strong
chlorine smell, which they suspected was from a disinfectant. They
conducted experiments to ascertain whether a corpse could be incinerated in a stove over the course of several days. They constructed a
furnace modeled after Pel's, cut up a human cadaver, and incinerated
it. They affirmed that Pel could have incinerated Boehmer's corpse in his
stove and that the symptoms of her illness, according to witnesses'
reports, were characteristic of arsenic poisoning. Brouardel and
L'Hôte observed that the case "raised numerous forensic questions."
In 1885 jurors convicted Pel of poisoning Buffereau, but not Boehmer,
likely on account of the lack of bodily remains and proof of poisoning.[88]

Around this time, the controversial Danval poisoning trial shook
forensic experts' general confidence in arsenic detection. In 1878 the
assize court of the Seine tried the pharmacist Gilbert Mordefroy-
Danval for poisoning his wife. The court called upon the doctors

Georges Bergeron and Emile Delens and the chemist L'Hôte. They detected traces of arsenic in the body of Danval's late wife and maintained it must have been ingested and administered in small, repeated doses. However, several other medical practitioners and scientists, including Jules Bouis who had been Danval's toxicology professor and Danval himself, strongly refuted their findings during the trial and noted that his wife displayed no symptoms of arsenic poisoning prior to death and no postmortem lesions. The physician Victor Cornil denounced Bergeron and Delens's autopsy as flawed, incomplete, and a disgrace. Nonetheless, the jury convicted Danval. The trial generated a great deal of controversy among medical professionals and the general public.[89] The Parisian police noted that Bergeron had become an object of "fierce hatred," particularly among fellow doctors. Considering Bergeron's reputation ruined, one commentator observed, "It would be better [for him] to retire and to leave matters of expertise to others."[90] Objections to Danval's conviction intensified after the biochemist Gabriel Bertrand and other scientists found small amounts of arsenic in the bodies of healthy organisms at the turn of the century. While scientists and doctors had rejected Orfila's flawed theory of normal arsenic decades earlier, a new scientific consensus emerged, confirmed by later studies, that people had small amounts of arsenic in their bodies from various sources, including water, air, food, and soil, which were comparable to the one milligram detected in Danval's late wife and a tiny fraction of lethal levels. After a lengthy appeals process, the French state reversed Danval's conviction.[91]

The highly publicized Danval cause célèbre evoked the cultural trope of the expert male poisoner, which emerged in the second half of the nineteenth century and stood in contrast to the figure of the female poisoner that loomed large in the French cultural imagination.[92] Although forensic doctors and the broader public commonly associated the crime of poisoning with female criminality, women did not constitute the majority of accused poisoners until 1847, after poisoning prosecutions had peaked. Commentators claimed that poison was "the weapon of the weak" and women's preferred weapon, since it did not require physical strength to wield it.[93] In 1863 Armand Fouquier's widely read *Causes célèbres* declared that people assumed that women committed more poisonings than men, since the "weakness of their sex does not permit them to take vengeance with open force." According to this logic, women's weakness led them to resort to the secret, hidden, and odious crime of poisoning. However, Fouquier claimed that poisonings were shifting from "the hands of women to the more able and experienced hands of men." He observed that learned men with training in medicine or chemistry commonly resorted to plant-based poisons due to the medicolegal difficulties in their detection. He cited the examples of Castaing's use of morphine and Pommerais's use of digitalis.[94] Adolphe Chapuis's 1888 treatise on toxicology similarly observed that a learned male poisoner, perhaps a doctor himself, would use poisons that would not leave easily detectable traces in order to assure his impunity. Chapuis was nonetheless convinced that such a poisoner would not escape justice. He declared, "But if the expert does not have sufficient means of isolating and identifying the poison, there is always, whether by indiscretion or a lack of foresight of the accused, sufficient evidence to secure a conviction."[95] Other doctors expressed varying degrees of confidence in the notion that science serving justice would triumph over science weaponized for criminal purposes.

The dominant narrative was that science would prevail and establish proof of poisoning, even for the most devious and well-planned crimes. In 1875 the journal *L'Union médicale* reported, "Intelligent and clever criminals will use little-known and difficult-to-detect poisons in vain...The cowardly poisoner, who silently kills, vainly reckons on the silence of the tomb. The medical examiner will make the corpse speak, and the torch of science will throw a dreaded glimmer on the mysteries of this unexpected death."[96] Many physicians and scientists attributed the decrease in criminal poisoning prosecutions in the late nineteenth century to scientific progress and criminals' fear of physicians' and chemists' abilities to detect poisoning.[97] Indeed, shifting patterns of criminal poisonings were most likely the product of these fears, which ultimately stemmed from growing public confidence in forensic expertise. At the same time, certain poisoning trials shook this confidence and exposed the limits of forensic medicine, while the science of poisoning – including its flaws, errors, and changing methodologies – unfolded before the public eye.

Throughout the nineteenth century, the field of toxicology was fraught with uncertainty and controversy. Poisoning investigations and trials were rife with conflicts and tensions among medicolegal experts, particularly between those in Paris and the provinces, and disagreements about standards of proof. Over the course of the century, rising numbers of doctors and scientists rejected the notion that symptoms and autopsy findings consistent with poisoning constituted proof of poisoning. Many of these medical men maintained that chemical proof of poisoning was necessary, since natural diseases, such as cholera, could mimic signs and symptoms of poisoning. However, doctors and scientists often struggled to furnish chemical evidence when they were convinced of poisoning on the basis of physiological and bodily evidence. Moreover, some medicolegal experts contested the chemical evidence their colleagues or rivals presented. Doctors and scientists nonetheless became more adept at detecting arsenic and other poisons by the mid-century. Criminals responded by shifting to poisons that were harder to detect, and criminal prosecutions for poisoning declined. Despite undetected crimes and wrongful convictions, many medical men proclaimed that they had triumphed over criminals in the struggle for justice. This said, conflicts over the relatively rapidly changing field of toxicology and its role in the courts still raised broader questions about the certainty of scientific knowledge and its utility in the pursuit of justice. Uncertainty and contestation about what constituted evidence for poisoning persisted throughout the century. Doctors' and scientists' interventions in poisoning trials at times inspired and at others eroded public trust in forensic expertise, yet they ultimately consolidated their authority during a crucial period in the rise of professionalization and expertise.

When examining the corpses of suspected poisoning victims, medicolegal practitioners sought to speak for the dead. But the living spoke for themselves and crafted narratives that were often at odds with those of medicolegal practitioners. Medical practitioners examining living persons insisted that not all men and women could be trusted and, moreover, that some were masters of deceit.

3

Deception and Detection

In 1813 François-Emmanuel Fodéré, the foremost figure in French legal medicine at the time, observed, "The art of feigning disease has been so perfected in the past twenty years that it is nearly as difficult to detect feigned diseases as to cure real ones."[1] People feigned illnesses in a number of contexts: accused criminals claiming insanity, jurors or witnesses claiming to be unable to appear in court, prisoners wishing to be transferred to a hospital or to defer their sentence, individuals feigning injuries to seek damages, and beggars soliciting charity. But the dominant reason for malingering was securing discharge or exemption from military service, following the introduction of mass conscription during the French Revolution. French medicolegal literature identified dozens of feigned conditions, and malingering at times took unusual or inventive forms. Medical men encountered malingerers who used animal parts, for example, a portion of beef or veal intestine or a sponge soaked in milk and blood, to simulate a prolapsed rectum, vagina, or, uterus.[2] In response to tales about people producing rats, moles, snakes, frogs, or lizards from their bodies, forensic doctors declared that any animal or animal parts expelled from a human body, for example a salamander from the rectum or vagina, must have been previously introduced into the bodily cavity.[3] However, commentators on malingering observed that they had entered a new age of increasingly sophisticated methods of deception yet insisted that medical practitioners were successfully combatting these methods with their own innovative tactics and wits.

A well-developed discourse on malingering first emerged during the period of the Revolutionary and Napoleonic Wars (1792–1815), and it evolved during the decades that followed. French revolutionaries' ideal of transparency found expression in medical men's efforts to uncover bodily truths and to expose malingering. These efforts intensified in the nineteenth century. Medicolegal literature discussed "simulated illnesses," which included completely feigned illnesses; illnesses "provoked by artifice;" illnesses whose symptoms were exaggerated; and faked illnesses that became real. This literature also attended to "dissimulated illnesses," conditions which people concealed, as well as imputed illnesses, those falsely attributed to a person. The latter was particularly common in the context of familial or spousal legal conflicts, for example, including claims that a parent was insane or mentally incompetent in order to obtain an interdiction for purposes of inheritance or that a spouse was afflicted with a venereal disease or impotent. Doctors often cited women's dissimulation of pregnancy as well as wet nurses and prostitutes' dissimulation of venereal diseases. Additionally, the rise of life insurance provided the impetus for individuals to dissimulate or conceal medical conditions for coverage.[4] Moreover, men eager to serve in the military, particularly as paid substitutes or volunteers, concealed conditions that would disqualify them from service; however, simulated conditions were far more common than dissimulated ones among military servicemen.[5] Men and women's motives and manners of deception varied widely in Revolutionary and nineteenth-century France and attracted the keen interest of medical practitioners seeking to expose them. Efforts to detect and expose deception were central to medicolegal thought during this period.[6]

The French medical discourse on malingering revealed medical men's abiding interest in detecting deception as well as the resourcefulness of malingerers. The more knowledgeable and vigilant doctors became in detecting malingering, the more medical knowledge people needed in order to malinger successfully and with increasing sophistication. Proof of malingering could be quite elusive and difficult to obtain, but doctors who published on the subject in medical journals and treatises expressed confidence in their own and their colleagues' ability to detect deception in uncertain cases. Some resorted to extreme measures. During the second half of the nineteenth century, medical practitioners debated whether their methods of detecting feigned conditions had gone too far. Doctors' interventions in detecting malingering played an important role in the professionalization of medicine during the late eighteenth and nineteenth centuries, as medical practitioners shored up their authority by filling an increasing number of juridical and administrative functions.

Malingering and Military Service

The demands of the Revolutionary and Napoleonic Wars stimulated the growth of the medical profession, and the French state heavily relied upon medical men to examine conscripts to exclude those unfit for military service during the Revolutionary and post-Revolutionary eras. An explosion of literature on malingering during this period focused on men's avoidance of military service and framed combatting malingering as a moral and national imperative for medical practitioners. Some works decried malingering men for shirking their civic duties and denounced them as violators of the social contract.[7] Other texts complained of medical practitioners who failed to unmask malingerers. An 1808 treatise on malingering lamented that some medical professionals during the Napoleonic Wars failed to recognize and fulfill their duty to expose malingerers, forgetting "the duties and dignity of their profession" or having been seduced by the "immoral" logic of those who viewed feigning illness as a just and "legitimate defense against the ever increasing invasion of conscription."[8] But French medical literature rarely discussed such doctors who were indifferent to or actively aided malingerers. Rather, it widely stressed the duty of doctors to unmask them. During the first half of the nineteenth century, many medical men sought to use their medical knowledge, self-proclaimed ingenuity, and a repertoire of techniques – including those that inflicted physical pain or emotional distress – to expose malingerers and ensure that able-bodied men served the French nation through military service.

Some desperate men, particularly during the Revolutionary and Napoleonic Wars, sought assistance from doctors, healers, and charlatans in order to simulate medical conditions that would disqualify them from military service, and a number of them experienced unintended permanent disability as a result. There were conscripts who

purchased substances from healers and charlatans that they could use
to fake illnesses to obtain medical discharge. Some *officiers de santé*
and those without any medical training, including a shoemaker, performed minor procedures on conscripts, such as piercing the scrotum
and forcing air into it through a straw in order to fake a hernia or
hydrocele, a collection of fluid in the scrotum, which disqualified men
from service.[9] In 1825 an *officier de santé* was condemned to five years
in prison for injecting an irritant into the scrotum that produced
serious medical complications in a man seeking to evade service.[10]
Artificial ulcers or other wounds produced with acids, alkalis, or other
corrosive or caustic substances often left young men hospitalized for
long periods of time, during which some succumbed to other illnesses.
A conscript in La Rochelle lost his leg, and a soldier in Cantal died
from sepsis after both faked an ulcer.[11] Medical professionals also
cited the case of a man trying to evade military service who became
blind as a result of a charlatan's efforts to induce ophthalmia and who
ultimately committed suicide.[12]

Other conscripts resorted to "feigning illness by provocation," and
the boundaries between induced illnesses, self-injury, and self-
mutilation were blurry. Some forms of 'provoked' illnesses were
fleeting, while others had lasting effects on the body. Some conscripts
destroyed their incisor teeth either by using acids, extracting them, or
filing them. The loss of incisor teeth was a disqualifying condition for
service, since it would prevent the soldier from biting off the end of his
cartridge in loading his musket. Additionally, the loss of fingers and
toes were common forms of mutilation among military men.[13]
Alarmed by the numbers of soldiers whose only injuries were the loss
of fingers at the battles of Lützen and Bautzen in 1813, Napoleon
suspected self-mutilation and launched an investigation. Dominique-
Jean Larrey, chief surgeon in Napoleon's *Grande Armée*, oversaw the
examination of over 2,000 suspiciously wounded soldiers. His forensic
investigation determined that the majority of wounds were not self-
inflicted. Many of the wounds were the product of soldiers' inexperi-
ence, particularly those of the second and third ranks who misdirected
their muskets and wounded men in the first ranks.[14]

Self-injury that rendered a person physically incapable of military
service constituted a criminal act, but during the Revolution and early
nineteenth century, it was unclear whether malingering was a crime. In

1832 the Court of Cassation declared that malingering men seeking to escape military service did not violate any law. Consequently, malingering rarely appeared in police and judicial records. Nonetheless, these records documented related criminal charges, including those that physicians, and more often surgeons or *officiers de santé*, faced for falsifying medical certificates to exempt or discharge men from military service as well as accepting bribes to do so.[15]

Doctors' efforts to detect malingering in the military involved examining men in active service as well as screening conscripts. Malingering offered active servicemen the possibility of hospitalization or obtaining leave (*congé*) or permanent discharge (*réforme*). Servicemen could also avoid chores, military exercises, or various assigned duties by faking anemia, fever, gastrointestinal illness, and other conditions.[16] One of the key sites where doctors encountered suspected malingerers prior to enlistment was at the *conseils de révision*. These draft boards consisted of three military officers and three doctors charged with examining conscripts to determine whether they had disabilities or conditions that granted them an exemption from military service. During the Revolutionary and Napoleonic eras, the French government pressured local officials to conduct medical examinations sparingly and to limit the number of medical exemptions given by the draft boards. Individuals and communities could exert pressure on local medical men to grant exemptions, and some young men from wealthy families received exemptions on improbable medical grounds.[17] In 1820 the military surgeon Pierre-Jean Moricheau-Beaupré lamented that some men secured exemptions by acquiring medical knowledge from local doctors who answered conscripts' questions concerning the conditions that they intended to fake. Moricheau-Beaupré and other medical men also complained that conscripts presented them with medical reports whose legitimacy they often could not judge, and their brief encounters with men at the *conseils de révision* often did not afford them the time necessary to determine whether they were faking conditions or not.[18]

Medicolegal literature discussed nearsightedness, deafness, and epilepsy as the most commonly feigned conditions but also reported unusual, less common cases. For example, publications on malingering recounted men faking polyps by inserting rabbits' kidneys or roosters' testes into their nasal passages or auditory canals. Some medical practitioners warned their colleagues to be cautious in diagnosing ozena, a rare disorder of the nasal passages, since malingerers feigned the condition by inserting stinking cheese into their nostrils.[19] Odor played a role in feigning and detecting various medical conditions, including excessive, putrid sweating, which disqualified men from military service. Those feigning the condition rubbed their entire bodies or just their feet and extremities with foul or putrid substances, including rotten cheese or fish. Doctors found this easily feigned condition easy to detect. In most cases, medical men could simply wipe off the substance, use a very strong soap, or bathe the person, causing the odor to dissipate or disappear.[20] Doctors and *officiers de santé* also encountered men who retracted their testicles into their abdomen through the inguinal canal, since the lack of one or both testicles disqualified them from military service. Some doctors maintained that it was easy to detect this stratagem, since men who lacked testicles were effeminate, small in stature, and had a shrill voice, whereas men who retracted their testicles were muscular, strong and displayed "all of the characteristics of virility."[21] Moreover, some men faked chronic ringworm or alopecia by using caustic substances that they acquired from medical practitioners to remove their hair.[22] Others purposefully infected themselves with ringworm to evade military service.[23] Medical men documented a vast range of simulated medical conditions that they encountered in the military.

Medical men noted how prevalent the problem of feigned nearsightedness had become since the advent of conscription. In 1813 Fodéré remarked, "It is curious to observe during the last twenty years how many young men have worn convex glasses in order to acquire nearsightedness; the condition, as much as they desire it, does not always develop, and many develop instead a weakened and defective sight, but not myopia." Fodéré and other medical men recommended that those who claimed nearsightedness should be given glasses designed for the condition and then instructed to take a vision test.[24] During the early nineteenth century, medical practitioners acknowledged how skillful and adept some men were in feigning nearsightedness or "the art of being nearsighted."[25] In 1821 the prominent military surgeons Pierre-François Percy and Charles Nicolas Laurent suggested that the proportion of men wearing glasses had quadrupled. They observed, "Never were there so many nearsighted men in France as during the conscription laws. Formerly, of a hundred young men, scarcely five wore glasses, then at least twenty."[26] These patterns persisted in the decades that followed, and medical men reported that nearsightedness was the most frequently feigned condition to appear before the *conseils de révision* throughout most of the nineteenth century.[27]

Doctors also contended with men faking other vision issues and were in some cases struck by malingerers' remarkable tenacity. Doctor Paul-Augustin-Olivier Mahon recounted the case of a soldier during the Revolutionary Wars who suddenly declared that he was blind and was then sent to the hospital. Medical practitioners there were convinced that he was faking, since they found that his pupil contracted perfectly. Nonetheless, the practitioners applied vesicatories that caused blistering and sutures to the eye. The soldier did not object to these measures and actually had been the first to propose them. The medical officers believed that he was malingering and wanted to try one last ordeal. They led him to the banks of a river and instructed him to march. He marched right into the river and was pulled out from the water. Still unable to prove that he was malingering, they granted him leave from the army. However, they warned that if he was feigning the condition, his ruse would be discovered when he returned to his hometown. They proposed granting him another period of leave if he confessed the truth. Once assured that the medical officers would keep their word, he took out a book and started reading.[28]

Doctors employed similar stratagems to expose other malingerers, including those who feigned deafness. Deafness was one of the most commonly feigned medical conditions but posed challenges for malingerers. An 1818 medicolegal thesis on malingering observed, "A thousand traps await the false deaf person."[29] Medical men themselves set many of these traps. For example, the military physician Salomon-Louis Laurillard-Fallot pretended to offer permanent discharge to a soldier feigning deafness and arranged for someone to congratulate the man on the success of his fraud on his way out of the hospital. Unsuspecting and proud of his success, he fell for the doctor's trap.[30] Medicolegal practitioners also advised making provocative statements or startling loud noises when least expected. Percy and Laurent, in their writings on malingering in 1821, recounted the case of a supposedly deaf man whom doctors placed in a room for soldiers accused or convicted of crimes in a hospital in Lille. Around midnight officials arrived and announced that he would be arrested for murder and theft.

He broke down in tears and cried out in protest, thus revealing that he heard their declaration.[31] Practitioners of military medicine commonly advised closely monitoring men suspected of feigning deafness.[32] During such monitoring, official instructions from the Ministry of War advised *officiers de santé* to clap loudly near the suspected malingerer at unexpected moments or while he slept.[33] In 1840 the physician Charles-Chrétien-Henri Marc justified the stratagem of doctors discussing in the presence of a suspected malingerer plans to burn the interior of his ear with a hot iron, which could lead to his protests and confession. Marc maintained that there was nothing cruel about this threat, since a person who was genuinely deaf would have heard nothing.[34]

Some medical men used threats, painful procedures, or opium when suspected malingerers claimed urinary incontinence. Many men invoked incontinence as grounds for medical discharge or exemption from military service, but it was a rare condition among young men. Percy, chief surgeon to Napoleon's *Grande Armée*, and Laurent estimated that fewer than one in a thousand men suffered from incontinence, but they had seen some fifteen conscripts at a time claiming incontinence in a recruiting depot.[35] Medical men distinguished real incontinence from feigned by observing whether urination occurred drop by drop in regular intervals, as in real incontinence, or in a stream, as in faked incontinence. To avoid this pitfall, malingerers increasingly feigned only "incomplete" incontinence, in other words nighttime bedwetting, rather than "complete" incontinence night and day. The latter was too difficult to feign, according to medical experts.[36] Fodéré recounted an "epidemic" of incontinence sweeping a hospital after a couple of soldiers had received medical discharge for the condition. He applied a vesicatory, a substance causing blistering, to the perineum of those claiming incontinence, which he claimed could treat the condition. Fodéré also tied a ligature to their penis, which was only to be removed by a person appointed for this purpose when they wished to urinate. According to Fodéré, those suffering from true incontinence experienced distension of the urethra above the ligature, and when it was removed for urination, the discharge took place drop by drop.[37] For alleged incontinence, Percy and Laurent prescribed urinary catheterization, by compressing the penis between two pieces of wood, or twenty lashes of the bullwhip, supposedly to strengthen the kidneys and tone the bladder.[38] Some military surgeons recommended giving a malingerer enough opium to make him sleep through the night and be unable to wet the bed by voluntarily urinating as on other nights.[39] Some medical men endorsed applying an actual cautery, a metal device such as a hot iron that uses heat to cauterize tissue, to the perineum.[40] Others remarked that this suggestion alone was enough to unmask the imposture. Doctor Emile Bégin acknowledged that using an actual cautery might seem cruel at first glance but defended it as an excellent means of treatment if the affliction was real and often necessary to unmask malingerers if not.[41]

Some doctors advocated a similarly aggressive approach toward feigned epilepsy, which in their estimation was commonly faked.[42] Medical practitioners observed that not all of the features of a seizure, most notably insensitivity, could be simulated. Accordingly, some medical men tried to detect malingering by testing the loss of sensitivity through various means, such as placing ammonia or stinking cheese under the nose, firing a pistol, or burning the body with boiling water, sealing wax, or actual cautery.[43] A soldier feigning epilepsy in a Besançon hospital had purportedly pricked and burned different parts of his body to render them insensitive and was therefore able to withstand a doctor applying sealing wax to his inner thigh but not the pain of the actual cautery the doctor subsequently used.[44] Some medical men recommended threatening large incisions, deep burns, and even castration to inspire enough fear to put an end to the seizures for good.[45] Despite such measures, doctors maintained that epilepsy remained commonly feigned, since its advantages were that seizures could be infrequent and faked at times when medical professionals were not present.[46] Nonetheless, some commentators observed that epilepsy was less frequently feigned by mid-century than at the beginning of the century, because the characteristics had become so well known that medical men would discover the ruse at the first seizure.[47]

Moreover, mental disorders were a major preoccupation of medicolegal experts, and medical practitioners working with soldiers were particularly concerned about nostalgia. In eighteenth- and nineteenth-century France, nostalgia was understood as a serious and deadly form of homesickness that claimed the lives of a great number of soldiers.[48] Medical men maintained that soldiers afflicted with true nostalgia experienced symptoms closely resembling those of melancholy, including a loss of appetite, weight loss, insomnia, listlessness, and apathetic indifference. Those suffering from nostalgia were taciturn, speaking little of the subject that preoccupied them: their homeland. Those feigning nostalgia spoke expansively on the subject, maintained their weight, and appeared to be in good health.[49]

While efforts to detect and expose malingerers in the military featured prominently in printed works, they rarely appeared in archival records, thus suggesting that in practice, many medical practitioners had likely been reluctant to report malingering, particularly those who took pity on men who were desperate to escape military service. Practitioners who had little sympathy for these men complained about colleagues who took the duty of detecting malingering too lightly. Percy and Laurent pointed to the problem of medical practitioners, namely *officiers de santé*, granting medical certificates to military servicemen feigning conditions that allowed them to take mineral waters in spa towns or to be hospitalized. They noted, "It is in times of war above all that we see the most of these impostures."[50] They lamented the social and financial costs of this problem, which entailed removing servicemen from their units; transporting and hospitalizing them, which often cost several hundred francs; and wasting resources that should have gone to those truly suffering. They considered the avoidance of military service altogether as an even graver problem and sought to impress upon *officiers de santé* the importance of exposing malingering.[51]

Moreover, some men hoping to avoid military service sought out lax or corrupt medical practitioners. Certain hospitals gained a reputation as places where men could easily obtain exemptions. Some conscripts approached doctor after doctor until they could obtain a medical certificate, while unethical medical practitioners sold drugs and caustic substances to men trying to simulate the signs and symptoms of diseases or accepted payment in exchange for a fraudulent medical certificate. In order to combat fraud and corruption, the prefect of the *département* of the Gironde in 1806 declared that the names of the medical practitioners serving on the *conseil de révision* would be announced only fifteen minutes before its hearing and that the doctors would change daily.[52]

Malingering had become a form of bodily resistance to the military and juridical power of the French state, and this resistance was an important force driving increasing medicalization and professionalization. But it is likely that some medical practitioners cared little for exposing malingerers and viewed them with sympathy, pity, or indifference, although evidence of these views is elusive. Authors who published on the subject generally characterized the task of detecting malingering as vitally important and challenging. Medicolegal authors generally expressed confidence in doctors' ability to outsmart even the most skilled and devious malingerers. Most of their accounts focused on their triumphs in successfully outwitting malingerers. They advised scrutinizing the actions, speech, and gestures of an individual suspected of malingering; calling upon him unexpectedly at different times of the day and night; and enlisting others to observe and keep him under surveillance. Marc maintained that there were many cases in which malingering would go undetected if not for doctors' "ingenious resources" and improvisations, which were the "fruit of [their] genius" rather than general medical principles.[53] Medical men exposing malingerers not only laid claim to expertise but also prided themselves on their ingenuity. These medical men viewed their detection of malingering as a testament to their talents and genius.

The Art of Faking It

Many civilians feigned illnesses in the same manner as men seeking to evade military service, although for different reasons. Common patterns in malingering emerged, but there was also a remarkable range and variety of practices that medical practitioners confronted in both military and civilian settings. In 1841 the forensic doctor Ollivier observed, "The examples of feigned illnesses provide one of the most curious chapters in the history of this science [of legal medicine.]"[54] The curriculum of medical schools featured instruction on methods of detecting numerous feigned diseases. As medical men acquired and disseminated more knowledge about malingering, malingerers continually refined their methods. French citizens applied their vernacular medical knowledge to fake conditions for various aims, while medical practitioners sought to expose their frauds.

Malingering played a role in medical charlatanism, which doctors denounced. Some malingerers sought out charlatans to provoke or simulate conditions, and charlatans also enlisted the help of malingerers to sell their remedies. These men and women feigned conditions that charlatans then "cured." Forensic doctors cited the example of a charlatan promoting a remedy for rabies with the aid of a person feigning a bout of that illness who then consumed a concoction the charlatan offered and was seemingly cured. Similarly, unscrupulous practitioners purportedly used people feigning scoliosis to prove the efficacy of a particular back brace.[55] Nonetheless, the primary relationship between medical men and malingerers was adversarial rather than collaborative.

Medical practitioners also took aim at malingering among beggars. Medical men reported that the most commonly feigned conditions among beggars were blindness and epilepsy. French law prohibited begging, classified in the Penal Code of 1810 as a misdemeanor punished by imprisonment. Article 276 prescribed six months to two years in prison for beggars who feigned wounds or illnesses. Most malingering cases among beggars did not involve criminal investigations, but in 1840 authorities launched an investigation into a fifty-year-old man who had been begging and been seen several times in the street suffering from seizures and vomiting blood. The man in question recounted that these conditions stemmed from him being shot in the stomach while serving in the military in 1815. Police sent him to a hospital, where a doctor concluded that he was faking his conditions. He was transferred to prison, and authorities learned that he had been previously convicted for begging while malingering. An examining magistrate summoned two doctors to conduct an examination. When the doctors instructed him to undress, a branch that was sharpened at one end and stained with blood fell from his clothes. They surmised that he been inserting the stick in his nostrils to cause bleeding, swallowing the blood, and then vomiting it. Their report led to him being sentenced to one year in prison.[56] Malingering posed risks but was a valuable means for some individuals to gain sympathy, private charity, or public assistance. The French state enlisted the help of doctors to distinguish between those deemed deserving and undeserving of charity and public assistance.[57]

Forensic doctors also denounced those who feigned injuries for financial gain. In 1841 the *Journal of Practical Medicine and Surgery* decried the emergence of "a class of individuals in Paris who make it their business to be run over by carriages belonging to wealthy individuals." These people sustained slight injuries and then feigned more severe ones in order to receive damages.[58] Ollivier published on this subject after a civil court in the *département* of the Seine called upon him to examine the injuries of a woman who had been knocked down by a carriage and hospitalized. The wealthy woman whose carriage struck her visited her at the hospital and offered her a considerable sum in compensation. A financial speculator approached the injured woman offering her even more money in exchange for power of attorney, which would allow him to extract even more compensation by having her feign more serious injuries. When Ollivier examined the woman, he found that the wounds on her legs were covered in a cold cream mixed with a blistering agent, which he discovered hidden in her bed and nightstand. As a result of Ollivier's report, the court rejected the woman's demand for higher damages.[59] During the final years of the nineteenth century, a new trend in malingering emerged. The industrial revolution had transformed France's economy and the nature of work, and industrial labor presented very real dangers for workers as well as opportunities for workers to fake workplace injuries. At the turn of the century, some physicians addressed the growing phenomenon of industrial workers feigning or exaggerating injuries from accidents to obtain compensation.[60] Other doctors noted that the rise of life insurance spurred some to fake death.[61]

Additionally, the problem of malingering appeared in prisons in a similar fashion to the military. The arrival of a new medical officer in a carceral institution often resulted in a spate of malingering among prisoners. Doctors also observed that malingering was most common among those with longer sentences who had already spent years in detention. The naval doctor Eugène Benoit maintained that these individuals at first lacked the audacity and courage to feign conditions, but after observing others' successes, they did so initially timidly and then more boldly. Benoit alleged that laziness was the sole motive for malingering in penal colonies, while individuals' motives in civilian and military life were varied.[62] Prisoners frequently feigned diarrhea and other gastrointestinal ailments in hopes of being transferred to a private hospital (*maison de santé*), where they could be more comfortable and escape more easily. Doctors noted that some prisoners indeed successfully escaped using this strategy.[63] Medical men at times collaborated with prison officers and enlisted prisoners as spies and confidential informants to detect malingering.[64]

Successful malingering to avoid military service emboldened some men to malinger in the legal arena. In 1828 doctors examined a man on trial for fraudulent bankruptcy to determine whether he was feigning madness. They concluded that the accused not only was feigning madness but also had previously feigned urinary incontinence for two years in order to obtain discharge from the military. He never again complained of the condition after his release from military service. The jury and the presiding judge concluded that the evidence clearly pointed to his malingering as well as his guilt.[65] In 1866 a prisoner seeking release reported mysterious illnesses over twenty times. Authorities learned that he had obtained military discharge two years earlier for a gunshot wound. Upon carefully reviewing his records, they determined that he had faked being shot by mutilating his left index finger.[66] Prior malingering in the military helped to affirm doctors' suspicions of malingering among the accused and condemned whom they examined.

While doctors understood the motivations of malingerers in the military and justice system, they were sometimes unable to discern a clear motive in other cases and were perplexed by certain feigned conditions. For example, the simulation of kidney or bladder stones often puzzled doctors. Doctors generally discounted people faking kidney stones on account of the pain involved in doing so; however, a woman at the Hôtel-Dieu in Paris confessed to introducing stones into her urethra, after the nature of the expelled stones – pebbles – raised suspicion.[67] Later in the nineteenth century, doctors linked the simulation of kidney stones with hysteria in women. In 1884 doctor Jules-Théodore Brongniart claimed that women were responsible for 80 percent of cases of feigned kidney stones and young boys accounted for the remaining 20 percent. He suggested that their motive was either laziness, attention seeking, or possibly sexual in nature, a form of "lechery." He asserted that sexual depravity was the primary reason why women faked kidney stones and inserted foreign bodies into their urinary tract.[68] When medical practitioners were at a loss to explain a motive, some attributed malingering to a person's desire for a prolonged hospital stay or for sympathy. Doctors also often linked malingering and hysteria, particularly among women.[69] Gabriel Tourdes, professor of legal medicine in Strasbourg, declared that certain hysterical women malingered with tenacity and consummate skill, "only for the pleasure of deceiving."[70]

Some doctors acknowledged that they risked misdiagnosing actual diseases as feigned, although such admissions rarely appeared in medicolegal publications. In the mid-nineteenth century the vast majority of physicians dismissed the secretion of colored sweat, typically black or dark blue, as a fraud. However, in 1861, a doctor from Brest presented to the Imperial Academy of Medicine his research on chromhidrosis, which came to be recognized as a rare condition characterized by the secretion of colored sweat.[71] Forensic doctors acknowledged their oversight but nonetheless insisted that some people simulated the condition, namely women using dyes and colored substances to carry out "feminine deceptions, either for the purpose of exploitation or without appreciable motive, with a rare audacity."[72] Even in cases in which the motive and proof of malingering were unclear, doctors nonetheless expressed confidence in their diagnoses.

Medical practitioners observed that people used various substances to alter their skin, eyes, and ears to feign certain illnesses. Those who feigned jaundice colored their skin yellow with a turmeric solution, saffron seeds, or lily stamens. Several medical publications discussed the case of an incarcerated women duping an *officier de santé* into releasing her from prison by using the yellow flowers of the perennial herb greater celandine to fake jaundice. In 1837 Laurillard-Fallot maintained that every military doctor had encountered feigned jaundice. He and other medical men maintained that they could easily expose these impostures by applying a soapy solution to the skin or by analyzing the malingerers' urine. Some malingerers sought to evade this method of detection by eating rhubarb to alter the color of their urine and artificially coloring their fecal matter with small doses of hydrochloric acid. Physicians observed that even the most resourceful malingerers were unable to simulate yellowed conjunctiva, the mucous membrane lining the inside of the eyelid and covering the white of the eye.[73] Some men and women feigned eye disease by applying irritants, such as tobacco and salt, to their eyes to provoke inflammation. By the late nineteenth century, doctors maintained that fewer people feigned partial or total blindness due to medical progress in ophthalmology.[74] Feigned deafness and ear diseases remained common, and in some cases doctors discovered small objects, such as a pea, inserted into the ear canal for this purpose. Others put pungent cheese in their ear canal to feign ear afflictions that were associated with bad-smelling pus. Additionally, a doctor suspicious of a man complaining of pus draining from his ear tasted the discharge and recognized it was honey.[75] Medical men maintained that careful examination would expose such ruses.

Various forms of malingering involved men and women introducing foreign objects into their bodies. Doctors reported that some people inserted a fragment of wood into their urethra to provoke inflammation.[76] Others faked anal fistulas by making a small incision near the anus and inserting a piece of a root from a plant into the wound. Some faked hemorrhoids by inserting the bladders of rats or small fish into their rectum. Medical men recommended using a needle prick to distinguish fake hemorrhoids from real ones, and suggested that feigned hemorrhoids were particularly common in the cavalry.[77] Malingerers employed similar techniques to fake rectal prolapse. For example, a soldier placed a small lamb's bladder into his rectum and positioned it to fall outside of his anus.[78] Laurillard-Fallot observed that another soldier who was aware of this case mimicked it a decade later using pig intestines although the doctor did not discuss how the soldier had acquired this knowledge. Another soldier complained to Laurillard-Fallot about rectal prolapse, but after the doctor recommended curing him with fire, he no longer spoke of the condition.[79] One doctor claimed that inserting animal intestines smeared with blood into the rectum was easier for men who had sex with men.[80]

Feigned swelling in the scrotum and groin was another form of malingering. Some malingerers inserted air or injected water into their scrotum, and others simulated scrotal or testicular disease through swelling resulting from bee stings or the application of leeches to the scrotum.[81] Doctors also cited cases of men using bee stingers to simulate hernias, namely inguinal hernias that produced a bulge in the groin area. One doctor in the *département* of the Indre-et-Loire reported that a man appearing before a *conseil de révision* declared that he had been suffering from an inguinal hernia for several years. The doctor observed acute inflammation in the scrotum. Upon closer examination, he noticed two shiny blackish points protruding from the skin of the scrotum. The doctor removed them to find that they were bee stingers, which he identified as the obvious cause of the inflammation despite the man's protestations.[82]

Blood or the appearance of blood played a central role in some men and women's attempts at malingering. Those who faked coughing up blood employed various techniques, including biting the inside of their cheeks, wounding their gums or naval cavity, sucking blood from small wounds to their fingers or forearm, or using blood obtained from bloodletting or an animal. Some men and women made superficial cuts in their skin or their gums and then used this blood to fake more serious bleeding. Others used a considerable quantity of animal blood to feign hemorrhaging. Medical literature instructed practitioners to identify the origin and nature of the blood, examine it under a microscope, and examine the organ that was the supposed site of the hemorrhage. Noting that doctors could be deceived, particularly by surface wounds that could be easily faked or self-inflicted, Tourdes cited the case of an aspiring holy woman whose faked stigmata duped a doctor, among others. However, a nun ultimately discovered a sharp instrument the woman had been using to make the small wounds and revealed her fraud.[83] Nonetheless, medicolegal literature generally presented trained practitioners as the only ones capable of unmasking such frauds.

Malingerers also faked the presence of blood in bodily fluids. Some vomited blood by swallowing and then regurgitating their own blood or animal blood, such as that of cattle or even pigeons.[84] Others faked blood in urine through various means. Some swallowed certain substances, such as prickly pear fruit, in order to turn their urine red. Those who prepared and consumed tinctures of cantharides for this purpose risked poisoning themselves. Medical men insisted that a careful examination of urine would expose the fraud. Medical practitioners declared that urine mixed with blood would yield a brown clot and yellow liquid when boiled.[85] Others called for a chemical analysis of the urine using reagents.[86] Medical men also reported that some malingerers injected blood into their bladder.[87] Others used a sharp object to cut the muscular layer of the urethra. Medical practitioners advised not only observing the suspected malingerer while urinating but also sequestering and strictly monitoring him.[88]

Medical practitioners favored the tactics of isolation and surveillance to detect many feigned conditions, such as diarrhea and dysentery. Those who faked these conditions commonly added urine and sometimes also blood to feces. Others used various suppositories, such as soap, to irritate the rectum or took purgatives, powerful laxatives. Medical men discovered such frauds in some cases by examining the person's feces for the presence of castor oil or other laxatives. Doctors recommended closely monitoring and placing these suspected malingerers in isolation.[89]

Medical men also relied upon surveillance to detect feigned insanity and typically confined suspected malingerers in the military or judicial system to an insane asylum for observation. Accused persons seeking to avoid criminal punishment constituted the vast majority of feigned insanity cases. Some practitioners expressed concerns that those who faked madness, particularly during confinement in an asylum, ran the risk of actually developing the condition for real. Several forensic doctors cited the case of two French sailors imprisoned on English pontoons who simulated madness for six months. By the time that they were freed, they had become truly insane.[90] In 1885 the physician Victor Parant argued that doctors could not prove that feigning madness was the cause of the sailors' subsequent insanity. According to Parant, doctors should not rule out other factors, including the physical and emotional suffering and deprivations the men endured as prisoners, as possible causes. Parant maintained that feigning madness for an extended period of time, months or even years, could result in actual madness – but it would not necessarily do so. Parant cited the case of a man who retained his full mental faculties after persistently feigning a series of disorders, including mania, imbecility, and epilepsy, for a year before being sent to the penal colony of New Caledonia.[91] While doctors debated the likelihood of a person feigning madness going insane, they generally agreed that it was a veritable risk. Some malingerers purportedly abandoned their attempts at feigning insanity due to their fears of becoming truly insane.[92]

The detection of feigned insanity was a central concern in the burgeoning field of psychiatry. Marc observed that one of the most serious and delicate functions of forensic doctors was determining whether insanity was real.[93] Combatting the notion that laypersons could evaluate sanity by using common sense, medicolegal practitioners and psychiatrists insisted that only those with formal medical training were competent to do so. Doctors advised that a medicolegal evaluation of sanity involved not only a direct examination of the person in question but also an indirect examination of all relevant documentation, including depositions, and personal background information. In an 1866 treatise on feigned insanity, psychiatrist Armand Laurent declared that evaluating sanity and detecting feigned insanity required not only specialized medical training and experience but also an understanding of the "world of criminals."[94] Practitioners of legal medicine maintained that a trained eye could easily detect crude attempts at feigning insanity. They observed that the public's misguided ideas about madness led malingerers to exaggerate symptoms, often by ridiculous or obviously affected speech and actions.[95] Medical men maintained that successfully feigning insanity was difficult. Doctors questioned how people without much learned medical knowledge or a certain degree of intelligence were able to feign insanity in a more sophisticated manner.[96] One answer was that they studied and imitated those whom they observed in the asylum.[97]

In the absence of malingerers' own frank accounts of their techniques and experiences, the medical literature of the period offers limited insight into how malingerers learned to feign various conditions. It seems that some based their tactics on observing those with the actual condition or other malingerers. Others may have learned from word of mouth and heard of other people's success in evading military service, escaping criminal punishment, or achieving some other aim. Clusters of people feigned the same condition in some military and carceral settings. Medical men documented "small epidemics" of certain diseases, such as night blindness or incontinence in military barracks or hospitals, in which the majority of those afflicted were faking the condition.[98] A highly uneven geographic distribution of documented cases of nearsightedness among conscripts suggests that many men were likely feigning the condition and hearing about successful malingering through word of mouth. For example, in the mid-nineteenth century, 51 out of every 100,000 men in the *département* of the Indre-et-Loire were exempted for nearsightedness, whereas the proportion was 1,181 out of 100,000 men in the Bouches-du-Rhône in southern France.[99] These statistics might have been shaped not only by regional patterns of malingering but also by individual, local, and regional variations in doctors' vigilance or lack of interest in exposing malingering.

Medical authors offered social commentary on patterns of malingering. In 1870 Edmond Boisseau, a professor of military medicine,
published a treatise on malingering, which became the most authori-
tative study of the subject in nineteenth-century France. According to
Boisseau, there were regional variations within France both in terms of
numbers of malingerers and in the nature of malingering. Boisseau
claimed that a disproportionate number were from Brittany and that
Bretons were tenacious malingerers. Additionally, those from
Normandy were scheming, Gascons had aplomb, and Parisians were
imaginative.[100] Lacassagne similarly maintained that the skills and
tactics of malingering persons varied across *départements*. He
claimed that "less educated *départements*" furnished unsophisticated
malingerers and "shameful deceptions."[101] For physician Prosper
Gentilhomme, the key social distinction was between those from the
countryside and those from cities. He maintained that those from rural
areas simulated illnesses that involved inertia and perseverance, such
as muteness, deafness, stuttering, paralysis, aphonia or loss of voice,
and blindness, and that doctors could easily detect their ruses when
poorly executed. In contrast, Gentilhomme maintained that urban
dwellers were more educated and more adept at malingering and that
they applied their intelligence to simulate a wide range of conditions.[102] Boisseau suggested that social class shaped patterns of malingering within the military. He observed that malingering was common
at military academies but rare among military officers and members of
elite military regimens, such as the Imperial Guard. In contrast,
he believed that malingering was common among ordinary soldiers,
particularly those serving in Africa. It is unclear whether Boisseau
attributed this phenomenon to soldiers' aversion to their assignments
in Africa or whether they were influenced by the so-called native
mendacity of colonial subjects.[103]

By documenting and drawing attention to the resourcefulness,
knowledge, and tenacity of individuals faking medical conditions,
doctors suggested that only trained medical professions were equipped
to detect malingering. Medical practitioners publishing on the subject
sought to advance and disseminate knowledge, build their own reputation, and elevate the medical profession and its public standing.
However, some medical men alluded to the dangers of malingerers
acquiring this knowledge and putting it to duplicitous use. Forensic

doctors Tourdes and Edmond Metzquer cautioned practitioners who questioned suspected malingerers about their symptoms with the intention of finding inconsistencies and contradictions. Tourdes and Metzquer warned, "It should be remembered, however, that some individuals have carefully studied the illness that they are faking." The doctors urged practitioners to be suspicious of the use of technical expressions and to be aware that some people feigned conditions for months or even years.[104]

Lay persons' expanding medical knowledge made them increasingly adept at malingering, and medical men suggested that only those with formal medical training could detect skilled faking. Both learned and vernacular knowledge shaped the practice of malingering, and these forms of knowledge evolved in tandem. For example, Tourdes observed that new forms of malingering developed alongside scientific progress. Some malingerers acquired the same surgical instruments and medical supplies as professionals.[105] However, the medical literature of the period insisted that doctors' diagnostic abilities would triumph over malingering. During the second half of the nineteenth century, debates about the legitimacy and ethics of their tactics and techniques raised the question of what lengths doctors should go to detect and unmask malingerers.

Medical Ethics and Proving Malingering

Medical men warned that failing to expose malingerers would damage a doctor's authority and reputation as well as the field of medicine itself. In 1798 Fodéré declared, "It is a great dishonor for medicine to be deceived."[106] Medical men who believed that detecting malingering was a matter of honor and justice implored their colleagues to "defend the interests of the state" by combatting increasingly sophisticated forms of malingering.[107] These medical men wanted to serve the state's interests by thwarting the efforts of French citizens to shirk their civic duties or to avoid criminal punishment by feigning medical conditions. These practitioners also wanted to keep their reputation as men of science intact by outsmarting malingerers and not falling for their tricks. Medical men set their own traps for malingerers. Some medical practitioners raised ethical objections and questioned the effectiveness of their colleagues' techniques to expose malingerers. Methods involving pain or anesthesia generated the greatest controversy. Over the course of the nineteenth century, medical men increasingly questioned whether the tactics of those who zealously sought to unmask malingerers were unethical, undignified, and even dangerous.

In the early nineteenth century, medical men expressed disdain for most malingerers yet sympathy toward those unfit for military service. Percy and Laurent expressed disgust and revulsion toward malingering, and they considered "the sad and strict necessity of revealing impostures" a moral and social imperative. On the one hand, these physicians wished to provide protection and care to those whose actual infirmities and physical limitations prevented them from fulfilling public duties, namely military service. On the other hand, they declared that they owed "nothing but contempt and severity to anyone who dares to imitate this state." Percy and Laurent denounced the cowardice and artifice of "this class of deceivers," who could capably serve in the military but instead shirked their duties. Nonetheless, they had sympathy for young men who were not suited for military service and resorted to feigning infirmities because they could not bear the idea of leaving their parents' home and loved ones.[108] These physicians sought the government's benevolence on behalf of "a class of men whose weak constitution makes them completely unfit for the profession of arms...without a beard and without the slightest appearance of virility, waiting miserably for permanent discharge or death." They maintained that such men who were unable to fulfill the ideal of martial masculinity were useless in the army and would better serve their country in other ways.[109] Nonetheless, they vigorously combatted the problem of feigned diseases to ensure that those who were fit to serve their country through military service did so.

Medical men's discussions of malingering revealed inherent tensions in their approaches. On the one hand, Percy and Laurent denounced the use of violence to detect malingering: "All violent means must be rejected as inexpedient, illegal, cruel, and dangerous. They are ineffective and disappointing and can only provide contradictory results."[110] On the other hand, these physicians advocated stratagems that inflicted discomfort or pain on suspected malingerers. Despite discouraging overly aggressive or painful treatments and threats, many early nineteenth-century medical practitioners maintained that these methods were excusable when one was sure of malingering or when the nature of the illness, if it were real, entailed the loss of sensitivity, for example a patient who lost all feeling in a paralyzed limb.[111] They also justified painful procedures that could be therapeutically beneficial for the purported medical condition.

This rationale led some practitioners to justify cauterizing or burning the bodies of those suspected of feigning madness and epilepsy. Some medical men maintained that most insane people were insensitive to external sources of physical pain. Consequently, certain medical practitioners were inclined to use pain to unmask feigned madness. In his 1835 treatise on feigned illnesses, Edouard Taufflieb cautioned that this was an unreliable method, since some malingerers would be able to withstand considerable pain, while some mentally ill individuals would be just as sensitive as perfectly healthy people.[112] Some medical practitioners, such as Bégin, justified using an actual cautery, specifically a hot iron applied to the arm, on those suspected of feigning seizures and considered the method almost always infallible. Defending these measures, Bégin wrote, "These painful experiments are often made necessary by the obstinacy of the alleged seizure and should be used even if one is convinced of the fraud, because it is not enough for the doctor to recognize these telltale signs, but he must convince the spectators … and above all oblige the malingerer to renounce his scheme, now exposed to everyone's eyes."[113] A spectacle could not only publicly reveal an imposture but also serve as warning to other malingerers.

Doctors justified such tactics as necessary to furnish clear proof of malingering. In 1829 two doctors examined Jean-Baptiste Gérard, who was arrested for murder and suspected of feigning madness and muteness. The doctors resorted to cauterization, which they claimed could potentially cure true insanity. They operated under the principle that the procedure could be beneficial if his madness and muteness were real and could break his silence if not. After a few sessions, Gérard spoke out, ending his period of muteness, and was ultimately convicted of murder by the assize court of Lyon and executed. Marc praised these doctors' methods and maintained that they cauterized the soles of Gérard's feet so carefully that he was able to walk to the prosecutor's office the following day. Marc insisted that the cauterization was justified, since jurors needed to be dazzled by very clear forms of proof, which the Lyonnais doctors provided.[114]

By the mid-nineteenth century, debates about the ethics and effectiveness of medical men's methods to unmask malingering crystallized
around the use of anesthesia. Some medicolegal practitioners championed anesthesia as an effective means of distinguishing feigned from
real diseases, including mental illnesses. French medical men quickly
put anesthesia to use in detecting malingering after the introduction of
ether and then chloroform as general anesthetics in the 1840s. In
1847 the surgeon Lucien Baudens reported using ether on two soldiers
to distinguish between real and simulated illnesses. The medical practitioners deemed one soldier a malingerer after his spinal curvature
disappeared under the effects of ether. They concluded that the other
soldier was not faking his ankylosis of the hip joint (an immobility of
the joint), since it persisted under full anesthesia.[115] Some medicolegal
experts advocated using ether to determine whether cases of paralysis
and contracture of limbs were real; however, in 1849 Henri-Louis
Bayard challenged the notion that a condition that disappeared under
anesthesia was necessarily feigned. He also objected to the use of
anesthesia to induce involuntary revelations. Bayard questioned the
accuracy and legal standing of such statements, pointing out that
physicians refrained from using narcotics or alcohol for such purposes.
He insisted that anesthesia should only be used if the person under
suspicion gave his free consent after being informed of the possible
consequences and that the doctor should remain liable for any adverse
effects, including death in rare cases.[116] Nonetheless, some practitioners advocated interrogating a person as he was going under or waking
from anesthesia as one of the best techniques for detecting malingering, particularly for stuttering, muteness, deafness, and epilepsy. In
1851 a French medical journal advocated using ether to unmask
feigned imbecility in the case of a seventeen-year-old in Lombardy
charged with raping and killing a seven-year-old girl.[117] Some medical
men recommended using chloroform at *conseils de révision*. An
1853 medical treatise that championed the use of chloroform maintained that other methods to identify malingering men seeking to
evade military service were, by comparison, exceedingly difficult,
time-consuming, and costly for the state.[118]

Ethical debates intensified as medical men's use of anesthesia to
diagnose malingering became more common. Some medical professionals supported the use of ether on suspected malingerers but

warned against chloroform as riskier and more dangerous; others rejected both. In 1866 Tourdes observed that a suspected malingerer's refusal to be anesthetized did not prove malingering, since they might simply fear anesthesia. Tourdes had moral qualms about using anesthesia to detect malingering and warned that a doctor could be held accountable for an anesthesia-related death in both criminal and civil courts. Tourdes maintained that anesthesia was generally an effective diagnostic tool on suspected malingerers but not a legitimate one, especially if used without a person's consent and against their will, which Tourdes likened to medieval torture.[119] In response to Tourdes and others who objected to anesthetizing suspected malingerers, Ernest Martino insisted that the use of chloroform was no more objectionable, and often less "cruel" or "barbaric," than other tactics, such as cauterization, seclusion, or depriving a malingerer of food until they gave up the ruse. Citing the army's medical supervisory council's 1862 directive that anesthesia only be used in military hospitals with "extreme reserve" on suspected malingerers whose conditions would exempt them from service, Martino argued that the French state did not insist upon the same degree of caution when using other means to detect malingering, including those that inflicted pain.[120]

Medical controversy over chloroform opened up broader debates about the ethics of methods to detect malingering. Practitioners of legal medicine had come to reject intoxication or the use of narcotics as investigative tools in legal proceedings, but issues surrounding doctors' wide-ranging tactics to diagnose malingering remained unsettled. Siding with Tourdes, Boisseau opposed most instances of doctors using chloroform as a diagnostic tool for feigned illnesses. Boisseau maintained that anesthesia always posed risks and should not be used to detect malingering. He warned against painful or dangerous measures that "more closely resemble torture than a method of treatment or investigation" and called for a complete ban on violent methods. He expressed confidence in the power of science to unmask malingering without recourse to painful or dangerous tactics. Moreover, he considered ruses and surprises to be more reliable than dangerous measures; however, he objected to certain kinds of surprises that were undignified for a doctor, such as setting fire to some straw around the bed of a malingering paraplegic. Boisseau also rejected the use of disciplinary methods to compel malingerers to capitulate, such as imprisonment or food deprivation, which he thought compromised the medical profession. He insisted that the role of doctors must be entirely distinct from that of military or judicial authorities.[121]

Ethical debates about the legitimacy of doctors' methods of exposing malingerers reached a zenith in the early Third Republic. Some forensic doctors declared that they should use every means at their disposal when dealing with a suspected malingerer. These methods included threats; close surveillance; surprises, such as shooting firearms near the malingerer; and subjecting them to cold showers, cauterization, electricity, or anesthesia.[122] An increasing number of medical practitioners objected in varying degrees to some of these measures, and the most widely opposed methods were those involving physical pain. An 1872 publication on simulated mental illnesses maintained that doctors had "unanimously rejected" painful means of exposing malingering.[123] The most contentious and divisive method was anesthesia. Some medical men who condemned the use of chloroform and other anesthetics to detect malingering warned of chloroform-related deaths. A doctor argued in 1887 that using chloroform to expose malingerers risked their death and was an illegitimate, "dangerous and unfair weapon that deserves to be relegated to oblivion."[124] However, some military medical practitioners continued to advocate administering chloroform to suspected malingerers, despite increasing pressure for the prohibition of this practice. Advocates insisted that the practice was not dangerous and was a useful diagnostic tool, particularly in the field of military medicine.[125]

Doctors also debated the role of pain in detecting malingering. The practice of cauterizing suspected malingerers with a hot iron became a point of contention. Some practitioners objected to the practice of cauterizing the perineum of men suspected of feigning urinary incontinence. The doctor and surgeon Jean-Jacques Fratini endorsed using opium on these men but objected to cauterization and unnecessary operations. He declared, "It is never permitted to mutilate or operate on one's fellowman to dispel doubts that may be ill-founded."[126] In 1870 doctor Adelphe Espagne noted that medical practitioners in the military had come to reject the "draconian measures" that Percy and Laurent had championed as a relic of the past, for example their recommendation of beating men suspected of feigning incontinence with a bullwhip.[127] Other doctors approved of performing painful procedures or operations on suspected malingerers as long as such treatments would treat or cure the real condition.[128] Nonetheless, pain became a less acceptable tool to diagnose malingering over the course of the nineteenth century, as medical men expressed confidence in the power of science to unmask malingering without recourse to painful or dangerous tactics.

Malingering had declined during the decades following the Revolutionary and Napoleonic Wars. Late nineteenth-century medical commentary observed an overall decline in malingering, at least within the military, with the exception of those who observed an uptick in malingering and self-mutilation following the French government's suppression of substitutes in 1872.[129] The reported decline in malingering was difficult to quantify or prove definitively. In 1882 Zuber observed that it was not easy to know the basis for reports that faked illnesses were becoming rarer in the army, based on the lack of statistical data. Even though he reported having observed a myriad of malingerers during his career as a military doctor among troops in Africa and at the military hospital Val-du-Grâce, Zuber was convinced that malingering had nonetheless become less frequent.[130] Most medical texts did not link the late nineteenth-century decline in malingering in the military to the absence of major wars, which had marked the preceding decades with the successive Napoleonic, Crimean, and Franco-Prussian Wars.[131] The outbreak of World War I would later reignite preoccupations with the problem of malingering.

This decline in malingering can most plausibly be attributed to shifting attitudes toward conscription and military service and greater awareness and refinement of medical men's methods of detection. Late-nineteenth-century observers tended to frame the decline in malingering in terms of either social or medical progress. Zuber maintained that improvements in the military and better educated soldiers led to this decline.[132] His publication appeared concurrently with the passage of the Ferry laws in 1881 and 1882 that created free and secular public schools, in which "moral and civic instruction" replaced religious instruction, and that made schooling compulsory for children between the ages of six and thirteen. Other doctors also attributed the decline in malingering to improved education and maintained that education fostered patriotism and deterred men from shirking their civic duties. Boisseau considered lack of patriotism the primary motive

for malingering in the military. He attributed the decline in malingering to better-educated soldiers and shifts in military culture that made
military service less burdensome.[133] Yet others attributed a decline in
malingering to scientific and medical progress, which enabled doctors
to unmask those who feigned illness more easily.[134] Tourdes maintained that progress in medical diagnoses had reduced the number of
conditions that people could plausibly simulate or dissimulate.[135]
However, doctors acknowledged that advances in medical knowledge
not only better equipped doctors to detect malingering but also
enabled people to feign conditions more effectively. Some observed
that malingerers had become more skilled, sophisticated, and scientifically informed as a result of a better educated citizenry and the
circulation of medical knowledge.[136] Nonetheless, the military doctor
Emile Duponchel insisted that medical and scientific advances out-
paced the innovations of malingerers and declared, "Science is ahead
of fakers."[137]

Medical men at the end of the century challenged the prevailing
view from the early nineteenth century that there was no harm in
assuming a condition was faked rather than real.[138] Fin-de-siècle
commentators complained that practitioners had often been too quick
to assume malingering and too readily offered a diagnosis of a feigned
condition in lieu of a more rigorous, scientific diagnosis. In
1890 Duponchel insisted that doctors needed to be vigilant in
detecting malingering but rejected the precept of assuming malingering. He dismissed it as not only outdated but also inhumane. Doctor
Charles Burlureaux similarly denounced it as being "as barbaric as
unscientific."[139] In 1896 the forensic doctors Tourdes and Edmond
Metzquer similarly insisted upon the importance of detecting malingering, while urging doctors, if they had any doubt, to treat the disease
as if it were real.[140] Physician Xavier-Paul Aubert observed that
doctors needed to strike a delicate balance of being on guard yet not
"suspicious to the extreme."[141] Viewing malingering as a failure of
patriotism, Aubert also urged doctors to reawaken ideas of honor and
patriotism in a soldier to inspire him to give up his ruse.[142]

There was no clear ethical code in medical interventions involving
suspected malingerers. Doctors' approaches and methods of decision-
making seemed to vary according to their perception of the social costs
of malingering in various contexts. Consequently, medical men

employed more drastic measures among soldiers, who lacked full autonomy over their bodies, than among civilians. Military physicians and surgeons weighed the interests of individuals against the needs of the military and of society. Medical practitioners who expressed disdain for malingering in the military often advocated aggressive approaches informed by not only professional norms but also their personal attitudes and convictions about military service. Medical men generally viewed feigned diseases, particularly insanity, in the criminal justice system as a serious threat. Some medicolegal practitioners recognized that what they considered to be proof of malingering would convince most fellow doctors but not the general public and jurors. Their awareness of the difficulties of reconciling evidence that was medically convincing with evidence that was legally convincing led them to seek confessions or seemingly incontrovertible forms of proof.

Doctors debated what constituted proof of malingering. Noting the limits of medical knowledge about the progression and treatment of a number of diseases, Duponchel challenged the notion that the disappearance or seemingly spontaneous healing of a condition constituted proof that it had been feigned. He also maintained that medical men should not assume a condition was faked if a drug or treatment for the condition had not succeeded. Moreover, he called for most of the earlier literature on feigned diseases to be completely rejected, since doctors authored these works at a time when many aspects of pathology were entirely unknown or misunderstood.[143] In 1896 Tourdes and Metzquer observed that proving the existence of a disease was easier and more straightforward than proving its nonexistence. A diagnosis based on the lack of signs of a disease was more uncertain than a diagnosis based on their presence. Tourdes and Metzquer noted that diagnoses were on surer footing when "the proof the fraud can be obtained directly by the discovery of the instruments or substances that were used to cause or to simulate the illness."[144] Tourdes, Metzquer, and Duponchel also cast doubt on confessions – if medical practitioners secured them with either threats or the promise of indulgence – as proof of malingering. They emphasized that doubt and uncertainty often factored into even the most careful examinations and attentive monitoring of suspected malingerers.[145]

Malingering occupied a prominent place in medicolegal thought and became an important battleground for doctors engaged in burgeoning debates about medical ethics. Debates about both the effectiveness and the ethics of medical men's methods to detect malingering intensified over the course of the nineteenth century. By the late nineteenth century, many commentators observed that medical practitioners had to shift their tactics in detecting malingering due to their declining effectiveness. For one, more knowledgeable and better-prepared malingerers meant that some of the tools and tactics that practitioners had previously employed successfully had become well known to malingerers. Consequently, they lost their effectiveness, since malingerers expected to be subjected to these tests and were on guard.[146] At the same time as doctors found that simple traps and elements of surprise were becoming increasingly ineffective, they also debated whether they should rule out other tactics involving pain and altered states of consciousness for ethical reasons. Debates over the ethics and effectiveness of anesthesia as a tool to detect faked conditions divided the medical profession. More and more medical men rejected its use to detect malingering and called for other diagnostic approaches rooted in careful observation. By the late nineteenth century, many medical men suggested that their approach to the problem of malingering had shifted and become more humane.

Acting on behalf of the state to expose malingerers and deceivers, medical men engaged in adversarial relationships with suspected malingerers in order to establish their authority and to enforce the law in the name of the public good. Detecting malingering in some respects became a sort of escalating competition between doctors and malingerers. While the science of detection had improved over the course of the nineteenth century, so had the methods of deceivers. Medical men's responses to suspected malingering also provided an impetus for debates about medical ethics; however, ethical concerns about doctors' methods of detecting malingering did not gain much traction or attract controversy until the latter half of the nineteenth century. Many doctors defended their far-reaching tactics, including the use of coercion, pain, and anesthesia as diagnostic tools, and their encounters with suspected malingerers served to enhance the public relevance of their profession. Medical literature insisted that exposing malingerers was essential to preserving doctors' authority and reputations. Malingering elicited strong condemnations from medical practitioners who publicly tackled the subject, but some practitioners were likely uneasy in their role as agents of the state. The latter either reluctantly applied or quietly refused to apply laws and regulations that they did not support or care to enforce. While most medical men viewed military service as the primary arena in which they combatted deception, some focused their attention on so-called deception and "ruses" among women in matters of pregnancy and maternity.

4

Reproductive Bodies and Crimes

In June 1834 in a small town in northern France, rumors that Célestine Fiévet, an unmarried agricultural worker, had secretly given birth sparked an infanticide investigation. Judicial authorities summoned a doctor to examine her. He determined that she had recently given birth, and the search for her child's body led to the discovery of Fiévet's placenta and then the infant's corpse. The doctor's autopsy report concluded that the child had been viable, born at term, and died by strangulation. The next day a second corpse was discovered in Fiévet's straw bed. She explained that she had previously delivered before term and her infant died during delivery. However, the medical examiner maintained that the infant had been born at term about a year and a half earlier. Authorities discovered another body three days later, and the medical expert determined that this child had been viable and born at term three or four years ago. Pressed by judicial magistrates, Fiévet confessed to have given birth to eight children, two whom she left at a foundling hospital and six who were still born or died naturally. However, authorities ultimately concluded that she had given birth to ten children: three of whom Fiévet placed in founding hospitals, a stillborn fourth, and the following six whom she killed. According to reports in the periodical press, Fiévet's trembling hands wiped away the tears streaming down her face during her trial before the Lille assize court that November. Swayed by the forensic evidence, the jury unanimously voted to convict without granting extenuating circumstances, thus sentencing her to death. On February 17, 1835, Fiévet was executed.[1]

Fiévet's trial was exceptional in some respects. Although infanticide was a capital crime in late eighteenth- and nineteenth-century France, executions of women tried for infanticide were fairly uncommon and became more and more rare over the course of the nineteenth century.[2] However, other aspects of the investigation and proceedings were fairly typical. For example, rumors about a concealed pregnancy and delivery were often the source of formal infanticide investigations, and the suspected woman was typically lower class and unmarried. Accused women generally denied giving birth until a doctor declared otherwise; at which point, these women typically admitted to giving birth but insisted that the child was stillborn or died naturally. Their narratives were frequently at odds with those of medicolegal experts who played an increasingly important role in the prosecution of infanticide and other reproductive crimes.

In late eighteenth- and nineteenth-century France, medical men seized opportunities to establish themselves as authorities on women's and children's bodies. While women, particularly midwives, routinely exercised medicolegal authority in early modern France in matters concerning female bodies, reproduction, and reproductive crimes, the Revolution diminished their role, and subsequent nineteenth-century French law generally excluded women from official roles as medicolegal experts. Male medical practitioners consolidated their authority through their interventions in investigations and prosecutions of reproductive crimes and other criminal inquiries involving the female reproductive body. These interventions included diagnosing pregnancy and recent delivery and examining infant corpses. Medical men grappled with the problem of managing uncertainty when scrutinizing women's bodies and the corpses of infants. This problem was particularly pronounced during investigations of infanticide. Forensic evidence was more essential in infanticide cases than in criminal proceedings for other reproductive crimes, such as abortion, in which often other evidence implicating an accused abortion provider could be sufficient to secure a conviction even in the absence of forensic evidence.[3] In many infanticide trials, forensic reports and testimony appeared to be the most decisive factor in shaping jury verdicts.

However, all-male juries often weighed forensic evidence against evaluations of the character and life circumstances of the accused, and the sympathies of jurors shaped the interpretation of forensic evidence as well as their verdicts. Medical men's role in the search for material proof and bodily evidence was often both crucial and problematic, and ambivalent social attitudes toward reproductive crimes shaped jurists' and juries' interpretations and weighing of forensic evidence.

The Female Reproductive Body and the Male Medical Expert

In 1813 forensic doctor Fodéré observed that there were no other aspects of legal medicine that involved "as much uncertainty" and required "more circumspection, knowledge, and wisdom from the doctor" than pregnancy and childbirth.[4] Practitioners of legal medicine faced considerable challenges in reproductive matters, particularly determining whether a woman who was suspected, accused, or convicted of a crime was pregnant or had recently given birth. During the French Revolution, jurists, doctors, and social commentators expressed concerns about women falsely declaring pregnancy in order to delay or avoid execution or other modes of punishment. During the nineteenth century, medicolegal experts more commonly scrutinized women's bodies to determine whether the woman in question had concealed her pregnancy or childbirth in cases of suspected infanticide or concealment of birth. This latter charge generally resulted from suspicions that a woman, typically unmarried, had kept her pregnancy and childbirth secret and committed infanticide, yet no body was found, and the cause of death was consequently unknown. Medical men positioned themselves as authorities on the female reproductive body but faced considerable uncertainty in detecting pregnancy and recent childbirth.

During the Revolution, some convicted women sought to benefit from longstanding legal norms that prohibited the execution of pregnant women. Although the revolutionary Penal Code of 1791 did not codify stays of execution for pregnant women, revolutionary penal practice upheld the tradition. French legal procedures differed from those in England, where the practice of women declaring pregnancy and receiving a stay of execution until giving birth was known as "pleading the belly." In English common law, a jury of matrons, composed of twelve women, was responsible for inspecting female bodies to determine pregnancy, from the medieval period until the abolition of the jury of matrons in 1879.[5] In France, women, particularly midwives, had played a significant role as experts on women's bodies before the courts under the Old Regime, but women's official roles as medical experts in legal investigations were marginalized during the French Revolution and then practically eliminated in the post-revolutionary era.[6]

Medical examinations of women charged with capital offenses became a particularly pressing issue after the creation of the Revolutionary Tribunal of Paris in 1793, which executed over 2,600 people. The National Convention had tasked it with judging suspected traitors, conspirators, and counterrevolutionaries without the possibility of appeal.[7] Condemned women's declarations of pregnancy generally resulted in the Revolutionary Tribunal summoning male physicians, surgeons, or *officiers de santé* and a female midwife to examine the woman. Confirmations of pregnancy led to a stay of execution, which in some cases saved the woman's life, particularly if her delivery occurred after the fall of Robespierre.[8]

An accused or condemned woman's declaration of pregnancy normally resulted in a medical examination to confirm her condition, and medical experts often struggled to interpret uncertain signs of pregnancy in these cases. Since medical practitioners considered most signs of the early stages of pregnancy uncertain and exceedingly difficult to determine authoritatively, faking pregnancy usually simply involved a woman's false declaration. It often served as an effective strategy, at least in the short term. Reluctance to execute pregnant women coupled with uncertainty over diagnosing pregnancy, particularly in its early stages, led many medical practitioners who examined women who were not exhibiting signs of pregnancy to call for another examination to be conducted at a later date, often after five months of reported pregnancy, in order to reach a definitive judgment.[9] Some women, notably Madame de Kolly, declared pregnancy repeatedly. After being condemned to death on May 3, 1793, Kolly declared that she had been pregnant since late February. The medical examiners could not confirm the pregnancy and called for a subsequent examination after more time had passed. On July 30, they found that Kolly did not appear six months pregnant, but she insisted that she had become newly pregnant in La Petite Force prison since the previous medical examination. The medical report concluded that it was impossible to determine at that point whether her new declaration of pregnancy was true or false. Another examination in August did not yield a confirmation of the reported pregnancy. Nonetheless, Kolly secured a stay of execution and awaited the next examination. In early November, Kolly reported that she had miscarried on September 20 and that she had proof. She offered a fetus to the medical examiners. They declared that the fetus appeared to be over four-and-a-half-months, whereas her purported pregnancy would have been around two months. Two *officiers de santé* and a midwife concluded that Kolly had faked her pregnancies and miscarriage. They denounced her "subterfuges." She was executed the following day, on November 4.[10] Two days earlier, the Revolutionary Tribunal tried Olympe de Gouges, the author of the *Declaration of the Rights of Woman* (1791), and condemned her to death. She declared to the authorities that she was three-weeks pregnant. Her medical examination indicated "equivocal symptoms" of pregnancy including a tightened cervix but was inconclusive due to the early stage. In contrast to Kolly, Gouges did not receive a subsequent examination and was immediately executed.[11]

After the fall of Robespierre and the end of the Revolutionary Tribunal, doctors and jurists continued to grapple with diagnostic, legal, and ethical issues involving pregnancy declarations – not only for stays of execution. In April 1795, the revolutionary legislature prohibited even the judgment of pregnant women in capital offense cases.[12] The Court of Cassation later explained in 1805 that the rationale for this policy was that a pregnant woman lacked the mental clarity necessary for her defense and that the stresses of a trial could potentially harm her unborn child.[13] The Penal Code of 1810 was silent on the issue, and some doctors lamented that it did not prohibit trials during pregnancy.[14] Nonetheless, forensic doctors' views about the diminished intellectual and moral faculties of pregnant women shaped legal practices and criminal defense strategies. Forensic doctors and psychiatrists debated whether women were legally responsible for crimes committed during pregnancy. Many maintained that the degree to which pregnancy diminished legal responsibility varied widely but generally agreed that pregnancy constituted an extenuating circumstance warranting lesser criminal sentencing.[15] Medicolegal questions surrounding the verification of pregnancy, the length of pregnancy, and the distinction between a "true" and a "false," or molar, pregnancy were also relevant to civil law. However, many doctors objected to a vaginal examination to determine whether a woman was pregnant in civil cases. Forensic doctors observed that a woman's consent was necessary for vaginal examinations to determine pregnancy, with the exception of women who declared pregnancy for a stay of execution.[16] Many jurists and doctors wished to err on the side of caution concerning medicolegal pronouncements that repudiated condemned women's pregnancy declarations. Doctor Auguste Lutard advised his colleagues, "The expert will ask for a reprieve each time the slightest doubt enters his mind."[17] Sharing Lutard's circumspection, forensic doctor Gabriel Tourdes lamented that some medical practitioners made "reckless" declarations that erroneously discounted women's pregnancies, which thus led to the executions of pregnant women.[18]

Although nineteenth-century medical men often expressed greater certainty about reproduction than their early modern predecessors, uncertainties surrounding the pregnant female body nevertheless persisted, as medical men acknowledged their difficulties in diagnosing pregnancy, particularly in its early stages.[19] Nonetheless, they employed new diagnostic tools and techniques as part of a broader shift to the anatomo-clinical method, which privileged medical men's physical examinations and clinical observations of pregnant women and minimized the importance of women's own accounts of their experiences of pregnancy. Medical men came to reject quickening, the moment when a pregnant woman felt the first fetal movements, as proof of pregnancy, since they maintained that self-reported quickening did not necessarily mean that a woman was pregnant, particularly in legal cases in which she had reason to lie about her condition.[20] Many nineteenth-century doctors identified their own perception of active fetal movements, auscultation of the fetal heartbeat using a stethoscope, and *ballottement*, a technique of feeling the rebound of the fetus following a sudden tap on a woman's cervix, as the most reliable signs of pregnancy. They also observed that detecting pregnancy during the first trimester was extremely uncertain but became more reliable around the fourth or fifth month.[21] Medical practitioners' certainty progressively increased as pregnancy advanced. But, Joseph Briand maintained in his 1821 treatise on legal medicine that no single sign was sufficient to conclude definitively that a woman was pregnant and that experts could only be very circumspect in the early stages of pregnancy. Briand cautioned that a woman in the later stages of a purported pregnancy could be inflating the volume of her belly with cushions or through other artificial means. She also could be concealing laundry that would show evidence of her monthly menstruation.[22] Recognizing the risk and problem of forensic doctors misdiagnosing pregnancy, particularly in women faking or concealing pregnancy, the physician Eusèbe de Salle proclaimed in 1835, "Nearly the only certain sign of pregnancy is childbirth."[23]

Medicolegal experts commonly examined women who concealed their pregnancy and recent childbirth in forensic investigations of infanticide, but they also rarely examined women who claimed to have given birth. This kind of medical expertise could arise from investigations of *supposition de part* or *substitution de part*, crimes that involved passing off a child as one's own or substituting another child for one's own. Legal and social commentary on these kinds of crimes stressed their gravity as threats to the social order. An 1802 medicolegal treatise on pregnancy advised doctors charged with this task to examine carefully both the woman and the child whom she purportedly delivered, particularly the child's umbilical cord stump, to determine whether the infant's age corresponded to how long ago the woman appeared to have or claimed to have delivered. The author also cautioned doctors not to mistake menstrual blood for lochia, the vaginal discharge after childbirth containing blood, mucus, and uterine tissue. He suggested that some women timed their false declaration with the start of their menstruation for this reason. He maintained that menstrual blood was "bloodier" and had an "animalistic odor," whereas lochia was more fluid and had an acidic odor.[24]

In the 1830s, Doctor Nestor-Joseph Pellassy des Fayolles conducted highly unusual, confounding experiments to determine whether a woman could plausibly fake childbirth and afterbirth. In 1833 Pellassy des Fayolles warned of the serious harms caused by a woman simulating pregnancy and childbirth and then passing off someone else's child as her own. His thesis presented to the medical faculty of Paris addressed the question of whether a woman could fake childbirth, a widely doubted possibility. He answered affirmatively. He experimented on twelve female cadavers and six live women to demonstrate that a placenta and umbilical cord could be introduced into the vagina. He explained that he had introduced a "fresh placenta" and umbilical cord with the aid of a speculum into the vaginal canal of these six live women, two of whom were pregnant, and reported that three of the women did not even perceive it. Pellassy des Fayolles did not comment on how surprising or implausible the women's supposed imperception would have been given that the average placenta is about nine inches long and weighs about a pound. He reported that after he removed the speculum, the placenta remained in one woman's vaginal canal for six hours. He claimed that she readily consented to the experiment, which he only briefly discussed. The primary message of his treatise was that doctors must be cautious and circumspect when investigating matters of pregnancy and childbirth. Pellassy des Fayolles insisted that even signs of pregnancy that seemed most certain were subject to possible error.[25] He republished his work five years later after the June 1838 arrest in Paris of two women, one of whom was a midwife, for the criminal act of infant substitution, presenting an infant as born of a woman who was not the mother. Pellassy des Fayolles noted the "diverse stratagems" and "ruses" that women could employ to simulate a pregnancy or recent delivery, including introducing foreign objects into the vagina for a prolonged period.[26] Alfred-Armand-Louis-Marie Velpeau's 1838 treatise on obstetrics, which referenced Pellassy des Fayolles's work, offered an account of a woman hospitalized in Tours and Paris who purportedly introduced rags into her vagina in order to simulate childbirth after having feigned pregnancy for nearly three years.[27] The question of feigned childbirth and pregnancy captured these physicians' imaginations.

   Other medical practitioners considered whether a woman might fake an abortion. Midwives, other medical practitioners, and pharmacists involved in abortions appeared more frequently in the courts on criminal abortion charges than the women they treated; however, the latter could also face criminal prosecution and serious punishment, namely imprisonment. Medicolegal experts, including Henri Legrand du Saulle, found it surprising that a woman would fake an abortion, since she would be identifying herself as guilty of or as an accomplice to a crime and could be severely punished.[28] Legrand du Saulle, however, pointed to Tardieu's involvement in one such case in September 1857, which Tardieu described as "unique in the annals of legal medicine."[29] The case involved a woman in Melun who reported that she had consulted a midwife to determine whether she was pregnant, after missing her period for three months and experiencing some light bleeding during the fourth month, and that the midwife had harmed her. The ensuing investigation revealed that the woman was actually working with another midwife to frame her professional rival for inducing an abortion without the woman's consent. Over the course of four days, the two accomplices produced blood clots, chunks of flesh, and a purported portion of the placenta, which they presented to a local doctor, Saint-Yves, as proof of the rival midwife's crime. The doctor believed that the so-called placenta was actually a sheep's spleen. Saint-Yves examined the woman and found no signs of recent pregnancy. The local prosecutor summoned Tardieu to weigh in, and he confirmed Saint-Yves's findings. The woman who had claimed to have been the "victim of the abortion" confessed, revealing that she had not even visited the midwife whom they had framed and had used her own menstrual blood and urine as evidence of a lost pregnancy and that her accomplice had supplied the pieces of flesh. Tardieu credited Saint-Yves's wisdom in suspecting the fraud and lauded both of their roles in bringing this unusual and "odious" fraud to light.[30]

In contrast to such exceedingly rare forms of medicolegal inquiry, medical experts commonly sought to determine whether women had concealed their pregnancy and childbirth, particularly during infanticide investigations. Some of these women produced purported evidence of menstrual blood as proof of their innocence. They resorted to various means of simulating menstruation to hide their pregnancy and childbirth. Jeanne-Marie Tessier, a mother of two who appeared before the Ille-et-Vilaine assize court for infanticide charges in 1864, sought to quash suspicions that she had been pregnant and killed her infant by reporting that she had merely experienced a temporary cessation of menstruation but her period had returned. She claimed to offer material proof of the return of her menses and placed a mass of blood and flesh in the hands of the mayor. The medical expert who had been summoned to examine Tessier reported without hesitation that she had recently given birth and that the substance that she provided to the mayor was her placenta, with its interior membrane carefully removed. He observed that she undertook these efforts "without a doubt with the hope of deceiving inexperienced eyes." Ultimately, the court convicted her of infanticide and sentenced her to fifteen years of hard labor.[31] Some women, particularly servants under the watchful eye of their employers, used blood that was not their own menstrual blood to stain their dirty laundry each month in order to make it seem as though they were menstruating and not pregnant.[32]

Some women, particularly those suspected of infanticide or concealment of birth, used various means to conceal or account for changes in their physical appearance during and after pregnancy. Some pregnant women resorted to mechanical or sartorial means of concealing their growing belly. In 1859 a twenty-seven-year-old domestic servant in Châteauneuf, seeking to conceal her pregnancy from her husband and community, claimed that she was suffering from a hernia. After being accused of and charged with infanticide, she revealed that she had "compressed the development of her waist with the help of a board she had a carpenter make, telling him that it would be used to hang a lamp."[33] Other women relied upon corsets to hide their pregnancy, while some simply used bulky clothing to disguise the size of their belly.[34] Women who concealed their pregnancy sometimes claimed to have other conditions, such as dropsy (involving bodily swelling due to an accumulation of excess water), to account for changes in their appearance or health.[35]

Most infanticide investigations that went to trial before the assize courts involved medical examinations of women who initially denied that they had been pregnant and had recently given birth. Women could in theory refuse a medical examination, but women tried for infanticide seemed to have rarely exercised their right of refusal successfully. Some medical experts seemed to have exerted strong pressure on women who expressed reluctance or objected to the examination.[36] Medical men primarily relied upon a pelvic examination and inspection of an accused woman's genitals to determine whether she had recently delivered. They evaluated other bodily signs of recent pregnancy and childbirth, focusing on the abdomen and breasts. Male medical experts scrutinized the appearance of abdominal skin and looked for linear hyperpigmentation or a brown line running vertically up the middle of the abdomen from the pubis to umbilicus, which commonly appears during pregnancy. They inspected the appearance of women's breasts and applied pressure on them to see whether they would secrete milk or colostrum. In some cases, experts also assessed milk or blood stains on the women's clothing, bedding, or mattress. A problem facing medical experts seeking to detect material traces of a recent delivery was that these signs could disappear fairly quickly. Fodéré contended that the signs of a recent delivery generally disappeared within eight to ten days.[37]

While medicolegal experts generally did not consider the signs of a recent delivery to be as uncertain as the signs of early pregnancy, some doctors clearly had difficulty in evaluating pregnant and postpartum women and committed diagnostic errors that risked or resulted in wrongful convictions. A medical expert concluded in an 1868 investigation that a woman who was accused of concealment of birth had very recently given birth. She was thus convicted and sentenced to six months in prison. The following month, she gave birth to a full-term infant. It therefore became evident that she had been wrongfully convicted.[38] A similar case occurred in 1896 when a doctor concluded that a woman accused of infanticide had recently given birth. Three days after his examination, she gave birth in prison. Her child died almost immediately, and she later demanded reparations from the doctor in the civil court.[39] The number of cases in which doctors misdiagnosed pregnancy and childbirth is unknown.

The female reproductive body presented uncertainties for male medical practitioners involved in criminal investigations and proceedings, particularly those involving reproductive crimes. As Revolutionary-era concerns about women's false declarations of pregnancy waned in the nineteenth century, medical experts more commonly scrutinized women's bodies to determine whether the woman in question had concealed her pregnancy in cases of suspected infanticide. Medical men during this period proclaimed and positioned themselves as authorities on women's bodies. However, the female reproductive body was relatively opaque to male practitioners and presented challenges to forensic doctors' efforts to uncover bodily truths and serve justice. Furthermore, many women actively sought to undermine these efforts in order to save their own lives.

The Forensics of Infanticide

In 1838 Charles-Prosper Ollivier d'Angers, member of the Royal Academy of Medicine, observed, "There is no question in the history of legal medicine that has been the object of a greater number of studies and experiments than that of infanticide." He noted that medicolegal expertise on infanticide required extensive knowledge and training in medical matters pertaining to childbirth, abortion, wounds, putrefaction, embryology, fetal anatomy, uterine diseases, and fetal viability.[40] However, not all of the medical practitioners who intervened in infanticide investigations and prosecutions had extensive training and experience in these fields. Medical practitioners often struggled to distinguish between stillbirth, natural death, and murder and to establish forensic proof of infanticide.

Medical experts played crucial roles in most stages of infanticide investigations, which often began after the discovery of an infant's corpse. People discovered infant cadavers in cesspools, latrines, bodies of water, or isolated areas. In the countryside, corpses were often found on the side of roads and in fields, gardens, and manure heaps. In cities and large towns, they were often found in rivers, canals, sewers, drains, and toilets.[41] Forensic doctors observed that the discovery of an infant corpse that seemed to have been hidden or discarded did not necessarily indicate that a child had been a victim of infanticide. The child could have been stillborn or died naturally. Physicians noted that some parents hid the bodies of their stillborn children simply to avoid the costs and burden of a burial.[42] Courts charged medical practitioners with examining found bodies.

Other investigations did not stem from the accidental discovery of a body but from suspicions of particular women. Scrutiny of women and their reproductive lives as well as gossip or "public rumors" often led to formal infanticide investigations and the active search for a body. Many of these searches resulted in the discovery of an infant's corpse hidden in the suspect's home, often in a fireplace or stove or in her room in a trunk, armoire, or underneath her bed. Community members typically communicated their suspicions to the authorities after observing what had appeared to be a woman's pregnancy ending without any mention of childbirth, loss, or a new baby. Surveillance and scrutiny of women's bodies extended beyond a woman's outward

physical appearance to signs of her menstruation or lack thereof.
Employers would notice whether the laundry and sheets of domestic
servants indicated either a lack of menstrual blood during a pregnancy
or bloodied clothing and sheets from childbirth.[43] Women, including
midwives, often alerted authorities about suspected cases of infanticide. For example, in 1864 in the Alpes-Maritimes, a seventy-one-year-
old woman approached a midwife and offered to pay her for a certificate stating that her thirty-year-old daughter's child was still-born. The
midwife was suspicious after examining the infant's corpse, and the
authorities charged both mother and daughter with infanticide.[44]

Some investigations did not culminate in infanticide prosecutions,
and medicolegal reports often determined how judicial authorities
proceeded and framed charges. When investigations yielded neither a
body nor a corpus delicti, judicial authorities could pursue lesser
charges of concealment of birth. In other cases, the discovery of the
cadaver of a presumably murdered newborn never resulted in the
identification of a suspect. Tardieu noted that over 1,200 unidentified
newborn cadavers arrived at the Paris Morgue from the mid-1830s
through the mid-1860s. He determined that about three-fourths had
been murdered.[45] When medical experts concluded in their autopsy
reports that the child died naturally, many of these investigations
ended without prosecution. When doctors could not determine the
cause of a child's death and the suspect had concealed her pregnancy,
authorities sometimes pursued concealment of birth charges rather
than infanticide. The ministry of justice also encouraged presidents
of the assize courts to pose to juries in infanticide trials the subsidiary
question of negligent homicide of a newborn, especially in cases when
medical evidence was lacking or inconclusive.[46] Additionally, investigating magistrates often chose not to bring infanticide charges before
the assize courts on account of inconclusive medicolegal reports. If
equivocal or inconclusive forensic evidence was coupled with strong
circumstantial evidence, jurists often charged defendants with negligent homicide or concealment of birth in the correctional courts that
tried less serious criminal offenses without juries. Moreover, even
when jurists found forensic evidence convincing, they would commonly resort to "correctionalization," the practice of reclassifying
crimes into lesser offenses tried by professional judges in the correctional courts, because of their concerns about juries' leniency toward

mothers accused of infanticide. In these cases, jurists sought to minimize the risks of acquittals for the crime of infanticide in the assize
courts by transferring charges of negligent homicide to the correctional
courts instead where judges were more likely to convict.[47]

Medical experts played a decisive role in determining whether the
crime of infanticide had been committed. Jurists charged them with
answering key questions, including whether the infant had lived or was
stillborn, and if the former, whether the death was due to natural
causes or was a violent death. Another central task for medical experts
was determining the age of an infant. To advance an infanticide case,
medical experts had to certify that the child was a newborn, commonly
understood legally as a child during the first three days of life. If the
expert concluded that the child was not a newborn, charges of infanticide did not apply.[48] Judicial authorities also instructed medical
experts to determine whether the time of the accused woman's delivery
corresponded to the presumed date of birth of the autopsied infant.
They sometimes were unable to offer an assessment due to the state of
the infant's cadaver, an inconclusive examination of the woman's
body, or both.

Judicial authorities also tasked doctors with determining whether
the child had been born at term and was viable. Doctors generally
identified a full-term birth in terms of the development of an infant's
body, particularly weight and height; the state of the skin; and the
degree of bone formation. The state of the cadaver, whether mutilated
or in a state of advanced decomposition, often presented challenges for
medical men. Some doctors assessed whether a mutilated cadaver was
a full-term newborn based on the measurements of the recovered
bones or the weights of recovered organs.[49] When forensic doctors
concluded that a cadaver was that of a newborn, they also had to
assess whether the newborn had all the characteristics of viability.
These characteristics included sufficient development of the organs to
sustain life and essential bodily functions as well as the absence of
congenital conditions or diseases that would compromise the life of the
infant.[50]

In addition to establishing viability, medical experts assessed
whether the infant had lived or was stillborn. Doctors considered
respiration as nearly the only sign constituting proof of life.[51] Many
women accused of infanticide insisted that their infant did not cry, thus

implying that the child had not breathed and that the child's death did not constitute infanticide. To assess proof of breathing or the lack thereof, doctors primarily relied upon the lung float test, also known as the hydrostatic test or docimasia. This autopsy procedure, developed in the late seventeenth century, entailed placing the lungs or portions of the lungs in water and observing whether they sank or floated. Doctors interpreted floating lungs as an indication that the infant had breathed independently of the mother and therefore died after birth.

Doctors debated to what extent the hydrostatic test constituted reliable proof of a live-birth and breathing. Some medical men identified various reasons that could account for floating lungs, aside from an infant's breathing. In 1801 doctor Emmanuel-Joseph Olivaud posited that artificial means of introducing air into lungs, for example an alarmed mother blowing air in her lifeless child's mouth, could penetrate the lungs of a dead child and produce a false indication of life.[52] Other forensic doctors suggested that lungs may also float due to putrefaction and infantile emphysema.[53] In 1805 medical experts in the *département* du Nord qualified their autopsy reports by noting that lung flotation did not constitute definitive proof that an infant had been born alive.[54] Nonetheless, some doctors were confident in the test as definitive. In 1838 Tourdes observed, "The docimasia...has an incontestable power, and despite the objections, nearly all theoretical, that those raise against it, it permits the medical practitioner in the vast majority of cases to confirm whether the child had or had not lived."[55] Tardieu objected, citing a case in which lungs initially sunk in a hydrostatic test but floated when tested days later after being preserved in a jar with alcohol. The preservation of lungs in alcohol, putrefactive gasses, artificial inflation, and freezing could all compromise the hydrostatic lung test.[56] An untold number of women who delivered a still-born baby may have been unjustly condemned for infanticide as a result of the test.

Additionally, medical experts sought to shed light on the question of how long ago an infant had died: hours, days, weeks, months, or even years before the discovery of the corpse. Medical experts evaluated postmortem rigidity, putrefaction, or the state of decomposition, in relation to the environmental factors that could affect these rates, including different temperatures and seasons. Some forensic doctors conducted experiments on cadavers to determine the effects and rates of decomposition under various conditions. For example, in the 1830s Orfila and Octave Lesueur experimented on cadavers by exposing them to open air, burying them, submerging them in water, surrounding them with fecal matter in cesspits, and placing them in piles of manure. Their findings suggested that many medical practitioners erroneously identified the time of death, particularly for infant bodies found in cesspits.[57]

During the years that followed, some forensic doctors turned to the newly developed field of forensic entomology to estimate time of death. Orfila and Lesueur were among the first medical experts to study the insects attracted to decomposing corpses, but they did not use these insects to determine time of death. The first application of forensic entomology to estimate the time of death in a criminal case occurred in 1850 following the discovery of a mummified infant cadaver in a chimney. Physician Louis François Etienne Bergeret's inspection of the mummified corpse revealed that insects had colonized it and devoured the internal organs. The court tasked Bergeret with determining the estimated date of death in order to identify a suspect. Bergeret used the life cycle of insects to estimate the date of death as two years earlier, although he mistakenly assumed that the complete metamorphosis of the insects took a year.[58] Subsequent studies on forensic entomology during the late nineteenth century included the pioneering work of Jean Pierre Mégnin. Mégnin, a veterinarian and researcher specializing in parasites, aided the forensic doctor Brouardel in a similar case involving the mummified body of a newborn discovered in a chimney in 1879. He subsequently conducted extensive forensic entomological research.[59] Forensic doctors' assessments of time of death, whether through forensic entomology or the science of human decomposition, were many times instrumental in identifying suspects and building the prosecution's case.

The most essential task for medical experts was identifying the potential cause of death – whether natural, accidental, or the result of violence. Medical experts examined cadavers for traces of violence, including those indicative of strangulation, wounds, and skull fractures. Tardieu identified suffocation as the most common method of infanticide. Forensic expertise was especially crucial for this manner of death, since it often did not produce outward signs of violence and required autopsies to yield proof. Tardieu influentially identified sub-pleural ecchymoses, or dark spots (Tardieu spots) found on lungs, as signs of suffocation. Tardieu enumerated various forms of suffocation: airways blocked by covering an infant's mouth and nostrils with a hand, bedding, or clothing or by thrusting a foreign object down the throat; sustained pressure on the chest or abdomen; deprivation of air in a confined space, such as a box, trunk, or piece of furniture; or burying alive. While some forms of suffocation could leave visible exterior traces of violence, such as nail and finger marks around an infant's nose and mouth, other forms of suffocation, such as using a pillow or bedding, might not. An autopsy could then reveal tiny hemorrhages on the lungs and the heart's pericardium, which Tardieu and other doctors viewed as indications of death by suffocation. However, some doctors did not view these signs as definitive proof of death by suffocation.[60]

Medicolegal experts also sought to determine whether traces of violence had been produced during life or after death. Fodéré noted that some perpetrators suffocated and inflicted violence on live infants by inserting straw, feathers, dirt, or even fecal matter into their mouths and nostrils. In other cases, the appearance of traces of violence on an infant's body might simply be the product of childbirth.[61] Tardieu similarly observed that obstetrical interventions could produce wounds during childbirth. However, he noted that some mutilations and wounds on infant corpses were intentional, fatal wounds made by sharp objects, including knives, razors, cleavers, scissors, and needles, while others were inflicted after death.[62] In some cases, animals, commonly pigs, inflicted postmortem wounds. Medical experts also detected marks from dogs, wolves, cats, birds of prey, rats, and various other carnivorous and omnivorous animals.[63] Some forensic doctors warned that traces of violence, such as a foreign object in the throat, might have been introduced after death in an attempt to simulate infanticide and to cast suspicions on the mother or other person charged with the infant's care.[64]

Medical men distinguished between infant death due to acts of commission, such as suffocation, smothering, strangulation, blunt head injury, or drowning, and death due to acts of omission, or the voluntary deprivation of the care necessary for the basic needs of the child. Medical experts and jurists understood infanticide by omission to include exposing a newborn to harmful cold or hot temperatures; depriving a child of air by not clearing airways obstructed by amniotic fluid, mucus, or blood; depriving a child of food; or hemorrhaging due to the failure to tie the umbilical cord.[65] Medical men debated whether a mother's neglect or negligence could be the product of her ignorance about the necessary care for a child. Doctors and jurists generally claimed that all women understood the importance of tying the umbilical cord. However, the extent of vernacular medical knowledge that some women, particularly those pregnant for the first time, actually possessed was unclear.

Medical authorities debated whether a mother's failure to tie her infant's umbilical cord would result in the child's death. Some doctors maintained that the absence of an umbilical cord ligature would produce fatal hemorrhaging. Others noted that medical knowledge on the subject had evolved. As Fodéré observed, the first doubts about the necessity of tying the umbilical cord emerged in the late seventeenth century, and during the eighteenth and nineteenth centuries, obstetricians and forensic doctors debated whether the absence of a ligature was always fatal.[66] Most nineteenth-century medicolegal publications that addressed the subject maintained that the absence of a ligature, whether by premeditated design or negligence, could produce fatal hemorrhaging but did not always result in death. Consequently, many forensic publications warned that the lack of a ligature was not sufficient reason for doctors to conclude that it was the cause of death, especially since this form of infanticide was extraordinarily rare.[67] Nonetheless, medical experts' written reports and courtroom testimonies in many infanticide trials attributed infant deaths to the lack of an umbilical cord ligature.[68] In most cases, medical men and prosecutors implied or asserted that a woman who failed to tie the umbilical cord intended to kill her child. The Parisian lawyer Charles-Claude Brillaud-Laujardière found fault with how easily and frequently some medical experts came to these conclusions. He argued that fatal hemorrhaging due to the absence of a ligature was exceedingly rare and nearly impossible under most circumstances.[69] In cases in which medical experts observed the lack of a ligature but did not identify it as the cause of death, they nevertheless noted in their reports that its absence was evidence of the lack of necessary care for the infant. This claim supported the case for negligent homicide. Some accused women insisted that they did not tie the umbilical cord simply because their child was stillborn or had already died of natural causes almost immediately after birth.

Forensic doctors expressed varying degrees of certainty in their findings, and some medical and legal professionals insisted that uncertainty should weigh in favor of the mother. Fodéré cautioned doctors not to make assumptions about the culpability of the mother in the absence of sufficient signs of voluntary violence on the infant's body.[70] Briand and Chaudé advised medical practitioners to ignore rumors or gossip about the accused and to interpret the facts of the case in the most favorable sense for the mother, whenever there was not sufficient proof against her. Medicolegal experts could introduce greater doubt in criminal trials due to the complexity of their findings. Briand and Chaudé insisted that this was rightfully so, since medicolegal reports that were nuanced and rigorous served as a bulwark against judicial errors and wrongful convictions. They and other forensic doctors lamented that some medical practitioners issued overly confident and erroneous forensic reports that exceeded the limits of their medical training and put the lives of innocent women at risk.[71] Lawyers expressed similar concerns about flawed forensic reports and the problem of proof. One observed in 1823, "The more serious a crime, the more the proofs must be strong and sure."[72] However, sure proof was rare in infanticide cases.

Moreover, jurists commonly decried the lack of competency, thoroughness, and knowledge of some medical experts. A jurist in Lille complained in 1810 that a doctor and an *officier de santé* performing an autopsy in a case of suspected infanticide by suffocation failed to examine the brain.[73] Often the reports of *officiers de santé* were not as clear and comprehensive as those of more highly trained doctors. In 1841 the president of the Nièvre assize court criticized the inadequacies of the reports by "ignorant" *officiers de santé*.[74] The following year the president of the Ille-et-Vilaine assize court complained of the "scandalous acquittal" of a nineteen-year-old woman who was accused of stuffing her child's mouth with dried leaves and throwing the child into a moat. The *officier de santé* whom the justice of the peace tasked with the autopsy did not perform the hydrostatic lung test or other standard procedures for infant autopsies. During and before the trial, he professed his lack of competence. The assize court president attributed the acquittal to the *officier de santé*'s incompetence and the failings of the justice of the peace.[75] In 1845 the president of the Haute-Garonne assize court complained about conflicting medical reports in an infanticide trial and the lacking qualifications of one expert, who "inspired little confidence when he said in court that he had never attended a birth in his medical career."[76] The public display of medicolegal incompetence through trial testimony before juries drew the ire of jurists.

Conflicting conclusions among medical experts increased the likelihood of acquittal in infanticide trials. In some cases, doctors disagreed about whether the child lived due to contradictory results from the hydrostatic lung test. The autopsy in an 1845 infanticide case heard at the Aveyron assize court indicated that the child had lived and breathed based on clear results from the lung test; however, the investigating magistrate ordered a second test, during which the lungs sank rather than floated, suggesting that the child had not breathed. The president of the assize court requested that a more learned expert, a professor of legal medicine in Montpellier, issue a third report. This report challenged the validity of the second test, since the lungs had been in calcium chloride, a caustic liquid, for twenty-six days between the first and second lung test.[77] Other disagreements concerned cause of death. In an 1845 infanticide investigation in Morhiban, the two medical experts performing the autopsy found bruising and a crescent-shaped mark, resembling a nail mark, on the infant's neck. Both concluded that asphyxiation by suffocation was the cause of death. However, one maintained that voluntary pressure from a person's hands was responsible for the lesions on the neck, while the other attributed the marks and bruising either to pressure from the pelvic bones during childbirth or to the weight of the mother's limb on the infant after birth. As a consequence of these conflicting medical views, the jury acquitted the accused of infanticide but declared her guilty of lesser charges.[78] Additionally, a jurist in 1859 complained about an autopsy report issued by an inexperienced *officier de santé* who found no traces of violence on the corpse. A doctor subsequently summoned to perform a new autopsy found that the child's skull had a triple fracture produced by blows to the head. The defense called another doctor who maintained that the fractures were due to strong pressure exerted during a difficult labor. The medicolegal testimony during the trial lasted four hours and caused confusion.[79]

Judicial magistrates lamented that uncertain, unclear, or conflicting medicolegal testimony could undermine the state's case and lead to an acquittal when jurists thought a conviction was in order. A common strategy of defense lawyers was to summon their own medical experts to contest the findings of the state's experts. Women charged with infanticide generally lacked the financial resources to fund their own legal defense, and the president of the assize court appointed an attorney for defendants in these cases. The French state paid the legal expenses, including the fees of medical expert witnesses. In some cases, defense lawyers secured medical experts who persuaded jurors of the validity of their findings more effectively than the experts whom the state called. Court-appointed medical experts at times struggled to explain forensic evidence to those lacking medical knowledge, a challenge that medicolegal literature of the period addressed.[80] A jurist complained about an infanticide trial before the Alpes-Maritimes assize court in 1864 in which the "hesitant declarations" as well as the appearance of the court-summoned doctor made a negative impression on the jury, particularly in contrast to the defense's medical expert.[81] In another infanticide trial at that court two days later, the defense summoned two doctors who contradicted the report made by the state's medical expert and insisted that there was an insufficient degree of certainty in the autopsy report. During the trial, the state's medical expert explained that less definitive formulations and terms such as "probable" were the norm in written medicolegal reports. The magistrate, who was convinced of the guilt of the accused, lamented that the jury nevertheless acquitted on account of the medicolegal debates. Jurors may have seized upon forensic uncertainty due in part to their sympathy for the defendant whose father impregnated her.[82] Nonetheless, jurists commonly expressed concerns about the deleterious effects of conflicting testimonies and a battle of experts in the courtroom sowing doubt among jurors.

While some jurors sympathetic to a defendant seized upon uncertainty in medical evidence as grounds for acquittal, others simply acquitted despite damning medicolegal evidence. Jurors often afforded more weight to their moral assessments of the accused or the circumstances of her plight than to the medical evidence indicating her guilt.

For example, a domestic servant, facing infanticide charges in 1841 after her master impregnated her, claimed that her baby died due to falling on the ground during delivery, but the medical experts attributed the infant's fractured skull to an act of violence. The president of the Nièvre assize court observed that the jurors in the trial did not give much weight to the doctors' findings and were more swayed by their sympathies for the defendant, particularly since her master would have had no legal paternal responsibility for the out-of-wedlock child.[83] In 1842 the president of the assize court at Lille complained of juries' leniency after jurors acquitted a twenty-year-old chambermaid, despite the conviction of the medical experts that violent blows to the head and a resulting skull fracture caused her newborn's death. However, the jurist reported that the accused's young age, her working-class status (like the vast majority of those accused of infanticide), her sadness and pain, "honest conduct," as well as the sorrow of her parents, from whom she hid her pregnancy, led jurors to ignore the medical evidence.[84]

Judicial magistrates and forensic doctors expressed grave concerns about the inadequacies of the forensic reports and testimonies of some medical practitioners. Jurists and juries grappled with inconclusive or conflicting reports of practitioners with varying degrees of expertise. Nonetheless, medical practitioners' autopsy reports often served as the most important determining factor in judicial authorities' decisions to prosecute infanticide cases and in many juries' trial verdicts. Tensions between doubt and certainty were at the heart of infanticide investigations, which could reveal as well as obscure the limits of forensic knowledge.

Medical Expertise and Mothers on Trial

Although many commentators decried infanticide as a heinous crime committed by monstrous mothers, others viewed it as a tragic and unfortunate response to bleak circumstances. The issue of infanticide was tied to the legal and social realities that constrained the possibilities for women, particularly poor unmarried women, and inhibited their ability to raise children in favorable circumstances. Jurors' sympathy for the plight of female defendants influenced their evaluation of forensic evidence and trial verdicts. The majority of women tried for

infanticide had concealed their pregnancy, and many initially denied
that they had given birth. A medical examination frequently led to
their admission of having given birth, but most accused women
insisted either that their child was stillborn or that the child died
naturally or accidentally. Forensic doctors sometimes found accused
women's narratives and defenses wildly implausible. While medical
experts' reports and evaluations of the plausibility of the accused's
claims carried weight in criminal proceedings, juries' attitudes toward
the broader social context of the crime and their sympathy for individual defendants were also crucial.

Infanticide stemmed from women's lack of access to other means of
controlling their reproductive lives given the lack of reliable contra-
ception, the criminalization of abortion, the absence of legal adoption
of children under twenty-one, and the difficulties of child abandonment. Infanticide in nineteenth-century France often effectively served
as a form of delayed abortion and was not only a reproductive but also
a survival strategy.[85] Many nineteenth-century commentators complained of policies that worsened the plight of unmarried mothers,
some of whom resorted to infanticide. For one, they decried the
Napoleonic ban on paternity suits (*recherche de paternité*), which
women had used to establish legal paternity and to claim child support
when the mother and father were unwed.[86] Moreover, many bourgeois commentators denounced the suppression of the *tours*, revolving
turnstiles in which abandoned children could be secretly and anony-
mously placed at foundling hospitals. A Napoleonic degree of 1811 had
ordered the establishment of *tours* through all French *départements*
and *arrondissements*. While supporters claimed that the *tours* saved
lives, opponents criticized the *tours* as an expensive social practice that
encouraged immorality and provided women an alibi for infanticide,
since a woman who killed and hid the body of her child could have
claimed to have left her infant in a *tour*. The suppression of the *tours*
began in the 1830s and continued through the late 1850s, amidst
ongoing, fierce debates on the subject. The closing of most *tours* made
child abandonment more difficult and anonymous abandonment
impossible. Supporters of *tours* argued that their suppression led to
an increase in abortion and infanticide, particularly exposure, which
involved leaving infants in an isolated place to die from hypothermia,
hunger, or an animal attack.[87] In 1838 a Parisian doctor, who insisted

that the suppression of the *tours* in Paris resulted in an increase in infanticide, recounted firsthand the horrific results of the exposure of infants, particularly when animals devoured infants' body parts.[88] In 1840 jurors in the Corrèze writing to the Minister of the Interior attributed an increase in infanticide cases to the suppression of the *tours*. They and other like-minded citizens suggested that the state should not merely prosecute women for infanticide but tackle underlying social problems and enact policies to alleviate the plight of women who could not care for their children.[89]

Infanticide was widely considered a crime of unmarried mothers abandoned by the men who seduced them. The majority of persons accused of infanticide were unmarried women from rural areas. One-third of those tried for infanticide were domestic servants.[90] Servants often concealed their pregnancies and deliveries, since an illicit pregnancy generally resulted in a servant losing her job. Servants were vulnerable to rape or seduction due to living apart from family and friends and sleeping in unlocked rooms that their masters and others could access.[91] Rape and seduction, the latter of which was associated with men's false promises of marriage, were generally considered extenuating circumstances in infanticide trials.[92] According to some nineteenth-century bourgeois commentators, the material conditions of working-class women and their romantic illusions led some to yield to "disastrous seductions," which could result in illicit pregnancies that ended in infanticide. Bourgeois men often understood women's recourse to infanticide as a means of avoiding the shame of illegitimate pregnancy and the burden of raising a child, particularly for those without the financial means to do so.[93] Many publications lamented the impunity of men who impregnated women and identified male irresponsibility for illegitimate children as a significant cause of infanticide.

Some commentators suggested that many juries either acquitted or granted extenuating circumstances to female defendants on account of their sympathy for the plight of unmarried women who resorted to infanticide, as well as their indignation over the impunity that men responsible for impregnating them enjoyed.[94] In contrast, juries showed little sympathy for the small number of men tried for infanticide. These men, particularly incestuous fathers who committed infanticide to destroy the proof of their crime, were often convicted without extenuating circumstances. The French state first introduced extenuating circumstances for infanticide in 1824 and expanded its scope in 1832, effectively decreasing the criminal penalty by two degrees. Those convicted of infanticide with extenuating circumstances faced hard labor or imprisonment for a minimum of five years, but those without extenuating circumstances faced the death penalty.[95] The rate of conviction for infanticide increased after the 1832 law on extenuating circumstances.[96] Juries widely – almost universally – granted extenuating circumstances to women convicted of infanticide. By 1836 the courts granted extenuating circumstances to 95 percent of those convicted of infanticide, and the proportion increased to 99 percent in 1840.[97] However, jurists complained that some juries continued to acquit guilty defendants to prevent them from going to prison. A jurist lamented in 1841 that even the most well-composed juries refused to convict women accused of infanticide whose guilt was clear.[98] Another jurist complained in 1864 that some jurors did not even view infanticide as a crime.[99]

Infanticide prosecutions in France peaked in the mid-nineteenth century. The average number of infanticide charges each year doubled between the 1820s and 1850s. Between 1856 and 1860, the assize courts tried over 1,200 persons for infanticide.[100] However, only a minority of allegations of infanticide culminated in prosecution. In some investigations, a body was discovered, but the culprit remained unknown. Many more cases of infanticide were presumably never detected or reported.[101] It is unclear whether or to what extent changes in the rates of prosecution reflected the actual incidence of infanticide. In 1868 the preeminent forensic doctor Tardieu suggested that the increase in infanticide prosecutions might not have been a product of a greater incidence of the crime. It might have been the result of prosecutors' greater efforts to investigate and to prosecute infanticide cases. He noted that the public prosecutor in the *département* of the Seine had been ordering autopsies for a greater proportion of the corpses in the Paris morgue. At the same time, the numbers of infant corpses reaching the Paris morgue were rising, and autopsies indicated that the majority of these newborns were victims of infanticide.[102] Autopsies and medicolegal reports played crucial roles in infanticide investigations and prosecutions but were not always decisive in juries' verdicts.

Some practitioners of legal medicine explicitly acknowledged that their assessments of the moral character of the accused, her efforts to hide her pregnancy, her degree of preparation for her child's birth, and the circumstances of her delivery shaped their forensic findings.[103] Doctors, legal authorities, and jurors generally interpreted an accused woman's lack of preparation for her infant as an indication of premeditated murder. Many of these women combatted this assumption by insisting that either they did not know that they had been pregnant or that they went into labor suddenly and earlier than they had anticipated. Medical men were highly skeptical of claims that a woman was unaware that she was pregnant until her delivery, particularly if it was not her first pregnancy.[104] In most infanticide investigations and trials, the findings of forensic experts were at odds with the accounts of the accused.

Women tried for infanticide commonly claimed that they had fainted at the time of delivery and found their child lifeless once they regained consciousness. Some women maintained that their child fell to the ground prior to their blacking out. Many doctors and lawyers argued that the impact from a fall would not produce fatal skull fractures in most cases, especially when a woman was crouching or kneeling, since the bones in an infant's skull were fairly soft and flexible. They advised doctors to examine whether the umbilical cord was torn or cut, since a ruptured cord would support a woman's claims about the force of her infant's fall.[105] Some medical men acknowledged that a woman could pass out during childbirth and her child could die during that time owing, for example, to severe hemorrhaging from a ruptured umbilical cord or suffocation under sheets, other bedding, or clothing.[106] However, medical experts in suspected infanticide cases tended to dismiss women's claims about blacking out.

Defendants often insisted that their child died as a result of other accidents or birth-related injuries, particularly the umbilical cord becoming wrapped around the baby's neck during delivery and cutting off the flow of oxygen. A number of medicolegal publications affirmed that the umbilical cord could become naturally looped around a child's neck and could result in death. The physician Négrier conducted experiments in order to demonstrate that the umbilical cord could produce substantial resistance around the neck, which he maintained

was enough to be fatal. Publishing his findings in 1841, he argued that
the assize court in Angers wrongfully convicted a woman for infanticide in 1838 as a result of the flawed autopsy report and testimony of
two physicians who erroneously maintained that the bruising on the
infant's neck was not caused by the umbilical cord during delivery but
by manual strangulation.[107] Other doctors advised taking care to
distinguish between strangulation that resulted involuntarily from an
umbilical cord wrapped around a child's neck and intentional strangulation constituting infanticide. Doctors and jurists expressed concerns that perpetrators of infanticide might disguise murder as a
natural or accidental death. Doctors often refuted the claims of women
tried for infanticide who reported that the umbilical cord accidentally
strangled their child, insisting instead that the defendants had used an
object, such as ripped fabric or a rope, to strangle the child.[108]

Women who said that they gave birth unexpectedly often reported
that they confused their labor pains with intestinal cramps or the need
for a bowel movement. Some women insisted that when they rushed to
a latrine, toilet, or outhouse in order to satisfy this need, they unexpectedly delivered a child who fell into the cesspit or sewers and whom
they were unable to retrieve. Investigating magistrates tasked medical
experts with determining whether the infant's death was due to an
accidental fall or intentional killing. Forensic doctors generally dismissed the notion that a delivery under these rare circumstances would
result in an infant's fatal, unintentional fall into a cesspit or
sewage pipes. Highly skeptical of claims about accidental death in
these scenarios, medical men typically concluded that criminal action
was at play.[109]

A number of these issues coalesced in an 1889 infanticide trial in
Paris in which the accused claimed to have been surprised by the pains
of childbirth when going to the toilet and that the child she delivered
fell into the latrine. When questioned about her lack of preparation for
the baby, the accused said that she planned either to commit suicide or
to go into hiding. The court called upon a doctor to issue a forensic
report, a plumber to provide an analysis of the dimensions and angles
of the latrine and pipes, and the midwife, who attended the three
previous births of the accused woman prior to her separation from
her husband, to testify. The midwife reported that the accused had
three prior normal deliveries, involving two to six hours of labor, and

maintained that the onset of intense childbirth pain would occur at the very least a minute before the expulsion of the infant. The presiding judge observed that this would be long enough for the accused to get off of the toilet seat and deliver her child on the ground. He also maintained that confusing the pains of childbirth with having a bowel movement would be improbable, given the accused woman's previous deliveries. Although the medical testimony in the trial implicated the accused, the plumbing expertise indicated that the dimensions of the latrine allowed for the possibility of the child falling directly into the cesspit. The jury acquitted her – part of a broader pattern of juries either disregarding damning forensic evidence or seizing upon any evidence that offered some degree of doubt in order to acquit sympathetic defendants.[110]

Juries' leniency in many infanticide trials was a product of jurors' sympathies for defendants and was a concern of some forensic doctors. Defendants often sought to present themselves as poor, hardworking women who were victims not only of seduction and abandonment but also broader social forces beyond their control.[111] In 1897 Brouardel observed that by the time an infanticide case went before the assize courts, usually months after the outrage following the discovery of an infant's cadaver, "the jurors, the judges, the public no longer see this cadaver. They have before them a poor girl, with a good reputation, who has been seduced and abandoned by an individual from whom justice demands no accountability; everyone feels sorry for her." It was then the forensic doctor's duty to speak for the dead and to describe the cadaver in clinical terms, avoiding "any expression that might betray one's personal assessment" of the case.[112] Brouardel argued that infanticide cases compromised doctors' reputations more often than any other medicolegal intervention – not on account of any unique medical challenges but due to the heightened public interest in infanticide and the emotionally charged debates about the issue.[113]

Jurors often seemed to consider an accused woman's emotional and mental state as well as her material conditions and social circumstances. Nineteenth-century attitudes toward infanticide revealed tension between a recognition of infanticide as, on the one hand, an understandable but tragic response to the bleak realities of the lives of poor, unmarried women and, on the other hand, such an atrocious, incomprehensible aberration from the meanings of womanhood that it

called into question the mother's sanity. Most infanticide cases that
went to trial did not involve a formal, extensive examination of the
mental state of the accused. Nonetheless, investigating magistrates
commonly asked doctors for their assessment of the mental and moral
state of the accused at the moment of the crime to determine whether
she acted with reason and was thus legally responsible for her actions.
The question of the mental state of infanticidal mothers became an
increasingly salient aspect of these debates over the course of the
nineteenth century, corresponding to the rise of psychiatry during this
period.[114]

Some women charged with infanticide reported, "I lost my head,"
and the success of such defenses varied. The more heinous or puzzling
the circumstances surrounding an infanticide case, the more likely
doctors, jurists, and defense attorneys were to raise the question of
the mental state of the accused. The question most often shaped
infanticide investigations and trials in which either the infants' bodies
had been especially mutilated, the accused did not take measures to
conceal the crime, or the accused seemed to lack an easily comprehensible motive, for example, if she were married. Defense attorneys
sometimes argued that defendants, especially those who killed their
infants in particularly violent ways, acted in a state of frenzy or mania
after childbirth, during which they were not conscious of or legally
responsible for their actions.[115] In 1842 the president of the Lille assize
court of decried the role of doctors in advancing and substantiating
this defense strategy. He remarked, "Doctors who generally see insanity everywhere are particularly convinced that mania always accompanies unmarried women's clandestine births."[116] In 1849 the
physician Jean-Pierre Beaude stressed the importance of medical
experts' roles in evaluating the mental or moral state of the mother
at the time of the crime. He maintained that puerperal fever, the pains
of childbirth, and the greater nervous sensibility that accompanied
pregnancy and childbirth could mean that she was not legally responsible for her acts or at least had mitigated responsibility warranting
extenuating circumstances.[117]

As interest in the relationship between childbirth and mental illness
heightened, some French physicians and psychiatrists adopted "puerperal insanity," or postpartum insanity, as a new diagnostic category
in the mid-nineteenth century. In 1851 doctor Matthieu Weill

identified puerperal mania as a state of frenzy in which "all maternal feeling disappears" and the mother might kill her child.[118] Some physicians suggested that this mental state could persist as long as several years or last as little as two minutes, meaning that a mother could become insane and kill her child during delivery, while almost immediately regaining sanity.[119] Doctor Louis-Victor Marcé's 1858 treatise on puerperal insanity maintained that some women were more susceptible or predisposed to puerperal insanity on account of heredity, older age, multiple pregnancies, their emotional or moral state during pregnancy, prior mental illness, the sex of their child, or a combination of these factors. Psychiatrists' views on puerperal insanity laid the foundation for legal defenses that could possibly exonerate an accused mother based on her mental condition and diminished criminal responsibility.[120]

The second half of the nineteenth century saw animated debates about puerperal insanity and its validity as a criminal defense strategy. Some doctors questioned the very diagnosis of puerperal insanity and opposed its use as a legal defense. Tardieu argued that the majority of psychiatrists too easily believed that women who killed their children, particularly around the time of birth, were not legally responsible for their acts and acted in a state of transitory insanity or the momentary aberration of their mental faculties. Tardieu lamented how commonly defense lawyers employed this defense, often with the corroboration of medical experts. He maintained that these women's reason and maternal instincts were intact in the vast majority of cases.[121] Medical interest in and debates about puerperal insanity and the sudden onset of "transitory mania" during childbirth, peaked in the 1870s.[122] Some psychiatrists denounced this notion of transitory insanity during childbirth as a dangerous forensic and legal principle, which could lead to the immunity of all newly postpartum mothers who committed infanticide regardless of how clear-minded they were in the act.[123] Skeptical about the diagnosis of transitory insanity among women who committed infanticide immediately after childbirth, the doctor Jules Chabanon warned of the possibility of women feigning postpartum insanity after committing infanticide. Nonetheless, he maintained that women, particularly seduced and abandoned young women, might be sane but have diminished "moral responsibility" as a result of the "state of physical and moral malaise that accompanies labor." Chabanon suggested that childbirth itself could be considered an extenuating circumstance.[124]

Legal defenses shaped and were shaped by the work of psychiatrists and other medical men. Some defendants initially denied having given birth but shifted to a defense of temporary insanity. In 1879 a nineteen-year-old domestic servant tried for infanticide in Paris confessed to strangling her child, only after learning that the autopsy report concluded strangulation and suffocation. She insisted that it was not premeditated but a result of her state of frenzy, or "violent exaltation." The jury acquitted her.[125] Another Parisian woman tried for infanticide cried, "I was desolate ... I was like a maniac...I no longer knew what I was doing."[126] In 1886 doctor Charles Vibert lamented how frequently defense lawyers argued before the courts that the defendant suffered from a fleeting period of mania during which she killed her child and was not legally responsible for her child's death. Vibert expressed reservations about these claims yet maintained that a woman's state of "moral and physical excitation" during childbirth could diminish her degree of responsibility.[127] Benjamin Bell, an English-born French psychiatrist and professor at the medical faculty of Paris, took seriously puerperal insanity defenses. Ball identified a difficult labor under "unfortunate moral conditions," such as secrecy, isolation, abandonment, and misery, as causes of transitory puerperal mania, a state he characterized by "infanticidal tendencies."[128] Some doctors and commentators linked puerperal insanity not only to the physical act of childbirth but also to aggravating social factors such as the stress of poverty.

The medical discourse on mental illness among women during and after childbirth both reflected and influenced popular attitudes toward infanticide and provided substantiation for accused women and their lawyers' invocation of the insanity defense. Deeply ambivalent attitudes toward infanticidal mothers ranged from outrage to pity. While some viewed these mothers as victims of social circumstances and seduction and abandonment, new psychiatric theories also presented women as victims of their own minds and bodies.[129] These views were likely in part responsible for the rise in acquittals during the fin de siècle. Furthermore, by the 1890s every person condemned for infanticide was granted extenuating circumstances, and the courts effectively stopped issuing death sentences for the crime.[130] Nonetheless, infanticide remained a capital crime during this period, despite calls to reduce it to a misdemeanor. In 1901, however, the French state abolished the death penalty for infanticide.

In the late eighteenth and nineteenth century, the French state increasingly relied upon male medical practitioners to play official roles in investigating criminal matters concerning female bodies, reproduction, and reproductive crimes, particularly infanticide. Many of them found the workings of women's reproductive bodies fairly opaque. Some accused and condemned women resourcefully used their vernacular medical knowledge and crafted narratives to further obscure bodily symptoms and evidence. These women's efforts presented challenges for the male medical experts who scrutinized women and infants' bodies during criminal inquiries and proceedings. Medical experts' conclusions were frequently at odds with the accused's or condemned's version of events, especially in infanticide cases. Medical evidence in infanticide investigations and trials commonly elicited criticism from other medical men or judicial authorities. Jurists ultimately accepted the increasingly influential roles that male medical experts played in these proceedings. Nonetheless, jurists often found fault with forensic reports and testimonies and complained of some medical experts' inability to clearly elucidate and convey the facts of the case and to persuade jurors. While jurors in some infanticide cases seemed to convict on the basis of forensic evidence, in other cases, jurors privileged their sympathies for the defendants over forensic findings. Although medical practitioners faced challenges in establishing proof, including proof of pregnancy and childbirth as well as proof of infant life and murder, they nevertheless consolidated their authority through their interventions in criminal proceedings involving women's reproductive bodies and lives. Let us now turn to medical men's efforts to establish their authority over sexually violated bodies, specifically those of children. Medical men's impulses to protect men from the threat of supposedly false accusations of sexual assault often led the courts to be more sympathetic toward mothers accused of infanticide than toward children who reported sexual abuse.

5

The Forensics of Sexual Crimes against Children

In 1850 Doctor Tardieu performed an autopsy on a thirteen-year-old girl, Eugénie Allier, whose body had been found in the Seine, and determined that she had been raped and strangled. Investigators suspected Jean-Georges Bixner, a Parisian textile designer who had sexually assaulted other girls, including his own daughter. Tardieu examined five girls who all recounted that Bixner had raped or molested them. Bixner's seven-year-old daughter ultimately revealed that her father had raped an eleven-year-old girl in her presence and murdered Allier. Bixner claimed that he was innocent and was unable to have sex due to a genital deformity. Tardieu affirmed that Bixner lacked a testicle but insisted that this did not prevent him from having sex. Consequently, the court convicted Bixner and sentenced him to death.[1]

Bixner's trial occurred during a period when the prosecution of sexual crimes against children was dramatically rising in response to gradually changing understandings of childhood and sexuality. The prosecution of sexual crimes against children was part of broader efforts for child protection during a period of industrialization, urbanization, and political upheaval, when many French men and women were concerned about threats to childhood and children's innocence. The growing prosecution of sexual offenses against children corresponded to an overall increase in prosecutions for crimes and misdemeanors against children, which tripled between 1830 and 1860. In 1832 the July Monarchy criminalized all sexual activity with children under the age of eleven. The increased prosecution of these crimes coincided with a period of French public policy dedicated to the care and treatment of children through welfare programs, social institutions, and legal reforms. During a period of anxiety about the declining birthrate and depopulation under the early Third Republic, the French state assumed greater responsibility toward children and passed a series of laws to regulate child labor; to make primary schooling free, secular, and compulsory; to protect nurslings, infants, and "morally abandoned" children; to punish parents who abused, beat, or starved their children; and to remove children from these homes.[2] Protecting children from sexual danger and bringing sexual predators to justice presented particular challenges shaped by the interplay of constructions of class, age, gender, and sexuality.

The history of sexual offenses against children in modern France cannot be understood without respect to the role of medical experts, who at times strengthened and at other times undermined efforts to bring offenders to justice. The conception of children as innocent and in need of protection from exposure to adult sexuality and sexual contact, particularly from predatory male sexuality, led to the greater willingness of the state to prosecute sexual crimes against children in nineteenth-century France.[3] But these prosecutions did not always translate into successful convictions of perpetrators of sexual crimes, in part due to contradictory and ambivalent understandings of childhood innocence and claims about the "precocious immorality" of some children. Additionally, medical experts' difficulties in detecting indications of sexual crimes also presented considerable challenges. Some doctors recognized that their negative findings were often the product of the ephemeral nature of such physical evidence. Other doctors concluded that a lack of bodily signs of sexual abuse in many instances was proof that the assault had never occurred. Medical men commonly equated a lack of physical traces of sexual crimes with false accusations. They widely challenged the veracity of children's accounts of sexual abuse in the late nineteenth century. By often discrediting or casting suspicion on these victims, medical experts presented themselves as the sole authority in matters of child sexual assault and used their scientific and medical authority to dismiss possible signs of assault as the product of unhygienic practices or immorality. Some medicolegal experts called into question the idea of childhood innocence that engendered new efforts to combat child sexual abuse. Medical experts' frequent negative findings led many to discount allegations as false and to maintain that children were not as innocent as they seemed. Medicolegal ideas and practices shaped and were shaped by assumptions about gender and class, including bourgeois anxieties about sexual behavior and exploitation, children's purity and innocence, and working-class immorality. The increasing influence of medicolegal expertise presented the possibility of enhancing the evidentiary basis for child sexual assault cases and strengthening efforts to bring offenders to justice; however, medical experts at times undermined these efforts by seeking to enhance their own professional position at the expense of sexual assault victims.

Morality, Medicine, and the Limits of Legal Protection

The equation of childhood and innocence that brought about legal and judicial changes regarding sexual crimes against children was the culmination of long-term changes in Western conceptions of childhood. At the heart of Philippe Ariès's influential and controversial account of childhood as a modern invention was the rise of the notion of childhood innocence. He argued that adults were not preoccupied with shielding or protecting children from sexual and lewd remarks and activities until the late seventeenth century, when modern notions of childhood emerged.[4] While scholars have challenged Ariès's account, it seems that an idea of childhood that was rooted in the doctrine of original sin had shifted by the late eighteenth century toward an Enlightenment model of childhood, primarily indebted to Jean-Jacques Rousseau's influential educational treatise *Emile*, which emphasized the natural goodness of children. A Romantic, sentimental model of the innate goodness and natural innocence of children dominated cultural constructions of childhood in France during the first half of the nineteenth century.[5] The cultural ideal of children's natural innocence included sexual innocence, and it heightened concerns about sexual offenses against children, which led to greater state efforts to combat the problem.

Nonetheless, attitudes toward children in nineteenth-century France were rife with ambivalence and contradiction. In her study of children arrested for crimes during the July Monarchy, Cat Nilan argues that attitudes toward children who failed to act in ways deemed appropriately childlike and innocent revealed the fragility of this sentimentalized cultural construction of childhood. The ideal of children's natural innocence contrasted with the notion of "precocious perversity," a term widely used to describe children accused of committing crimes, including sexual offenses against younger children.[6] What is remarkable about the discourse on sexual offenses against children in nineteenth-century France is that journalists, jurists, medical experts, jurors, and others applied the label of "precociously perverse" not only to young criminal offenders, including perpetrators of sexual crimes against children, but also to the victims themselves of sexual assault. On the one hand, medical experts' interventions in criminal investigations and proceedings were the product of a commitment to protect children from sexual crimes. But, on the other hand, their mobilization of the concept of "precocious perversity" discredited some of the children who reported sexual abuse, which aided offenders' efforts to evade justice. Even after French legislators modified the penal code to protect all children under a specified age from any sexual activity with adults, the practical application of the law involved investigators, jurists, jurors, and medical experts, whose attitudes toward children were shaped by notions about age, class, and gender, leading some to conclude that certain children were not truly innocent and were thus undeserving of legal protection.

The discourse on sexual crimes against children also stressed the dangers of false accusations. Fodéré, one of the first French authors to publish on the forensics of sexual assault, wrote about his examination of a nine-year-old girl whose mother reported that she had been raped in an inn and accused several men in Martigues of the crime in 1808. After examining the girl in the presence of two *officiers de santé*, the justice of the peace, and the court clerk, Fodéré reported that he found her hymen intact and was unable to introduce his finger into her vagina. However, he noted a small red wound near her vulva, which decreased in size and redness over the course of the examination. Fodéré concluded that the mother had inflicted the wound on her daughter and warned doctors against women and children's false accusations and self-injury to simulate bodily signs of an assault.[7] Fodéré declared that many women and girls were "perverse enough to dare claim that they were taken by force when they gave themselves voluntarily."[8] Fodéré's warnings about children and their mothers' false accusations and simulations of sexual assault resonated with many doctors. Consequently, Fodéré and like-minded doctors were prone to dismiss the indications of sexual assault or to suspect that such signs were faked or self-inflicted in many cases.[9]

Early nineteenth-century prosecutions of sexual offenses against children involved questions concerning consent and violence. Fodéré considered sex with a child a consensual act and not a crime if the child was pubescent and intelligent, as he noted in his 1813 treatise.[10] At that time, rape – defined exclusively in terms of vaginal penetration – and indecent assault with violence were the only legal categories of sexual offenses against children. Defense lawyers often used the absence of physical violence as an effective defense, leading juries to acquit when evidence of physical violence was lacking – which was frequently the case.[11] However, in the absence of medical evidence of physical violence, the Paris assize court convicted the teacher Marc-Paul Paris for the indecent assault of girls whom he taught, on account of "moral violence." Paris's suicide attempt and self-mutilation of his testicles in prison seemed to confirm his guilt. Nonetheless, in 1821 the Court of Cassation overturned the verdict due to the lack of physical violence and discounted the juridical validity of moral violence.[12] In 1827 the *Journal du droit criminel* (Journal of Criminal Law) lamented that most indecent assaults committed on children occurred without physical violence but were no less odious. The journal implored courts to recognize moral violence exercised on children and "the purity of their childhood"; otherwise offenders would continue to sexually abuse children with "perfect impunity." In response to the 1827 acquittal of a music teacher who molested several young male students, the *Gazette des tribunaux* observed that the lack of explicit protections for children from indecent assault in the absence of physical violence was "a distressing lacuna in the law."[13]

Ultimately, these concerns culminated in legal changes in 1832 that made the indecent assault of children without violence a crime. Physical violence was not necessary to constitute a sexual crime against a child; "moral violence" and the categorical incapacity to consent applied to children under eleven.[14] This 1832 law modifying the penal code also introduced extenuating circumstances to French jurisprudence, in part as a remedy to the problem of juries acquitting

the accused due to the severity of the punishment. Conversely, aggravating circumstances could apply to the crimes of indecent assault
without violence, indecent assault with violence, or rape, if the
offender was a parent, teacher, or in another position of authority
over the child.[15]

Although the 1832 law made children under the age of eleven
categorically unable to consent to sexual activity, the fraught issue of
consent and innocence made its way into cases involving sexual crimes
against children. Some men suggested that physical, social, or intellectual maturity was more important than age in considering whether a
particular child should be considered a "true child" in need of legal
protection against sexual contact. Even when doctors reported scientific or medical proof of sexual assault, some juries acquitted the
accused because they did not consider the child, in most cases a girl,
truly an innocent victim. In these cases, the defense maintained and
jurors seemed to accept that the child either consented to sexual
activity or was simply undeserving of legal protection on account of
their immorality or lack of innocence. Although medical experts were
convinced of the guilt of a man accused of indecent assault before the
Loir-et-Cher assize court in 1839, the jury ultimately acquitted the
accused on the basis of debates during the trial about the "perversity"
and "depravity" of the victim – a six-year-old girl. The president of the
court's account of the trial suggested that the young girl's look and
smile seemed to have troubled jurors.[16] In an indecent assault trial
before the Aube assize court in 1839, jurors perceived a supposed lack
of innocence on the part of the victim due to her language, dress, and
precociousness. The jury understood that legislators crafted article
331 of the penal code to protect innocent children from sexual contact,
but the jurors did not see such innocence in the girl, who was three
days shy of her eleventh birthday – the legal age of consent. The jury
consequently acquitted the accused.[17] Jurors evaluating an indecent
assault case in the Seine-Inférieure in 1846 wrestled with similar issues,
since they deemed a ten-and-a-half-year-old victim morally fallen despite her young age. The forty-five-year-old man accused of assaulting
her was from a wealthy family with an excellent reputation and had
many allies, including some of the jurors who asked if they could
testify about the girl's "precocious immorality" and "shameful liber-
tinage." The president of the court noted that while the issue of the

child's immorality prominently figured into the trial, the jury adhered to the penal code and convicted the accused. The jurist expressed his own concerns about depravity among the working classes but observed that jurors were ultimately coming to accept the new legal principle and to appreciate that the younger a child was, the less possible it was for them to consent.[18]

Under the Second Empire, the law of May 13, 1863 raised the age of legal protection for the indecent assault of children without violence to thirteen. Legislative debates over modifying the age specified in Article 331 of the penal code acknowledged that the number of sexual crimes against children appearing before the courts was rising sharply. Legislators and legal commentators observed that many children were vulnerable to predatory sexual acts and worried that predators might wait until the very day a child turned eleven to act with impunity. They lamented that not every child was physically or intellectually capable of fully informed consent by the day that they turned eleven. Raising the legal age to thirteen was a response to the recognition of the danger of sexual abuse of eleven- and twelve-year-olds and the varying paces of their moral, intellectual, and physical development.[19]

However, many bourgeois jurors refused to apply these legal protections to working-class child victims from "an already corrupted social milieu."[20] In 1859 a jury in the Bouches-du-Rhône acquitted a man accused of sexually assaulting two girls aged eight and ten, since jurors believed that the girls were "so corrupted" that they had "provoked" the assault and subsequently lied about it.[21] In 1863, months after French legislators extended legal protections to children to the age of thirteen, jurors acquitted a twenty-year-old man in Marseilles of the sexual assault of a twelve-year-old-boy, despite eyewitness testimony. Jurors considered the advanced state of the boy's physical development to have put him on a par with the accused despite their age difference. They saw the victim as "even more corrupted" than the accused, whose family's "excellent reputation" aided his acquittal.[22] In reference to an 1863 case involving a butcher who had sexually assaulted two girls in a slaughterhouse, the president of the Bouches-du-Rhône assize court observed, "The attitude and morality of the victim exercise a great influence on the minds of juries." The jurist noted that there was "no doubt of the accused's guilt," based on the details the children provided during the investigation; however, the "precocious depravity" of the victims and other children who testified as witnesses became a focus during the trial.[23] Judicial records rarely explain why exactly jurors, medical examiners, or jurists viewed certain children as "corrupted" or "precociously perverse," but their coded language and assessments were generally class-based. In 1867 a public prosecutor addressed the issue of the supposed immorality of some children subjected to sexual crimes and suggested that sexual predators might target children with already "depraved morals." He claimed that it was "easier and less dangerous" for offenders to target children who were "already corrupted."[24] The prosecutor's remarks about child immorality obscured the social dimensions of these crimes, in which upper-class and bourgeois offenders often seemed to enjoy the presumption of innocence among their peers and likely targeted lower-class children in the hope of acting with impunity.

Nonetheless, greater acceptance of the notion that children were categorically unable to consent to sex, coupled with an expanded age range of legal protection, contributed to the dramatic increase in prosecutions of sexual crimes against children. The number of these trials relative to the overall population of France rose more than fivefold from the 1820s through the 1870s. During the late 1820s, on average 133 persons, or 4.2 per million population, were tried annually for the rape or indecent assault of children. When the prosecution of these crimes peaked in the late 1870s, this figure had risen to 809 persons, or 21.9 per million population, annually. The ratio of trials involving child victims to adult victims of sexual crimes was six to one, and nearly one out of five of all persons tried before the assize courts faced charges of rape or indecent assault of children.[25]

Medical evidence was a crucial consideration for investigating magistrates in framing charges. If a medical expert did not conclude that the victim of a reported rape showed clear bodily signs of rape and vaginal penetration, magistrates almost always chose to either drop the case or downgrade charges to either attempted rape, indecent assault, or public indecency. Prosecutors and jurists commonly downgraded criminal accusations even when forensic evidence corroborated rape complaints in order to improve their chances of a conviction by transferring lesser charges to the correctional courts tried by professional judges. The president of the Puy-de-Dôme assize court observed in 1841 that many cases were too risky to try as rape in the assize courts due to juries' reluctance to convict, either because of their incredulity that a rape had really occurred or because of the notion that the verdict might further shame the victim.[26] Magistrates commonly lamented juries' indulgence toward those accused of rape. The pursuit of lesser charges might have also stemmed from jurists' suspicion that forensic evidence might not be enough to persuade jurors to condemn men who seemed respectable. Furthermore, many men distrusted children's testimony, even when medical experts corroborated it. Some doubted whether children truly could be raped, on account of the physical difference between adults' and children's bodies and sexual organs. Medical experts who admitted the possibility proposed various ages at which rape would be physically possible. For example, Adolphe Toulmouche, a doctor in Rennes, insisted in 1856 that vaginal penetration of a girl under thirteen was impossible.[27] The notion that the rape of girls was possible became more widely accepted in the latter part of the nineteenth century. There was no legal category of rape, only indecent assault, for boys violated by adult men.

The degree to which forensic experts' reports and testimonies were decisive in the prosecution or conviction of those accused of sexual assault is difficult to quantify. Forensic expertise in many cases seemed crucial to the decisions of the magistrates who conducted the investigative proceedings that preceded a criminal trial. The relative weight that jury members attached to experts' reports and testimonies cannot be known in most cases. Presidents of the assize courts and other jurists sometimes offered their impressions of jurors' assessments of experts' interventions. Jurists observed that some experts' reports and testimonies were much clearer and more cogent than others. Many trials involving sexual crimes against children, particularly those involving incest or sodomy, were closed trials. The lack of openness and publicity for these trials was a cause of concern for some doctors who wanted press coverage of the proceedings and medical reports to inform those who might be called as medical experts. In 1847 the journal *Annales d'hygiène publique et de médecine légale* advocated for public trials and lamented that doctors lacked the opportunity to study indecent assault in practice. Nonetheless, they served as experts in cases where the court summoned them to shed light on questions that they were unequipped to answer.[28] This concern about medical professionals' lack of knowledge and training was particularly salient in the first half of the nineteenth century, when medicolegal literature paid scant attention to sexual crimes against children and many medical practitioners lacked appropriate education and training in detecting the signs of sexual assault.

Some medical experts expressed moral judgments about the children they examined and presented these moral assessments as objective scientific or medical evidence. Doctor Louis Pénard questioned the morality of two girls whom he examined in 1851 after they reported that their father had raped them. Pénard found that fourteen-year-old Eugénie had a broken hymen. He surmised that the way it was broken indicated "guilty abandon," but he did not explain what would have distinguished it from a hymen broken by rape. Eugénie insisted that no man had touched her except for her father, who had violently assaulted her a year earlier, but Pénard reported that the state of her genitals and her developed intelligence led him to believe otherwise. Circumstances that Pénard did not specify led him to believe that the father was "not the cause of her deflowering." He also examined Eugénie's thirteen-year-old sister, Victorine, and drew the same conclusions. Victorine's hymen was broken, but it was Pénard's "profound conviction" that this "deflowering was accepted by her" from a man other than her father. Pénard later recounted that the presiding trial judge chastised and "rudely warned" him that he was exceeding his mandate and medical role by focusing more on moral questions than on medical ones and by defending the accused. While Pénard did not retract his position, he later observed that sticking to the material facts would avoid such judicial clashes.[29] Tardieu, the leading expert on sexual forensics in France who analyzed over six hundred cases of sexual abuse in his treatise on indecent assault, advised medical experts to discuss only medical matters. Doctors should exclude any declarations of those involved, since they were in no position to verify them. Tardieu exhorted doctors to stick to the material facts and not to offer any moral impressions, which would make them a witness rather than an expert.[30]

Medicolegal literature advised doctors to proceed with great caution when children, particularly young girls, seemed to present the signs of venereal disease or sexual assault. This literature counseled doctors to be extremely skeptical of parents' claims that their children had been sexually assaulted. It also cautioned against viewing unusual genital discharges and vaginitis as signs of assault. Medicolegal experts emphasized the prevalence of vaginitis in young girls, especially those of the lower classes, that was unrelated to sexual assault.[31] While vaginitis in young girls could indeed be the product of unsanitary practices, skin conditions, allergic reactions, or other causes, it could also be the result of trauma or a symptom of a sexually transmitted infection, which many doctors dismissed. Doctor Alfred Fournier warned that it could be difficult or even impossible for doctors to distinguish naturally occurring cases of vaginitis from those faked, provoked, or caused by a sexual crime.[32] In the absence of bacteriological techniques, doctors' diagnoses of venereal disease generally involved the visual interpretation with the naked eye of vaginal discharges and symptoms like lesions, rashes, and chancres.[33]

Doctors routinely discounted claims of sexual assault and attributed discharges or abnormalities in the appearance of a child's genitals to masturbation instead. Masturbation, or onanism, became an increasingly prominent issue among doctors who frequently determined that masturbatory habits rather than sexual assault caused the inflammatory lesions or genital deformations that they observed. Tardieu asserted that doctors could ably distinguish between various causes but acknowledged that doctors often had difficulty determining whether genital irritation or abnormalities in young girls should be attributed to masturbation or assault. He maintained that cases of "inveterate onanism" in girls often involved an enlarged or swollen clitoris, an enlarged and reddened opening of the hymen, and a pale redness to its edges and to the vulva's mucus membrane, as well as a pale discharge.[34] Tardieu warned of the dangers of doctors mistaking the signs of masturbation as evidence of sexual assault. Tardieu referred to his experience examining a fourteen-year-old girl who another medical expert concluded had signs of syphilis and a broken hymen after her father repeatedly sexually assaulted her. Tardieu observed that the girl had large breasts and attributed her "precocious" development to masturbation. He observed that her hymen was distended and deformed. Tardieu suggested that its condition might be mistakenly viewed as partially torn, but he did not consider her deflowered. He declared that masturbation, or "the excesses of onanism," was responsible for the state of her hymen and vaginal discharge, which the previous doctor misinterpreted as venereal disease.[35] Medical experts frequently offered their assessments of whether children had "bad habits," meaning masturbation, sometimes at the request of the examining magistrate. Their medicolegal reports commonly reached positive conclusions. Pénard observed that medical experts frequently concluded that children had not been assaulted but simply practiced masturbation.[36] Léon-Henri Thoinot, professor of legal medicine in Paris, noted that masturbation in boys might lead to general fatigue and an abnormal development of the penis, which might be mistaken for the signs of sexual assault.[37]

Doctors' pronouncements on child masturbation were doubly pernicious. First, doctors' preoccupation with masturbation likely led some to discount veritable signs of sexual assault as indications of masturbation instead. Their reports served as evidence in the judicial arena that the reported sexual crime had not occurred. Second, claims about a child's masturbatory habits called into question the morality of the child, since the discourses on masturbation during the period equated the practice with immorality.[38] The medical expert in a child sexual abuse trial in the Lot-et-Garonne in 1863 declared that the ten-year-old girl whom he examined masturbated habitually and that this proved her "precocious immorality." Those involved in the investigation and trial questioned the moral character of both the child and her mother.[39] Assessments of a child's morality were pivotal in many investigations and trials of sexual offenses.

Doctors who offered their moral assessments of the children they examined often called into question the victims' and parents' reputation and credibility. When doctors privileged their own notions of a child's morality over physical evidence, magistrates at times intervened to stop doctors from flagrantly overstepping their boundaries. By concluding that a child habitually masturbated or presented no signs of sexual assault, a medicolegal expert could undermine the state's case against the accused, leading to their acquittal. Nonetheless, doctors' reports that a child had been deflowered, sodomized, or infected with a venereal disease did not always lead to convictions. In many criminal trials involving sexual offenses against children, jurors who were confronted with damning forensic evidence weighed it against matters of reputation for the accused, accuser, and the parents or family involved. Doctors and others commonly called into question victims' and their families' reputation and morality, which were decisive in trial outcomes. Reputation at times outweighed forensics.

Sexual Offenders and the Signs of Assault

Medical experts' interventions in investigations and prosecutions of sexual crimes against children were embedded in relations of social dominance and subordination. A wide range of cases, including those involving family members, domestic servants, neighbors, employers, teachers, clergymen, and strangers, appeared before the courts and commonly entailed forensic examinations of the accused and accuser. Doctors' assessments of forensic evidence were often bound up in their narratives and anxieties about the perceived immorality of the working classes. Constructions of gender difference, childhood, sexuality, and class shaped not only medicolegal discourse and practice but also patterns of prosecution as well as attitudes toward sexual offenses against children.

Forensic doctors' examinations of the bodies of accused sexual offenders could bolster the prosecution's case. Medical experts searched for any distinctive bodily features that the victim identified. Tardieu recounted a case in which a member of the Congregation of Christian Brothers had been accused of sodomizing children entrusted to his care. One of the boys said in his deposition, "On his pecker, there were little spots." Tardieu's examination of the accused revealed superficial skin eruptions on his penis that corroborated the boy's statement.[40] In multiple later publications, Lacassagne, chair of legal medicine and toxicology at the medical faculty of Lyon, discussed the investigation of a man who reportedly assaulted two girls. The girls said that he had shown them "a fat finger" and said that he would make them "see the devil." A medical examination of the accused revealed a tattoo of a devil on his penis. Lacassagne noted that distinctive marks, such as a tattoo, tumor, or lipoma in or near the genital region, could compel a confession or demonstrate the guilt of the accused.[41] In some cases, accused sexual offenders attempted to alter the appearance of their genitals to evade justice. In 1866 in the Seine-et-Marne, an accused offender claimed to have a venereal disease that proved his innocence, since the victim was not infected. The medical expert examining the accused determined that he simulated the symptoms of syphilis by placing a layer of snuff under his foreskin in order to produce inflammation.[42] Other offenders claimed impotence and various medical conditions that prevented them from having sex, such as large hernias, venereal diseases, or genital malformations including hypospadias, a condition in which the opening of the urethra is on the underside of the penis. Forensic doctors expressed great skepticism about claims of impotence among accused sexual offenders.[43]

Less commonly, doctors also evaluated the mental state of the accused. For example, psychiatric questions became an issue in the 1843 case in the Eure-et-Loire of Roch Ferré, a thirty-year-old primary school teacher accused of indecent assault. During his interrogation, Ferré defended his sexual contact with his students as natural and in their own interest. Invoking Socrates and Alcibiades, Ferré maintained that sexual contact was a way of gaining his students' confidence and was an expression of a tender and reciprocal love between them. Ferré insisted that his system of education would civilize the people of the countryside and that he should be regarded as a benefactor of humanity rather than the object of hatred and injustice. The three doctors summoned by the examining magistrate noted that Ferré had received military discharge in 1836 for "religious monomania." The forensic doctors affirmed this earlier diagnosis of insanity and determined that Ferré lacked the full use of his mental faculties. They deemed him not criminally responsible.[44] Forensic doctors came to a different conclusion in the 1875 at the assize court of the Rhône's trial of Edouard Cronfault, who purportedly sexually assaulted at least seventeen of his students. The religiously devout Cronfault confessed that at the time he thought that molesting students was no different than masturbation or sex outside of marriage, since they were all wrong and sinful. During the course of the investigation and legal proceedings, Cronfault acknowledged that he had made a serious mistake and had come to understood its gravity. The forensic doctors declared that Cronfault was sane and responsible for his actions. The jury sentenced him to twenty years of hard labor.[45]

While the burgeoning field of psychiatry powerfully shaped forensic medicine and the courts, it did not radically transform ideas about people who sexually violated children. The emergence of forensic psychiatry in the first half of the nineteenth century was tied to the

5

rise and fall of the notion of monomania, in which the affected individual's mind was understood to be pathologically preoccupied with a single idea (*idée fixe*) but was otherwise rational and sound. Accordingly, doctors characterized monomania as a hidden mental disorder whose detection and understanding required the expertise of psychiatrists.[46] However, these doctors did not theorize adults' desire for sex with children within this framework. During the second half of the nineteenth century, the notion of hereditary degeneration powerfully shaped psychiatry, social thought, and the French cultural imagination, particularly through the novels of Emile Zola and the writings of the physician Bénédict-Augustin Morel.[47] Some French doctors, psychiatrists, and sexologists medicalized sexual "abnormality" and "perversion" as symptoms of degeneration. Medical men also ushered in a shift in which sexual acts or behaviors were converted into identities, most notably in the terms of homosexuality and the construction of the homosexual, or sexual "invert," as a "species" and an identity, as Michel Foucault and others have argued.[48] Given the proliferation of classificatory systems of sexual perversions and mental diseases in late nineteenth-century France, one might mistakenly assume that the child molester, later termed pedophile, would emerge as a distinct category during this same time.[49]

However, the medicolegal discourse of the period did not generally include child molesters in experts' taxonomies. It is unclear whether doctors viewed men's sexual contact with girls as a form of perversion that was a natural, though morally objectionable, variation from normative heterosexuality, in contrast to homosexuality, or "sexual inversion," as a fundamentally abnormal deviation. Most medical experts did not offer explanations for why individuals committed sexual offenses against children. Those who did tended to eschew medical or psychiatric explanations based on pathologies among offenders and favored social or environmental explanations that emphasized immorality among the working or "dangerous" classes. These explanations aligned with the dominant model of criminology in France, associated with Lacassagne, which viewed criminal behavior as a product of social environment, as opposed to the Italian physician and criminal anthropologist Cesare Lombroso's view of the "atavistic born criminal."[50]

Foucault, in his work on the construction of the "abnormal" individual and the history of sexuality, controversially offered the example of Charles-Joseph Jouy, who was arrested for sexually assaulting Sophie Adam, an eleven-year-old girl, and subjected to psychiatric evaluations that resulted in his confinement to an asylum for the rest of his life.[51] In a medicolegal report submitted to a jurist in Nancy and subsequently published in 1868, Henry Bonnet and Jules Bulard discussed Jouy's arrested, childlike mental development and "lack of sufficient mental self-possession to resist by himself certain tendencies" or dangerous "bad instincts."[52] Foucault used Jouy as an example of how increasingly elaborate systems of control and disciplinary power were brought to bear on what Foucault considered a trivial sexual encounter involving a "somewhat simple-minded" man who "obtained a few caresses from a girl." For Foucault, the case's significance was "the pettiness of it all; the fact that this everyday occurrence in the life of village sexuality, these inconsequential bucolic pleasures, could become, from a certain time, the object not only of a collective intolerance but of a judicial action, a medical intervention, a careful clinical examination, and an entire theoretical elaboration."[53]

Feminist scholars have objected to Foucault's trivialization of child sexual assault and his description of this incident as "inconsequential," "barely furtive pleasures of simple-minded adults and alert children." In his lectures in *Abnormal*, Foucault noted that a second incident occurred in which "Jouy dragged young Sophie Adam (unless it was Sophie Adam who dragged Charles Jouy) into the ditch alongside the road to Nancy. There, something happened: almost rape, perhaps. Anyway, Jouy very decently gives four sous to the little girl who immediately runs to the fair to buy some roasted almonds."[54] By using problematic language that undermined the eleven-year-old girl's status as a victim of sexual assault by a forty-year-old man, Foucault reproduced elements of the nineteenth-century discourse on sexual offenses against children that cast suspicion on the victim, implying that she was not truly innocent and deserving of legal protection but was sexually precocious and a consensual partner. Sophie Adam ultimately bore the brunt of these attitudes. After her mother found her clothing covered in blood and stains following the rape, she alerted her husband, who complained about his undisciplined daughter.

According to the medicolegal report summarizing the case, "revelations" among townspeople of Sophie's "immorality" led to her confinement in a house of correction until she came of age.[55]

While some aspects of the Jouy case were exceptional, in many
ways it was representative of child sexual assault cases in nineteenth-
century France, particularly with respect to the operation of age, class,
gender, and power. Although the accusations against the offender
were taken seriously and resulted in legal proceedings, these proceedings involved calling the morality of the child victim into question and
prosecuting the crime as an indecent assault rather than rape. The
accused was not a member of the social elite but a farmhand.
Bourgeois offenders seem to have wielded their social and cultural
capital more effectively to evade prosecution and act with greater
impunity than their social inferiors.[56] Many instances of sexual
assault, particularly those involving accusations against elites, never
culminated in a trial. Some that did go to trial resulted in acquittals,
particularly when the defendant and witnesses cast aspersions on the
moral character of the victim or their family. About one-fourth of
defendants charged with sexual crimes against children were acquitted
each year.[57] Acquittals were particularly common when bourgeois
men faced charges of sexually assaulting lower-class victims, but most
cases that went to trial involved an accused and accuser both of
working-class origins. Most defendants were working-class men, especially day laborers, although many cases involved more socially ele-
vated teachers, clergymen, or relatives. Women were also among the
ranks of the accused, but usually fewer than ten women faced charges
each year. Women made up only about 1 percent of those accused.[58]

Male relatives were among the most common perpetrators of sexual
crimes against children, and forensic experts attributed the frequency
with which fathers or male relatives committed sexual abuse to the
material and moral conditions of the lower classes. Medical experts
were keenly aware of their social status and those of the subjects
whom they examined. Doctor Henry Coutagne observed that those
whom he examined in these sexual assault cases "belong[ed] exclusively to an inferior social milieu."[59] Thoinot claimed that fathers'
sexual assault of their daughters almost always occurred in poor
households where all family members shared a bedroom, sometimes
even a bed. A father would retire in the evening after drinking and

assault his daughter, and the accusation might emerge only long afterward.[60] When fathers appeared before the courts on charges of assaulting or raping their daughters, they frequently faced conviction and severe punishments in cases where forensic evidence corroborated the charges. Pregnancy resulting from fathers' sexual assault of their daughters also provided evidence. Although fathers facing these accusations generally denied paternity, jurors frequently dismissed these denials. Widespread concerns about hereditary degeneration during the late nineteenth century provided further impetus for conviction.

Female relatives were much rarer offenders, and the expert discourse on child sexual assault presented mothers' sexual assaults of their children as nearly unfathomable. In a rare reference to this kind of abuse, Tardieu expressed revulsion toward a young mother who stuck her fingers very deeply into her daughter's vagina as well as her anus several times each day. Tardieu observed that the child had a broken hymen and genital deformations, including a large, dilated vagina and an enlarged anal orifice, that were consistent with these assaults. The mother justified these "monstrous practices," as Tardieu put it, as being in the interest of her child's health and cleanliness. Rejecting the mother's account, Tardieu suggested that she was driven by sexual impulses instead of hygienic concerns. The daughter recounted that her mother's acts woke her in the middle of night and sometimes lasted an entire hour, while her mother breathed heavily and was bathed in sweat. Tardieu also discussed a case, drawn from the German medicolegal authority Johann Ludwig Casper, concerning a mother who inserted fingers and stones into her ten-year-old daughter's vagina and claimed that she did so to prepare her daughter for sex.[61] Motherhood was widely viewed as the natural vocation for women, and many considered a mother's sexual abuse of her child, regardless of any ill-conceived justifications, as one of the most unnatural and heinous acts imaginable.

Although the expert discourse on sexual assault focused on men's sexual crimes against girls, Tardieu wrote about a number of cases of men assaulting boys. He suggested that increasing urbanization and industrialization made greater numbers of boys vulnerable to sexual predators. Tardieu observed a growing phenomenon of children coming to Paris for work and then becoming victims of sexual assault by their employers whose beds they shared, "because of the promiscuity that prevails in the poorest dwellings of the capital."[62] In 1862 Tardieu examined two apprentices, aged fourteen and sixteen, who were attacked by two older men employed in the same workshop. Tardieu observed a notable enlargement of the anal sphincter in the older apprentice and anal tears and redness in the younger apprentice, who had been sodomitically assaulted five or six times.[63] Tardieu expressed concerns about working children's vulnerability to sexual assault. He also advanced the notion that there were identifiable physical signs of habitual "passive pederasty," concerning the appearance of the buttocks and anus, and "active pederasty," concerning the size and appearance of the penis, which could aid medicolegal investigations of sodomitical sexual assaults.[64]

In general, medicolegal experts downplayed the prevalence of sexual offenses against boys. Most medicolegal publications and authors – with the exception of several forensic doctors, such as Thoinot – remained silent on the issue. In his late nineteenth-century forensic treatise on sexual assault, Thoinot claimed that boys were rarely subject to sexual crimes. Thoinot maintained that when these rare assaults did occur, the perpetrator was, as a general rule, a woman.[65] Archival evidence and court records do not substantiate Thoinot's claim. Although criminal charges involving the sexual abuse of girls were more common than criminal charges involving boys, the sexual abuse of boys was not rare, and most often males were their abusers. Estimates of the proportion of boys identified as victims in sexual assault trials have varied widely, but it seems to have been around one-third.[66] The actual prevalence of these kinds of assaults, which were likely the most underreported kind of sexual offense, is impossible to quantify accurately.

The archival record reveals much more about the prevalence of sodomitical assault than printed works do, but the judicial archives nevertheless have considerable lacunae. Sometimes medical reports and testimonies were absent from judicial records. The reasons for their absence were generally not articulated, but presumably the medical examination had not occurred. Some parents or children might have refused to consent to a medical exam in these cases, particularly those involving sodomy and the ignominy associated with it. Boys' bodies might not have been subjected to the same degree of scrutiny as those of girls. Medical examinations of young girls with torn hymens yielded clearer findings than those of children involved in sodomitical assaults. In 1880 Coutagne observed that physical evidence was rare in sodomitical assaults on children of either sex, since the resistance in the child's anal region was less than in an adult's and any physical sign of an assault would rapidly disappear. Coutagne's work suggested that forensic experts who intervened in sodomy cases involving children would be unable to detect minor injuries due to rapid healing of the anal region.[67]

The problem of nonexistent or fleeting medical evidence was even more pronounced among boys whom women sexually assaulted. Thoinot observed that women's sexual assault of boys generally left no trace except in cases of the transmission of venereal disease.[68] In 1895 Pierre-André Lop published the only forensic study in nineteenth-century France devoted exclusively to male victims, in which he argued that women's sexual offenses against boys were not as rare as one would tend to believe. Every year at least one or two of these cases went before the courts in France. These cases usually involved venereal disease transmission. Lop discussed a case of a three-year-old boy whose parents brought him to the hospital for stomach pains, but Lop and other doctors observed that the boy was suffering from urethritis, an intense inflammation of the urethra with pus-like discharge. They determined that he had contracted gonorrhea. His twenty-year-old aunt also appeared to have gonorrhea. A microscopic examination of her vaginal pus detected the recently discovered gonococcus bacteria. She ultimately confessed to sexually assaulting her nephew. Lop maintained that urethritis had an infectious etiology and was always the product of direct transmission through sexual contact. Lop insisted that doctors should question children who presented the condition about their sexual activity and subject any adults implicated to thorough examination and testing.[69] Lop analyzed a few other cases of women's sexual offenses against boys but failed to acknowledge that the most common sexual crimes against boys were those committed by adult men. His study was part of a broader pattern of most medical experts eliding or minimizing the status of boys as vulnerable victims of predatory male sexuality and sexual violence.

Despite the increasing prominence of both medical experts and sexual crimes against children in the courts, the problem of doctors' lack of sufficient training and education on sexual assault persisted. In the late nineteenth century, Brouardel declared that it was troubling that some doctors had never seen a hymen and even more distressing that such doctors assumed official roles as experts. Brouardel insisted that the lack of training in sexual forensics was a much-needed area of reform in medical education and the practice of legal medicine.[70] Most doctors did not check for signs of sexual assault unless specifically instructed to do so. Doctors conducting autopsies routinely failed to examine the anus and vagina. Despite concerns about doctors' lack of knowledge of and attentiveness to the signs of sexual assault, medical experts played a growing role in these criminal cases.

Most investigations of sexual offenses had negative or inconclusive forensic findings and pitted the word of the victim against that of the accused. In some cases, multiple victims came forward to testify to the abuse, particularly against teachers or clergymen. Usually a considerable number of victims coming forward bolstered the legal case. But some forensic experts suggested that the number of accusers was irrelevant in cases in which all the children involved were unreliable or lying, as the doctors asserted. Lacassagne's study of a cleric charged with exposing himself to children illustrated an increasingly prominent feature of the discourse of sexual assault: doctors' insistence on the pervasiveness of false allegations.

Fear of False Accusations in the Fin de Siècle

In 1889 the court of Chambéry charged Joseph François Barbier, known as Father Bérard, with indecent exposure. The witnesses were four girls, aged thirteen to fifteen, who reported seeing Father Bérard with his robe lowered, legs outstretched on a chair, and penis exposed, seemingly peeking out of a pocket of his robe. The girls affirmed that they had definitely seen "a man's thing." The court convicted Father Bérard of public indecency and sentenced him to six months in prison. In 1890 the case went to the appeals court in Lyon. The defense attorney enlisted Lacassagne to answer a number of questions: Could a small penis reach a considerable length in a state of erection, and could the accused stick his penis ten centimeters out of the pocket of his robe while in a sitting position? Should the testimony of children, especially girls, in matters of sexual assault be trusted? Lacassagne conducted experiments that proved, in his eyes, that the girls had lied. Lacassagne used Father Bérard's chair, a capuchin robe, and a replica of the confessional to determine that the penis length needed to be twenty-five to thirty centimeters under the conditions the girls described. Lacassagne noted that the average length of a flaccid penis was nine centimeters, fifteen centimeters in a state of erection, and that Father Bérard's penis was small and seemingly atrophied.[71] The court acquitted Father Bérard. Forensic doctors in the late nineteenth century commonly cited Lacassagne's study as proof of children's propensity to lie and the unreliability of their testimony.

While Lacassagne maintained that the girls who accused Father Bérard had made an innocent mistake, medical experts at the end of the nineteenth century insisted that children were not as innocent as they seemed. Notions of children's natural innocence had shaped the dominant cultural representations and understandings of childhood during the first half of the nineteenth century, although the notion of precocious perversity nonetheless challenged this model. By the final decades of the nineteenth century, the Romantic, sentimental model of childhood innocence was waning. Medical experts offered some of the most strident attacks on the model of natural childhood innocence, which emphasized children's purity, candor, and ingenuousness. They claimed that children commonly falsely reported sexual offenses. Doctors used the terms perversity, corruption, deceit, and dissimulation when describing these children. Doctors' claims about children's false reports of sexual assault were part of ongoing debates within the medical profession about child psychology, children's propensity for lying, and false allegations.[72]

Claims about the prevalence of false accusations and the importance of the role of experts in exposing these allegations as baseless were a focal point of most published forensic studies on rape or indecent assault. In 1898 Thoinot claimed that sexual assault allegations rarely went to trial because of the frequency of false accusations, alleging that less than 20 percent of formal accusations were justified. The courts dismissed 60–80 percent of formal accusations, whether prior to, after, or in the absence of a forensic medical exam, as investigations of sexual crimes frequently resulted in an *ordonnance de non-lieu*, meaning that there would be no trial and prosecution. Thoinot observed that forensic examinations resulted in negative conclusions in the vast majority of cases. In his own experience, it was always negative. It seems that Thoinot interpreted the lack of forensic evidence as an indication or proof that a charge was baseless, despite medical experts routinely acknowledging the difficulty in detecting fleeting or nonexistent physical evidence.[73] Other experts, such as Henri Legludic, drew similar conclusions, construing negative findings in forensic examinations as evidence of children's false allegation, particularly girls who reported sexual offenses. Legludic claimed, "Often my reports demonstrate, by their negative conclusions, the falseness of [the girls'] assertions."[74]

Forensic experts discussed a number of reasons for false accusations, some of which they identified as deliberately malicious, for example, lying about sexual assault for the purposes of blackmail. Lacassagne and other forensic experts advanced the increasingly widespread notion that many sexual assault charges were simply attempts at blackmail.[75] The fear of female exploitation of vulnerable men animated the medicolegal discourse on sexual assault. Doctors expressed fears of being falsely accused themselves and possibly blackmailed. Paul Bernard warned fellow doctors, "One must never forget that doctors share with clergymen the sad privilege of being more especially subject to the malicious suppositions and calumnies of children and hysterical women."[76] Doctors urged their colleagues to take preventive measures to minimize the likelihood of becoming the victim of a false accusation and not examine a child alone. In his 1886 treatise on sexual assault of girls, Bernard claimed that young girls in Paris, particularly along the Champs-Elysées, and in other large cities commonly resorted to "rape blackmail."[77] A doctor in Lyon in 1888 declared, "We all know how frequent rape blackmail (*chantage au viol*) is."[78] The claims that women and girls were lying about assault were tied to notions of female duplicity and the exploitation of men. It is highly improbable that so-called rape blackmail attempts were as widespread as doctors claimed, given the lack of evidence. But, attempts at blackmail would have been most likely and plausible in cases of men having sex with male prostitutes, especially boys, who might blackmail their clients, a phenomenon that Tardieu had earlier observed.[79] In the courts, defendants mobilized the myth of rape blackmail to discredit victims. For example, a roofer charged with sexually assaulting two young apprentices in 1860 claimed that the boys were lying for financial gain.[80] Almost all the authors who published studies about sexual offenses against children in nineteenth-century France addressed the issue of extortion and blackmail, but it was not until the 1880s that authors foregrounded the issue and stressed its pervasiveness.[81]

Forensic doctors warned how easily children could imitate or simulate the signs of sexual assault. Even if a doctor determined that a child who reported having been raped had a broken hymen and was consequently deemed deflowered, Pénard and others maintained that it could be the child's own doing. Forensic doctors observed that sexual intercourse was the most common cause of "defloration" but maintained that masturbation could produce the same results. Insisting that a torn hymen could be a result of a child's masturbation, Pénard claimed that the child's "onanism" might not be for sexual pleasure but have the perverse aim of a blackmail attempt.[82]

Experts cautioned against viewing genital infections as indications of venereal disease, and they claimed that children or their parents might provoke or simulate the symptoms to take advantage of well-to-do men and falsely impugn male honor. In 1880 the Parisian physician Fournier, a leading specialist in syphilis at the time, wrote about the supposed problem of young children faking venereal disease. Fournier outlined a formula that he thought children or their parents widely used to blackmail innocent men. It consisted of selecting a rich man; creating the conditions under which he would be left alone with the child; provoking an inflammation of the vulva through the use of an irritating substance, friction, or violence that would be analogous to what would result from a sexual assault; and then accusing him of sexual assault with great anger and indignation, accompanied by the threat of going public or going to the courts unless he would provide financial compensation. Fournier presented a cautionary tale in which "an excellent and perfectly honorable man, a father...absolutely incapable (I will gladly act as a guarantor) of any ignominious action, allowed himself to be caught in a trap of this kind." Fournier maintained that the young girl in question was from a poor, disreputable family and claimed that the lesions on her vulva were likely the product of the disease of scrofula, not venereal disease. The accused maintained his innocence but said he did not wish to go to court, so he made a payment to the victim's family, which Fournier described as "a ransom to vile exploiters." Fournier viewed claims of men sexually abusing lower-class children with great skepticism. He and other doctors seemed to identify much more strongly with their social peers accused of assault than they did with the victims. To substantiate his claim that allegations of sexual crimes against children were often fabricated attacks on innocent men, Fournier published a widely cited report on an eight-year-old girl who reported sexual abuse. Fournier found her to be "literally bathed in a yellow pus oozing from her vagina." Fournier noted that he had never seen a vulva in such a condition. He noticed that the child repeated her account of a rich old man sexually assaulting her with little variation and in a manner that seemed rehearsed. Trying to gain the child's confidence and friendship, Fournier enticed her with treats, coins, and a doll. The girl then purportedly confessed to him that the man had not touched her genitals but that her mother had taken a polishing brush to them and instructed her daughter to tell no one. Fournier considered this moment "a triumph" that resulted in the suspension of the investigation. He expressed little concern for the sexually abused child but great pride in "safeguarding the honor, liberty, and interests of an innocent [man]," which he saw as one of the foremost duties of medical experts.[83] Medical experts upheld notions of male honor not only by fashioning themselves as protectors of women and children through helping to bring male sexual predators to justice but also by seeking to expose false charges against honorable bourgeois men.[84]

Forensic doctors identified other reasons, besides blackmail, for supposedly false accusations and so-called simulations of the signs of sexual assault, including vengeance or the desire to rid oneself of a father or guardian. These doctors often insisted that mothers were ultimately to blame. Fournier, for one, insisted that some girls falsely accused their fathers of sexual assault to free themselves from their fathers' authority and more easily pursue a life of debauchery. Some forensic doctors also claimed that a woman seeking vengeance on a cheating partner or seeking to get rid of her husband might accuse him of child sexual abuse and that her child might lie accordingly. Moreover, medical experts maintained that some mothers framed innocent men by provoking vaginitis in their daughters with an irritant.[85] But, these doctors also observed that false accusations might arise inadvertently from a worried mother presuming, on observing that her child had an inflamed vulva or vaginal infection, that she had been assaulted and had contracted a venereal disease. The alarmed mother might ask leading questions of her child whose suggestibility might prompt allegations of sexual abuse. Fournier cited the example of an anxious mother, who, seeing that her nine-year-old daughter's inflamed vulva was oozing yellow pus, asked questions that led the girl to report that a man had touched her. After the accused man was arrested, the girl continued to be pressed with questions and then declared that he had not touched her. She said that she and a playmate had been touching each other and her playmate instructed her to blame the man instead. Fournier lamented, "A man's honor can find itself at the mercy...of a child's precocious perversity."[86] Fournier and others suggested that while innocent children needed masculine protection from sexual offenses, bourgeois men needed their own protection from women and children, particularly girls, whom they assumed were lying about sexual assault. Doctors, investigators, male jurors, and the public often gave the benefit of the doubt to bourgeois men and dismissed their accusers' accusations as false. Bourgeois men's anxieties about female agency, particularly in response to the emergence of the "New Woman," who challenged traditional gender norms, heightened their concerns about threats to male authority. Consequently, these concerns and anxieties shaped the findings and writings of medical men, which not only discredited women and children but also reinforced patriarchal domination more broadly.

The figure of the lying child loomed large in the discourse on sexual offenses against children during the 1880s and 1890s, at a time when childhood was increasingly central to psychiatry. Children's propensity for lying figured prominently in a number of forensic studies of this period and in debates among the members of the Medico-Psychological Society, France's premier psychiatric association.[87] In his 1887 study on children's false judicial testimony, Doctor Auguste Motet declared that children's lies had an "astonishing resemblance" to the lies of women with hysteria. [88] Motet drew upon Charles Lasègue's 1881 study of lying among hysterical women and children, including the case a ten-year-old boy who accused a man of sexual abuse in quite detailed terms, but the accused, a "perfectly honorable" man, vehemently denied it. During the investigation, the boy recanted. Lasègue declared that the boy had fabricated the accusation as a result

of leading questions that his worried mother asked after he had
returned home an hour later than usual. His parents had him point
out where the sexual assault occurred. According to Lasègue, the boy
pointed arbitrarily to the accused's house.[89] Brouardel maintained that
children lied about sexual assault on account of their highly suggestible nature. He presented the techniques he used to demonstrate how
easily and commonly children would falsely accuse an innocent man of
sexual assault. Brouardel reported that he would ask two- and three-
year-old girls with vaginitis, "Who did this to you?" When the girls
hesitated, Brouardel suggested the name of a man, for example, a
foreign diplomat. They replied, "Yes, it was him." They would repeat
the name when Brouardel later followed up with them.[90] These
accounts became widely cited as proof of children's ease in inventing
narratives of sexual abuse and as justification for experts' privileging
the word of "honorable" men over that of children.

The expert discourse on sexual offenses against children raised
broader questions about children's nature and moral education.[91] In
some respects, this discourse represented a backlash to the notion that
children were naturally innocent and in need of adult protection
during this perilous and fragile period. Brouardel declared, "We often
speak of the innocence of children; nothing is more false."[92] Children
were easily molded and suggestible, meaning that pernicious influences
could easily corrupt children. Failed moral environments usually had a
specific class location in the minds of forensic doctors: the lower
classes. There was also a gender dimension. Forensic doctors suggested
implicitly or explicitly that girls were more prone to deceive than boys.
Legludic claimed that many young girls were poorly raised and lied
about sexual assault on account of their "perversity."[93] Addressing the
Medico-Psychological Society in 1882, Eugène Dally maintained that
lying developed earlier in young girls than in boys. He claimed that
lying was more common among French children than British, but
others disputed this claim. Dally also claimed that a child is "essen-
tially a liar" and that malice was the usual source of children's lies.[94]
The physician Claude-Etienne Bourdin argued that all children were
inclined to lie by nature and did so for a variety of reasons, whether for
the pleasure of doing harm, vengeance or hatred, or avoiding a duty or
punishment.[95] Insisting that children were often neither truthful nor
innocent, a number of doctors described some children as perverted

and wicked and attributed their lies to their base natures. Lacassagne warned of children's "perversity, [whether] acquired or subconscious" as well as their "wickedness and meanness."[96] Bourdin distinguished between children whose lies were innocent innovations and "wicked" children who used lies as weapons for personal advantage or to harm others. Bourdin insisted that children, like adults, lied on account of greed, hatred, hostility, vengeance, and jealousy. He sought to "strip from childhood the halo of sincerity with which it has been so unjustly crowned" and declared that it was up to doctors "to destroy the myth of the infallible sincerity of the child."[97]

Forensic doctors asked whether or to what extent a child's word should carry weight in the judicial arena. Some discounted children's accounts altogether and insisted that the only reliable evidence was forensic.[98] Paul Bézy, who studied hysteria in children, declared in 1893 that children's testimonies "were subject to error and dominated by lies and, if not declared invalid, must be at least seriously controlled."[99] Legludic declared that the longer he practiced forensic medicine, the more distrustful he became of children's accounts.[100] When children who were under pressure to recant their accusations did so, experts generally interpreted it as proof that the child had initially lied. Medical writings on child sexual abuse commonly insisted that doctors should omit what they heard from children, which could be lies, from their medicolegal reports. Several forensic studies of sexual crimes against children instructed medical practitioners to focus on medical and bodily matters by closing their ears and opening their eyes.[101] These works insisted that children's accounts of sexual assault could not be trusted. They also acknowledged doctors' difficulties in recognizing material proof in cases involving sexual crimes against children. The implication was that neither children's bodies nor their words could furnish reliable proof of sexual abuse, and this notion made the prosecution of sexual crimes against children all the more difficult.

The inability of medical experts to detect signs of sexual crimes against children stemmed both from the nature of the crimes, as many of these acts left no discernible traces, and from the state of medical and scientific knowledge of the time. While doctors increasingly turned their attention to sexual offenses against children and acknowledged the difficulty or even the impossibility of recognizing material proof in numerous cases, many concluded that their negative findings often constituted proof that these crimes had not occurred and that these allegations were false. By the end of the nineteenth century, there was a new emphasis on forensic chemical analysis as a more reliable form of evidence than bodily examinations or children's testimonies. Chemists' or pharmacists' analyses of stains on clothing or bedding that were suspected to be blood or semen nevertheless presented considerable challenges. These challenges persisted even after the physician Albert Florence introduced new techniques of identifying seminal fluid using iodine in the 1890s in Lyon, with additional protocols for inspecting stains, blood, vaginal discharge, and semen.[102] The prosecution of sexual crimes against children declined in the late 1880s and early 1890s, as medical experts cast greater suspicion on child victims and publicly advanced the notion that children lied about abuse.[103] Still, sexual crimes against children appeared before the courts and figured into public consciousness to a much greater degree than at the beginning of the century.

The prosecution of sexual offenses against children and doctors' roles in these cases revealed conflicting views of childhood innocence and sexuality that engendered ambivalent atittudes toward these crimes. Medical experts routinely cast moral judgments on children, particularly working-class girls, identified as victims of sexual crimes. Although many bourgeois men sought to protect vulnerable women and children, they also sometimes showed excessive sympathy to male perpetrators of sexual violence in an attempt to preserve their reputation, status, or power.[104] The prosecution of sexual crimes against children often pitted these competing impulses against one another. Influenced by bourgeois attitudes toward male honor and notions about the "immorality" of the working class, medical men often advised not attaching much weight to children's claims and proceeding with great caution. They maintained that children's accounts of sexual assault could not be trusted and warned that malicious women and children could easily destroy men's reputations and those of their families. By discounting children's accounts, doctors laid claim to their exclusive ability to evaluate proof of sexual abuse. Furthermore, by discrediting children identified as victims of sexual crimes, medical men shaped attitudes toward sexual assault that presented long-lasting challenges to the pursuit of justice.

Conclusion and Epilogue

Beginning in 1893, a series of grisly murders of teenage shepherds alarmed authorities and the French public. In one of the earliest cases of criminal profiling, the investigating magistrate Emile Fourquet saw a pattern in these crimes and created a profile of the murderer that he sent to public prosecutors across France. In 1897 authorities arrested Joseph Vacher, a former soldier and vagabond, after he attempted to sexually assault a woman who was gathering wood in a field in the Ardèche. The local investigating magistrate thought Vacher matched the description that Fourquet had circulated. Fourquet then interrogated Vacher, who ultimately confessed to murdering eleven persons, mostly adolescent farmers and shepherds. However, authorities suspected that he had killed at least fifteen people. Vacher, known as "the French Ripper," "the South-East Ripper," and "the killer of shepherds," had "horribly mutilated" the bodies of most of his victims, some of whom he had also raped. Vacher's highly publicized trial before the assize court of the Ain in 1898 raised the question of his sanity and criminal responsibility. He insisted that he committed his acts in a state of frenzy. He claimed that he tore off the genitals of one of his victims, a sixteen-year-old boy, with his teeth in a state of blind rage. But, doctor Lacassagne insisted that the autopsy revealed that the victim's wounds had been made with a cutting instrument. Vacher suggested that his mental afflictions stemmed from being bitten by a rabid dog during childhood and subjected to deleterious quack cures. Lacassagne argued that Vacher was trying to feign insanity.[1]

According to Lacassagne and the four other doctors who examined Vacher's mental state, his murders were the methodical work of a "monstrous criminal" – not an impulsive madman.[2] Jurors declared Vacher guilty, and he was executed on December 31, 1898.

Medicolegal expertise played a crucial role in the Vacher trial, at a point when the authority of medical experts in French courts had become relatively well established. The trial brought together a number of the issues developed in the preceding chapters. These include the popular fascination with gruesome murders and mutilated bodies, the centrality of autopsies in murder investigations, forensic doctors' concerns over malingering, their increasing attention to the signs of sexual assault, and the greater influence of medicolegal reports and testimonies on juries and judicial verdicts. Indeed, Lacassagne was a respected medicolegal authority whose testimony was decisive in the Vacher case and whose confidence at times belied the uncertainty inherent in forensic medical practice during this period.

From the late eighteenth to the late nineteenth century, medical men carved out spaces for themselves in the judicial system and the administration of law, while managing uncertainty in their quest to provide proof and reliable scientific evidence. Medical experts had had more limited roles under the Old Regime, but Revolutionary reforms created new opportunities for medical professionals to exercise greater authority in the legal arena. However, these opportunities were restricted to male surgeons, doctors, and *officiers de santé*, whose abilities and scope of medicolegal knowledge varied widely. While some medical men eagerly seized opportunities to practice legal medicine, others were deeply uneasy in their role of medicolegal expert. Medical practitioners also debated what constituted proof, particularly for medicolegal tasks that involved considerable uncertainty, such as evaluating signs of death, causes of death, evidence of poisoning, malingering, signs of early pregnancy, and evidence of sexual assault. In addition, the concerns of medical men and of the public about certain medicolegal matters shifted throughout this period. For example, the issues of malingering in the military and the detection of early pregnancy had become less salient by the end of the nineteenth century. In contrast, anxieties about the detection of plant-based poisonings, the mental state of infanticidal mothers, and false accusations of sexual assault had intensified. Moreover, as forensic knowledge became popularized, men and women seeking to evade the law used their vernacular knowledge to make the tasks of medical experts even more challenging. Despite these challenges, many practitioners expressed confidence in their work and in the field of legal medicine, as they sought to elevate the public profile of their profession.

Over the course of the nineteenth century, there was more practical instruction in legal medicine for medical students, a proliferation of medicolegal publications, greater awareness of forensic medicine, a wider range of questions that medical experts answered for the courts, and a more decisive role that medical evidence played in prosecutorial decisions, legal defenses, and judicial verdicts. Medical experts' written reports often determined investigating magistrates' decisions about bringing cases to trial and framing charges. However, the weight that jurists and juries gave to medical evidence in verdicts and sentencing varied, and medical expertise tended to play a complicated and contested role in jury trials in the assize courts. Juries also evaluated forensic evidence in relation to circumstantial evidence, "moral proofs," and their own sympathies. The stature of individual medicolegal experts, the nature of forensic evidence, the kind of criminal offense and punishment, the social status and comportment of both victim and accused, and other factors all shaped the role of medicolegal expertise across different investigations, trials, and legal matters. As defense attorneys' reliance on their own experts' reports and testimonies grew, contradictory medical evidence further complicated and sometimes obscured answers to medicolegal questions. The president of the assize court in Riom observed in 1845, "Medical science in the assize courts is usually less a means of discovering the truth than a cause of obscurity."[3] Despite controversies among experts and denunciations of flawed forensic evidence, public esteem for practitioners of forensic medicine nonetheless rose on the whole from the late eighteenth to the end of the nineteenth century.

The Vacher trial was not only testament to the growing stature of the medicolegal expert but also a harbinger of new trends, such as the emergence of scientific systems of identifying criminals at the fin de siècle. The field of "anthropometry," or human measurement, took distinct shape in the late nineteenth century. During the 1880s, the Parisian police officer Alphonse Bertillon applied anthropometry to law enforcement to create an identification system, also known as *bertillonage*, or the Bertillon system, based on physical measurements, photography, and record-keeping. In 1897 authorities took anthropometric measurements of Vacher's limbs; recorded other physical data about his body, including his scars, weight, height, and eye color; and analyzed x-ray images of his head. Bertillon's anthropometric identification system entailed recording this information on cards with photographs, and these identification cards became the first mugshots.[4] In the 1890s Bertillon became an international celebrity, due in part to his testimony as a handwriting expert in the Dreyfus affair. He initially resisted the introduction of fingerprint identification, but fingerprinting ultimately superseded the Bertillon system as the primary method of identification at the turn of the century. Bertillon, like Lacassagne, also turned to analyzing ballistics and trace evidence at crime scenes. Their works were part of a broader shift toward the emergence of forensic science.

The twentieth century saw the rise of trace-oriented forensic science that supplemented the practice of body-centered forensic medicine. In 1910 Bertillon's disciple Edmond Locard established the first forensic science laboratory in Lyon. Locard refined the study of fingerprints and developed a theory about the transfer of trace evidence between objects, which became known as Locard's exchange principle. His notion that "every contact leaves a trace" became the guiding principle of forensic science across the globe.[5]

The authority and influence of forensic doctors and scientists in twentieth- and twenty-first-century France stem from the acceptance that medicolegal experts gained over the course of the nineteenth century as well as from subsequent medicolegal reforms. These reforms included better remuneration and the creation of national and regional official lists of experts who were well established and respected in their field of expertise. In contemporary criminal investigations, the examining magistrate for serious crimes or the public prosecutor for lesser crimes gathers pretrial evidence, compiles a dossier containing all the investigative materials, and appoints experts from an officially approved list to provide written reports for the dossier in cases needing forensic or other expert analysis. Professional judges in France generally have confidence in the experts whom they appoint from official lists. These judges determine civil and criminal verdicts, with the exception of felony criminal cases tried with juries at the assize courts.[6] Experts' positions tend not to be highly contested, and the French public and the courts generally place considerable trust in forensic experts.

Matters of medicolegal reform and public confidence in experts have followed a different trajectory in America, with its adversarial common-law system. Efforts to replace coroners, whose roles in death investigations have generated controversy, with medical professionals have had limited or mixed success. In 1877 the state of Massachusetts established the medical-examiner system in which physicians, pathologists, or forensic pathologists conducted death investigations. During the decades that followed, other states and counties moved to the medical-examiner system. Yet many states and counties retained systems in which coroners, who usually held elected public office, conducted investigations into deaths. Consequently, death investigations in the United States, carried out either by coroners or medical examiners, became highly varied, depending on the particular legal and political contexts across the states and counties.[7]

Medical, legal, and scientific professionals in the United States have engaged in ongoing debates about what constitutes reliable forensic and other scientific evidence. In 1923 the US Supreme Court's *Frye v. United States* decision set standards for the admission of scientific evidence, including forensic evidence, in US courtrooms. The *Frye* standard, known as the "general acceptance test," required that the courts only admit expert opinion based on scientific principles and techniques that a sufficient proportion of the relevant scientific community accepted. The *Frye* "general acceptance test" remained the dominant standard for determining the admissibility of scientific evidence until 1993. The 1993 *Daubert v. Merrell Dow Pharmaceuticals* decision transformed trial judges into gatekeepers and evaluators of admissible scientific expert testimony and evidence.[8] The *Daubert* standard has attracted scrutiny and criticism from some commentators concerned about judges' competence in understanding and evaluating scientific evidence.[9] In contrast to American law and its adversarial common-law tradition, France's largely inquisitorial legal system lacks such evidentiary rules.

Both American and French citizens today have high levels of confidence in forensic expertise. While some commentators have expressed grave concerns about the scientific reliability of forensic evidence and "junk science" in the courtroom, criticism of flawed forensics in the courts has been a relatively elite discourse standing in contrast to popular attitudes toward forensics. Television and popular media portrayals of forensic science and crime-scene investigation as seemingly infallible have helped engender favorable popular attitudes toward forensic expertise. Commentators in recent years have also lamented that jurors' misguided expectations of forensic science and their overconfidence in the reliability of forensic evidence have adversely impacted criminal prosecutions, a phenomenon that has been termed the CSI effect. First described and theorized in the 2000s, the CSI effect maintains that the great popularity of the *CSI: Crime Scene Investigation* television franchise and other related crime dramas has changed the way jurors evaluate forensic evidence. These shows have led jurors to demand more forensic evidence in criminal trials and to have unrealistically high expectations of forensic science. The theory posits that these jurors are more likely to overvalue forensic evidence and to acquit in cases lacking various kinds of forensic evidence, even if other evidence of guilt is overwhelming.[10]

Conversely, jurors have become more likely to convict on the basis of forensic evidence, particularly DNA evidence. DNA was first used to identify and convict offenders in the United Kingdom and the United States during the mid-1980s and in France during the 1990s. The late 1980s and early 1990s saw judicial challenges to the admissibility of DNA evidence in American courts. A consensus eventually emerged around reliable methods and techniques for DNA testing to identify or rule out individuals as perpetrators, when biological evidence, such as saliva, blood, hair, semen, or tissue, was present and collected at a crime scene. DNA testing became increasingly central to criminal prosecutions. It also became a tool for post-conviction exoneration. From 1989 to 2019, DNA testing proved the innocence of 367 wrongfully convicted persons in the United States. These DNA exonerations have shed light on the unreliability of witness identification and confessions as forms of evidence. The Innocence Project has found that eyewitness misidentification was involved in over two-thirds of DNA exonerations in the United States. Additionally, nearly half of DNA exonerees had been originally convicted on the basis of flawed, misapplied forensic science.[11] While DNA testing itself is not immune from error, forensic genetics is generally considered the most accurate and scientifically sound field of forensic science today. The scientific community and courts have found other forensic techniques unreliable, including those involving the analysis of bite marks, blood spatter, firearm and tool marks, hair, and fibers. Nevertheless, television crime shows commonly depict these methods as infallible. Moreover, even forensic evidence generated from techniques deemed acceptable could be either compromised by human error, fabricated, subject to cognitive bias, overstated by experts, or misunderstood by jurors.

As these issues come into focus, forensic scientists may face greater challenges to their expertise and authority; however, forensic science has not come under attack to the same extent as other domains of expertise. A declining respect for expertise, seen most clearly in the rejection of scientific findings on climate change and vaccination, has led some commentators to observe a current "crisis of expertise" or "the death of expertise."[12] Many commentators also argue that Donald Trump and his administration engaged in a "war on expertise."[13] Although respect for expertise is generally more robust in France, the country has been experiencing aspects of this crisis and had the lowest levels of confidence in vaccinations for any country worldwide prior to the COVID-19 pandemic.[14] The pandemic put national and political differences in attitudes toward scientific and medical expertise into stark relief, yet public trust in science and scientists increased globally during this period.[15] Varying degrees of confidence in or distrust of medical or scientific authorities and the validity of their claims have profound implications for matters of justice, individual and public health, the environment, and public policy. The role of experts and expertise in society and policy making presents increasingly pressing issues in our own times.

Relatively favorable yet nuanced attitudes toward expertise in France are in part the product of the historical struggle of scientists and medical practitioners to establish their authority in the legal arena. France was in many respects at the forefront of legal medicine throughout the late eighteenth and nineteenth centuries. But, practitioners and the public grappled with the problem of proof and the question of what constituted reliable evidence. Forensic medicine offered the promise of reliable forms of legal proof and justice served. However, medicolegal findings did not necessarily establish the objective facts of a case. Rather, these findings were often the product of controversial techniques, contested scientific claims, and the moralizing judgments of medicolegal practitioners. Nonetheless, medical experts' claims to authority gained general public acceptance, and the rise of forensic medicine has both bolstered and undermined the pursuit of justice.

Notes

Introduction

1 Véronique Campion-Vincent, "L'œil révélateur," *Cahiers internationaux de sociologie* 104 (1998): 58.
2 Sandra Menenteau, "L'art d'improviser: La pratique des autopsies médico-légales au XIXe siècle," *Histoire des sciences médicales* 2 (2012): 154.
3 Maxime Vincent, "Applications de la photographie à la médecine légale," *Annales d'hygiène publique et de médecine légale* series 2, vol. 33 (1870): 239–51; Campion-Vincent, "L'œil révélateur," 61.
4 Archives de Paris (ADP) D2U8 223, Letter from Arsène Beauvais, June 27, 1887; Archives de la Préfecture de Police de Paris BA 83. On the Pranzini affair, see Aaron Freundschuh, *The Courtesan and the Gigolo: The Murders in the Rue Montaigne and the Dark Side of Empire in Nineteenth-Century Paris* (Palo Alto: Stanford University Press, 2017).
5 Bruno Bertherat, "Les mots du médecin légiste, de la salle d'autopsie aux Assises: l'affaire Billoir (1876–1877)," *Revue d'histoire des sciences humaines* 22, no. 1 (2010): 124.
6 Isabelle Coquillard, "Des médecins jurés au Châtelet de Paris aux médecins légistes: Genèse d'une professionnalisation (1692–1801)," *Histoire des sciences médicales* 46, no. 2 (2012): 133–44; Cathy McClive, "'Witnessing of the Hands' and Eyes: Surgeons as Medico-Legal Experts in the Claudine Rouge Affair, Lyon, 1767," *Journal for Eighteenth-Century Studies* 35 no. 4 (2012): 489–503; Christelle Rabier, "Defining a Profession: Surgery, Professional Conflicts and Legal Powers in Paris and London, 1760–1790," in *Fields of Expertise: A Comparative History of Expert Procedures in Paris and London, 1600 to Present*, ed. Christelle Rabier (Newcastle: Cambridge Scholars Publishing, 2007), 85–114; Stanford Emerson Chaillé, *Origin and Progress of Medical Jurisprudence, 1776–1876: A Centennial Address* (Philadelphia: Collins,

1876), 4; Frédéric Chauvaud, *Les experts du crime: La médecine légale en France au XIXe siècle* (Paris: Aubier, 2000), 12.

7   The first chairs were Paul Augustin Olivier Mahon in Paris, Clément François-Gabriel Victor Prunelle in Montpellier, and François Fodéré in Strasbourg. Eusèbe de Salle, *Traité de médecine légale et jurisprudence médicale* (Paris: Gautret, 1838), 8.

8   For classic studies on the Paris school of medicine, see Michel Foucault, *The Birth of the Clinic: An Archeology of Medical Perception* (New York: Vintage Books, 1975); Erwin Ackerknecht, *Medicine at the Paris Hospital, 1794–1848* (Baltimore: Johns Hopkins University Press, 1967).

9   Roger Magraw, *France, 1800–1914: A Social History* (London: Routledge, 2002), 271.

10 The law of 19 ventôse an XI (March 10, 1803).

11 For recent scholarship on the history of modern forensic medicine beyond North America and the United Kingdom, see, e.g., Ian Burney and Christopher Hamlin, eds. *Global Forensic Cultures: Making Fact and Justice in the Modern Era* (Baltimore: Johns Hopkins University Press, 2019); Chauvaud, *Les experts du crime*; Frédéric Chauvaud and Laurence Dumoulin, eds. *Experts et expertise judiciaire: France, XIXe et XXe siècles* (Rennes: Presses universitaires de Rennes, 2003); Daniel Asen, *Death in Beijing: Murder and Forensic Science in Republican China* (Cambridge: Cambridge University Press, 2016); Katherine Watson, *Forensic Medicine in Western Society: A History* (New York: Routledge, 2010); Bruno Bertherat, "La morgue de Paris au XIXe siècle (1804–1907): Les origines de l'Institut médico-légal ou les métamorphoses de la machine" (PhD diss., Université Paris 1, 2002); Sandra Menenteau, *L'autopsie judiciaire: Histoire d'une pratique ordinaire au XIXe siècle* (Rennes: Presses universitaires de Rennes, 2013); Michel Porret and Fabrice Brandli, *Les corps meurtris: Investigations judiciaires et expertises médico-légales au XVIIIe siècle* (Rennes: Presses universitaires de Rennes, 2014); Michel Porret, *Sur la scène du crime. Pratique pénale, enquête et expertises judiciaires à Genève (XVIIIe–XIXe siècles)* (Montreal: Presses de l'Université de Montréal, 2008); José Ramón Bertomeu-Sánchez and Augustí Nieto-Galan, eds. *Chemistry, Medicine, and Crime: Mateu J.B. Orfila (1787–1851) and His Times* (Sagamore Beach, MA: Science History Publications, 2006); and Khaled Fahmy, *In Quest of Justice: Islamic Law and Forensic Medicine in Modern Egypt* (Berkeley: University of California Press, 2018); Lorraine Chappuis, et al., *Faire parler les corps: François-Emmanuel Fodéré à la genèse de la médecine légale moderne* (Rennes: Presses universitaires de Rennes, 2021).

12 On coroners and death investigation, see, e.g., Ian A. Burney, *Bodies of Evidence: Medicine and the Politics of the English Inquest, 1830–1826* (Baltimore: Johns Hopkins University Press, 2000); Jeffrey Jentzen, *Death Investigation in America: Coroners, Medical Examiners, and the Pursuit of Medical Certainty* (Cambridge, MA: Harvard University Press, 2009); James Crail Mohr, *Doctors and the Law: Medical Jurisprudence in*

Nineteenth-Century America (New York: Oxford University Press, 1993); and Katherine Watson, Medicine and Justice: Medico-Legal Practice in England and Wales, 1700–1914 (Abingdon: Routledge, 2020).

13 Mohr, Doctors and the Law.

14 Tal Golan, Laws of Men and Laws of Nature: The History of Scientific Expert Testimony in England and America (Cambridge, MA: Harvard University Press, 2007); Tal Golan, "Revisiting the History of Scientific Expert Testimony," Brooklyn Law Review 73, no. 3 (2008): 879–1033, see especially pp. 880–81.

15 On psychiatry in France, see Jan Goldstein, Console and Classify: The French Psychiatric Profession in the Nineteenth Century (New York: Cambridge University Press, 1987); Robert A. Nye, Crime, Madness, and Politics in Modern France: The Medical Concept of National Decline (Princeton, NJ: Princeton University Press, 1984); Pierre Darmon, Médecins et assassins à la Belle Epoque: La médicalisation du crime (Paris: Seuil, 1989); Ruth Harris, Murders and Madness: Medicine, Law, and Society in the Fin de Siècle (Oxford: Clarendon Press, 1989); Marc Renneville, Crime et folie: Deux siècles d'enquêtes médicales et judiciaires (Paris: Fayard, 2003); Laurence Guignard, Juger la folie: La folie criminelle devant les Assises au XIXe siècle (Paris: Presses universitaires de France, 2010); and Laure Murat, The Man Who Thought He Was Napoleon: Toward a Political History of Madness, trans. Deike Dusinberre (Chicago: University of Chicago Press, 2014).

16 Chauvaud, Les experts du crime; Chauvaud and Dumoulin, Experts et expertise judiciaire.

17 Cathy McClive, "Blood and Expertise: The Trials of the Female Medical Expert in the Ancien-Régime Courtroom," Bulletin of the History of Medicine 82, no. 1 (2008): 86–108; Julie Hardwick, Sex in an Old Regime City: Young Workers and Intimacy in France, 1660–1789 (New York: Oxford University Press, 2020), 157–62.

18 James M. Donovan, Juries and the Transformation of Criminal Justice in France in the Nineteenth and Twentieth Centuries (Chapel Hill: University of North Carolina Press, 2010), 14, 46.

19 On Revolutionaries' opposition to transcribing testimony, see Laura Mason, "The 'Bosom of Proof': Criminal Justice and the Renewal of Oral Culture during the French Revolution," Journal of Modern History 76, no. 1 (2004): 29–61.

Chapter 1

1 Archives nationales de France, Pierrefitte-sur-Seine (AN) BB/24/2010/1; Mathieu [Mateu] J.B. Orfila, "Mémoire sur la suspension, lu à l'Académie royale de médecine, le 6 octobre 1840," Mémoires de l'Académie royale de médecine (Paris: Baillière, 1841), 9:234–76.

2 Ambroise Tardieu, Etude médico-légale sur la pendaison, la strangulation, et la suffocation, 2nd ed. (Paris: Baillière, 1879), 67–74.

3 Article 27 of the law of 19 ventôse year XI.

4 Sean M. Quinlan, "Apparent Death in Eighteenth-Century France and England," *French History* 9, no. 2 (1995): 27–47.

5 On "apparent death" or death verification in nineteenth-century France, see Anne Carol, "Une histoire médicale des critères de la mort," *Communications* 97, no. 2 (2015): 45–55; Anne Carol, "Le 'médecin des morts' à Paris au XIXe siècle," *Annales de démographie historique* 127, no. 1 (2014): 153–79; Anne Carol, *Les médecins et la mort, XIXe–XXe siècle* (Paris: Aubier, 2004); Stephen Sawyer, "A Question of Life and Death: Administrating Bodies and Administrative Bodies in Nineteenth-Century Paris," in *Fields of Expertise: A Comparative History of Expert Procedures in Paris and London, 1600 to Present*, ed. Christelle Rabier (Newcastle: Cambridge Scholars Press, 2007), 291–315; Martin Pernick, "Back from the Grave: Recurring Controversies over Defining and Diagnosing Death in History," in *Death: Beyond Whole-Brain Criteria*, ed. Richard M. Zaner (Dordrecht: Kluwer Academic Publishers, 1988), 17–74; and Jan Bondeson, *Buried Alive: The Terrifying History of Our Most Primal Fear* (New York: W. W. Norton, 2001).

6 Jean-Baptiste Desgranges, *Supplément au Mémoire sur les moyens de perfectionner l'établissement public formé à Lyon en faveur des personnes noyées, etc.* (Lyon, 1790).

7 Anton Serdeczny, *Du tabac pour le mort: Une histoire de la réanimation* (Paris: Champ Vallon, 2018); Francis Trépardoux, "Les secours aux noyés dans la ville de Paris, 1772–1831: Composition des boîtes de secours en ustensiles et médicaments," *Revue d'histoire de la pharmacie* 84, no. 312 (1996): 370–73.

8 Jules Parrot, *De la mort apparente* (Paris: Delahaye, 1860), 72; Charles Vibert, "Respiration artificielle," in *Nouveau dictionnaire de médecine et de chirurgie pratiques* (Paris: Lahure, 1882), 31:314–15.

9 Suzanne Necker, *Des inhumations précipitées* (Paris: Impr. royale, 1790).

10 Carol, "Le 'médecin des morts,'" 154; Carol, *Les médecins et la mort*, 190–93; Sawyer, "A Question of Life and Death," 294.

11 J. B. Monfalcon, "Inhumations," in *Dictionnaire des sciences médicales*, ed. Adelon, Alard, Alibert, et al. (Paris: Panckoucke, 1818), 25:171–72, 179–80, 187–88, quotation on p. 188.

12 Marie-François-Xavier Bichat, *Recherches physiologiques sur la vie et la mort* (Paris: Brosson, year VIII [1799]); Félix Gannal, *Mort réelle et mort apparente* (Paris: Coccoz, 1868), 26–31; M.-J.-B. Orfila, *Secours à donner aux personnes empoisonnées ou asphyxiées, suivis des moyens propres à reconnaître les poisons, et les vins frelatés, et à distinguer la mort réelle de la mort apparente* (Paris: Feugueray, 1818), 189–90.

13 Charles-Chrétien-Henri Marc, "Inhumations," in *Dictionnaire des sciences médicales* (Brussels: Dewaet, 1829), 8:310, 314–15. Alessandro Volta invented his "pile," the first battery, in 1799.

14 C.-F. Tacheron, *De la vérification légale des décès dans la ville de Paris, et de la nécessité d'apporter dans ce service médical plus de surveillance* (Paris: Gobin, 1830).

15 Prosper Touchard, *Aperçu général des précautions prises en France avant l'inhumation des citoyens morts* (Tours: Placé, 1833), 13.

16 Jean-Sébastien-Eugène Julia de Fontenelle, *Recherches médico-légales sur l'incertitude des signes de la mort: Les dangers des inhumations précipitées* (Paris: Rouvier, 1834), 9.

17 Alphonse Devergie, "Mort," in *Dictionnaire de médecine et de chirurgie pratiques*, ed. Gabriel Andral, Louis Jacques Bégin, Philippe Frédéric Blandin, et al. (Paris: Méquignon-Marvis, 1834), 11:544.

18 Eugène Bouchut, *Traité des signes de la mort et des moyens de prévenir les enterrements prématurés* (Paris: Baillière, 1849), x.

19 "Sur les morts apparentes et sur les moyens de prévenir les enterrements prématurés," *Annales d'hygiène publique et de médecine légale*, series 1, vol. 40 (1848): 108–109.

20 "Sur les morts apparentes," 102; Jules-Antoine Josat, *De la mort et de ses caractères: Nécessité d'une révision de la législation des décès pour prévenir les inhumations et les délaissements anticipés* (Paris: Baillière, 1854), 76–82, 310–19; Bondeson, *Buried Alive*, 168–70; Carol, *Les médecins et la mort*, 180.

21 "De la valeur de l'acupuncture du cœur proposée par M. le docteur Plouviez comme moyen de distinguer la mort réelle de la mort apparente," *L'Union médicale*, no. 131, October 31, 1861.

22 Léon Collongues, *Traité de dynamoscopie, ou Appréciation de la nature et de la gravité des maladies par l'auscultation des doigts* (Paris: Asselin, 1862); Bondeson, *Buried Alive*, 149.

23 Barrangeard, *Extrait de divers mémoires publiés depuis très-longtemps par le docteur Barrangeard, sur le danger des inhumations précipitées et sur la nécessité de constater avec soin tous les décès sans aucune exception* (Lyon: Jaillet, 1863), 4, 10–11, quotation on p. 4.

24 Bondeson, *Buried Alive*, 170–71; J. Rambosson, "Les inhumations précipitées et les moyens de les prévenir," *Le Correspondant* 80 (Paris: Douniol, 1869): 303.

25 Alphonse Devergie, "Inhumations précipitées: Rapport fait au nom du conseil de salubrité du département de la Seine," *Annales d'hygiène publique et de médecine légale*, series 2, vol. 27 (1867): 322–27; Carol, *Les médecins et la mort*, 206.

26 Gabriel Tourdes, "Mort (médecine légale)," in *Dictionnaire encyclopédique des sciences médicales*, series 2, vol. 9 (Paris: Masson, 1875), 603–604; *L'Union médicale*, no. 151, December 19, 1867; Alphonse Devergie, "Des signes de la mort: Etude de leur cause, appréciation de leur valeur," *Annales d'hygiène publique et de médecine légale*, series 2, vol. 41 (1874): 380–405; *Archives générales de médecine* (Paris: Asselin, 1878), 1:630. The Prix Dusgate also commonly appeared in print as the Prix Dugaste.

27 Devergie, "Inhumations précipitées," 306.

28 Tourdes, "Mort," 688.

29 Tourdes, "Mort," 603.

30 Marc, "Inhumations," 315.
31 Charles-Chrétien-Henri Marc, "Grossesse," in *Dictionnaire des sciences médicales* (Paris: Panckoucke, 1817), 19:531–46.
32 Nathalie Sage-Pranchère, "La mort apparente du nouveau-né dans la littérature médicale (France, 1760–1900)," *Annales de démographie historique* 1 (2012): 127–48.
33 Tourdes, "Mort," 619.
34 Maze, *"L'Egalité devant la mort," signes de la mort et moyens de prévenir les inhumations précipitées* (Paris: Noblet et fils, 1892).
35 Carol, *Les médecins et la mort*, 212; B. Gaubert, *Le péril des inhumations précipitées en France: Société des chambres mortuaires d'attente de la ville de Paris* (Paris: Chevalier-Maresq, 1895), 117–19; Jules Eugène Rochard, *Traité d'hygiène publique et privée* (Paris: Doin, 1897), 547.
36 Jean-Baptiste-Vincent Laborde, *Le traitement physiologique de la mort: Les tractions rythmées de la langue, moyen rationnel et puissant de ranimer la fonction respiratoire et la vie, détermination expérimentale du mode d'action, ou mécanisme du procédé* (Paris: Alcan, 1894), quotation on p. 168; Jean-Baptiste-Vincent Laborde, "Application de la méthode des tractions rythmées de la langue," *Bulletin de l'Académie de médecine*, series 3, vol. 42, no. 33 (1899): 273–88, quotation on p. 287; Carol, *Les médecins et la mort*, 182.
37 *L'Union médicale*, no. 112, September 13, 1888; Frédéric Dufour, *La constatation des décès en France au point de vue des inhumations prématurées et des morts criminelles* (Poitiers: Blais et Roy, 1899).
38 Vanessa Schwartz, *Spectacular Realities: Early Mass Culture in Fin-de-Siècle Paris* (Berkeley: University of California Press, 1999), 58; Bruno Bertherat, "La mort en vitrine à la morgue à Paris au XIXe siècle (1804–1907)," in *Les narrations de la mort*, ed. Régis Bertrand, Anne Carol, and Jean-Noël Pelen (Aix-en-Provence: Presses universitaires de Provence, 2005); Bertherat, "La morgue de Paris."
39 Mathieu [Mateu] Joseph Bonaventure Orfila, "Cadavre," in *Dictionnaire de médecine*, ed. Adelon, Alard, Alibert, et al. (Paris: Béchet jeune, 1822), 4:24–27.
40 Paul Brouardel, *Du service des autopsies médico-légales à la morgue* (Paris: Asselin, 1878), 9.
41 In the *départements* of the Vienne and the Deux-Sèvres, doctors performed half of autopsies in domestic settings. Sandra Menenteau, "Dans les coulisses de l'autopsie judiciaire: Cadres, contraintes et conditions de l'expertise cadavérique dans la France du XIXe siècle" (PhD diss., Université de Poitiers, 2009), 648–56.
42 Records of the registers of morgue are housed at the Archives de la Préfecture de police de Paris in the LA series.
43 Schwartz, *Spectacular Realities*, 50, 53–55; Alphonse Devergie, "La morgue de Paris," *Annales d'hygiène publique et de médecine légale*, series 2, no. 49 (1878): 52–54.

44 Adolphe Guillot, *Paris qui souffre: La basse geôle du Grand-Châtelet et les morgues modernes* (Paris: Roquette, 1887), 219.

45 Rochard, *Traité d'hygiène publique*, 549.

46 Ambroise Tardieu, "La morgue: Les morts violentes, crimes et suicides," *Paris Guide*, part 2, *La vie* (Paris: Lacroix, 1867), 2003–4.

47 Devergie, "La morgue de Paris," 52; Bertherat, "La morgue de Paris," 94–96.

48 Guillot, *Paris qui souffre*, 218; Rochard, *Traité d'hygiène publique*, 550.

49 Tardieu, "La morgue," 1996–2005; Schwartz, *Spectacular Realities*, 53–58; Bruno Bertherat, "La morgue de Paris," 174–78, 427, 68.

50 Tardieu, "La morgue," 2002.

51 Tardieu, "La morgue," 1997; Firmin Maillard, *Recherches historiques et critiques sur la morgue* (Paris: Delahays, 1860), 118; Devergie, "La morgue de Paris," 61.

52 *A Handbook for Visitors to Paris*, 2nd ed. (London: John Murray, 1866), 196.

53 On crime and its representations in nineteenth-century France, see Dominique Kalifa, *Crime et culture au XIXe siècle* (Paris: Perrin, 2005); Dominique Kalifa, *L'Encre et le sang: Récits de crimes et société à la Belle Epoque* (Paris: Fayard, 1995); and Dominique Kalifa, *Les Bas-fonds: Histoire d'un imaginaire* (Paris: Seuil, 2013).

54 Devergie, "La morgue de Paris," 61, also cited in Schwartz, *Spectacular Realities*, 69.

55 Bruno Bertherat, "Visiter les morts: La Morgue (Paris, XIXe siècle)," *Hypothèses* 19, no. 1 (2016): 377–90; Schwartz, *Spectacular Realities*, 72.

56 ADP, D2U8 59; *Gazette des tribunaux*, March 15, 1877; *Gazette des tribunaux*, March 16, 1877; Georges Bergeron, "Quelques explications relatives à l'affaire de la femme coupée en morceaux (affaire Billoir)," *Annales d'hygiène publique et de médecine légale*, series 2, vol. 49 (1878): 134–37; Bertherat, "Les mots du médecin légiste"; Schwartz, *Spectacular Realities*, 71–76; Louis Ravoux, *Du dépeçage criminel au point de vue anthropologique et médico-judiciaire* (Lyon: Storck, 1888), 54–56.

57 ADP D2U8 7.

58 AN BB/24/2045.

59 *Gazette des tribunaux*, July 29–30, 1878; *La presse illustrée*, April 21, 1878; ADP D2U8 75.

60 Thomas Cragin, *Murder in Parisian Streets: Manufacturing Crime and Justice in the Popular Press, 1830–1900* (Lewisburg, PA: Bucknell University Press, 2006), 166; *Le cadavre de la rue du Pré-Maudit: Arrestation de l'assassin* (Paris: Aubert, 1880).

61 AN BB/24/2048/2.

62 Investigators also found Menesclou's notebook of songs containing the following verses that Menesclou admitted to composing the day after Deu's death: "I saw her, I seized her. I am now angry with myself, and happiness was but an instant. In my blind rage, I did not see what I was

doing." ADP D2U8 102; AN BB/24/2048/2; Ravoux, *Du dépeçage criminel*, 68–74; Archives de la Préfecture de police de Paris BA 1612.

63 Charles Lasègue, Paul Brouardel, and Auguste Alexandre Motet, "Affaire Menesclou," *Annales d'hygiène publique et de médecine légale*, series 3, no. 4 (1880): 440.

64 Bibliothèque municipale de Lyon Fonds Lacassagne, MS 5250; Alexandre Lacassagne, "De la mensuration des différentes parties du corps dans les cas de dépeçage criminel," *Archives d'anthropologie criminelle* 3 (1888): 158–63; Alexandre Lacassagne, "Du dépeçage criminel," *Archives d'anthropologie criminelle* 3 (1888): 229–55; Ravoux, *Du dépeçage criminel*, 190.

65 *Le Figaro*, June 26, 1901.

66 Lacassagne, "Du dépeçage criminel," 231.

67 AN BB/18/1921.

68 Paul Descoust, Adhémar Robert, and Jules Ogier, "Expériences sur la combustion des cadavres," *Annales d'hygiène publique et de médecine légale*, series 3, vol. 31 (1894): 533–53; *La Liberté*, December 19, 1893.

69 Claude-Nicolas Le Cat, *Mémoire posthume sur les incendies spontanés de l'économie animale* (Paris: Migneret, 1813); Meghan K. Roberts, "Spontaneous Human Combustion and Claude-Nicolas Le Cat's Hunt for Fame," *Journal of Modern History* 93, no. 4 (2021): 749–82.

70 Aimé Lair, *Essai sur les combustions humaines produites par un long abus des liqueurs spiritueuses* (Paris: Gabon, 1800); D. Chirac, *Considérations sur la combustion du corps humain* (Paris: Didot jeune, 1805); Alphonse Devergie, *Médecine légale, théorique et pratique*, 2nd ed. (Paris: Baillière, 1840), 2:341–64; Guillaume Dupuytren, "Combustion humaine spontanée," in *Dictionnaire de médecine et de chirurgie pratiques*, ed. Gabriel Andral, Louis Jacques Bégin, Philippe Frédéric Blandin, et. al. (Paris: Méquignon-Marvis, 1830), 5:367–82; M.-J.-B. Orfila, *Leçons de médecine légale* (Paris: Béchet jeune, 1823), 1:729–33; M.-J.-B. Orfila, *Leçons de médecine légale*, 2nd ed. (Paris: Béchet Jeune, 1828), 2:559–64.

71 N. A. Gavrelle, *Recherches sur les combustions humaines spontanées* (Paris: Didot le jeune, 1827), vi.

72 Ambroise Tardieu and Rota, *Relation médico-légale de l'assassinat de la comtesse de Goerlitz, accompagnée de notes et réflexions pour servir à l'histoire de la combustion humaine spontanée* (Paris: Baillière, 1851); Alphonse Devergie, "Mémoire sur la combustion humaine spontanée," *Annales d'hygiène publique et de médecine légale*, series 1, vol. 46 (1851): 383–432; Ernest Alcide Lecourt, *Etude médico-légale sur la combustion du corps humain* (Paris: Imprimerie générale de la presse, 1881), 13; J. L. Heilbron, "The Affair of the Countess Görlitz," *Proceedings of the American Philosophical Society* 138, no. 2 (1994): 284–316.

73 See, e.g., Paul Brouardel, *Etude médico-légale sur la combustion du corps humain* (Paris: Baillière, 1878); Lecourt, *Etude médico-légale sur la combustion du corps humain*.

74 Gabriel Tourdes, "Combustion humaine spontanée," in *Dictionnaire encyclopédique des sciences médicales* (Paris: Asselin, 1876), 19:269–292.

75 Oscar Amoëdo, *L'art dentaire en médecine légale* (Paris: Masson, 1898); Fabrice Brandli and Michel Porret, *Les corps meurtris: Investigations judiciaires et expertises médico-légales au XVIIIe siècle* (Rennes: Presses universitaires de Rennes, 2014), 30. For an earlier medicolegal work on teeth, see Albert Dumur, *Des dents: Leur importance et signification dans les questions médico-légales* (Lyon: Pastel, 1882).

76 *L'Eclair*, August 29, 1892, as cited in Schwartz, *Spectacular Realities*, 58.

77 François Chaussier, *Recueil de mémoires, consultations, et rapports sur divers objets de médecine légale* (Paris: Barrois, 1824), ix.

78 Chaussier, *Recueil de mémoires*, x–xi.

79 Alphonse Devergie, *Médecine légale, théorique et pratique*, 3rd ed. (Paris: Baillière, 1852), 1:x.

80 Charles-Alexandre-Hippolyte-Amable Bertrand, *Manuel médico-légal des poisons* (Paris: Croullebois, 1817), 350–51.

81 Charles-Chrétien-Henri Marc, "Introduction," *Annales d'hygiène publique et de médecine légale*, series 1, vol. 1 (1829): xxxiv.

82 Menenteau, "L'art d'improviser," 153.

83 Orfila, "Cadavre," in *Dictionnaire de médecine*, ed. Adelon, Alard, Alibert, et al. (Paris: Béchet jeune, 1822), 4:24.

84 *Congrès scientifique de France, seconde session tenue à Poitiers, 1834*, vol. 2 (Poitiers: Saurin, 1835), 153.

85 Devergie, *Médecine légale, théorique et pratique* (1852), 1:xiv.

86 *Gazette des tribunaux*, March 23, 1855, also cited in Frédéric Chauvaud, "Le déplacement des figures," in *Experts et expertise judiciaire: France, XIXe et XX siècles*, ed. Frédéric Chauvaud and Laurence Dumoulin (Rennes: Presses universitaires de Rennes, 2003), 231.

87 Charles Vibert, *Précis de médecine légale* (Paris: Baillière, 1886), 36; also cited in Chauvaud, "Le déplacement des figures," 239.

88 Emile Pereyra, *Quelques réflexions sur l'insuffisance du jury en matière de médecine légale* (Bordeaux: Faye, 1842), 14.

89 Vibert, *Précis de médecine légale*, vi.

90 Charles-Chrétien-Henri Marc, "Politique (médecine)," in *Dictionnaire de médecine* (Paris, 1827), 17:316–17.

91 Adolphe-Victor Paillard de Villeneuve, "Rapport," in *Dictionnaire de médecine usuelle à l'usage des gens du monde* (Paris: Didier, 1849), 9:723.

92 Paillard de Villeneuve, "Rapport," 722–23.

93 Devergie, "Des signes de la mort," 382, also cited in Chauvaud, "Le déplacement des figures," 230.

94 AN BB/20/114–15.

95 As cited in Laurence Dumoulin, "Du quasi vide juridique à la reprise en main," in *Experts et expertise judiciaire: France, XIXe et XXe siècles*, ed. Frédéric Chauvaud and Laurence Dumoulin (Rennes: Presses universitaires de Rennes, 2003), 56, fn. 27; François Cambrelin, "Les médecins sont-ils tenus d'obtempérer aux réquisitoires qui leur sont adressés par les officiers

de police judiciaire quand il s'agit de la recherche des preuves d'un crime ou d'un délit?," *Annales d'hygiène publique et de médecine légale*, series 1, vol. 24 (1840): 419.

96 Vibert, *Précis de médecine légale*, 14; Joseph Drioux, *Etude sur les expertises médico-légales et l'instruction criminelle d'après les projets du Code d'instruction criminelle et les législations étrangères* (Paris: Pichon, 1886), 14.

97 François-Emmanuel Fodéré, *Traité de médecine légale et d'hygiène publique, ou de police de santé* (Paris: Mame, 1813), 1:liii.

98 *Congrès scientifique de France*, 154.

99 Archives départementales des Bouches-du-Rhône (hereafter ADBR) 2U 1/1331.

100 Annick Tillier, *Des criminelles au village: Femmes infanticides en Bretagne (1825–1865)* (Rennes: Presses universitaires de Rennes, 2001), 42.

101 AN BB/20/120.

102 AN BB/20/226/2.

103 Pereyra, *Quelques réflexions sur l'insuffisance du jury.*

104 Drioux, *Etude sur les expertises médico-légales*, 21, 37.

105 Paul Brouardel, "De la réforme des expertises médico-légales," *Annales d'hygiène publique et de médecine légale*, series 3, vol. 11 (1884): 367–68, 370–71.

106 On the rates set in 1811, see Alphonse Devergie, *Médecine légale, théorique et pratique* (Brussels: Dumont, 1837), 1:19–22. For complaints about these rates, see AN BB/20/133; Société de médecine légale de France, "Organisation de la médecine légale en France," *Annales d'hygiène publique et de médecine légale*, series 3, vol. 11 (1884): 169–71; Brouardel, "De la réforme," 362–64; Charles Desmaze, *Histoire de la médecine légale en France* (Paris: Charpentier, 1880), 321; Drioux, *Etude sur les expertises médico-légales*, 37–39; Henry Coutagne, *Des réformes les plus urgentes des honoraires médico-légaux* (Lyon: Association typographique, 1890); M. E. Horteloup, *Du droit de réquisition des médecins-experts par la justice* (Paris: Baillière, 1890), 36–46, 52.

107 Alexandre Lacassagne, *Les médecins-experts devant les tribunaux et les honoraires des médecins d'après le décret du 21 novembre 1893* (Lyon: Storck, 1894).

108 Ernest Chaudé, "Rapport sur les droits et les devoirs des médecins appelés en justice comme experts," *Annales d'hygiène publique et de médecine légale*, series 2, vol. 44 (1875): 379; Frédéric Chauvaud, "L'essor des spécialités," in *Experts et expertise judiciaire: France, XIXe et XXe siècles*, ed. Frédéric Chauvaud and Laurence Dumoulin (Rennes: Presses universitaires de Rennes, 2003); Drioux, *Etude sur les expertises médico-légales*, 19–21; Gabriel Tarde, "Les actes du Congrès de Rome," *Archives d'anthropologie criminelle* 3 (1888): 77.

109 H.F. Rivière, *Lois usuelles, décrets, ordonnances, avis du conseil d'état, et législation coloniale*, 27th ed. (Paris: Chevalier-Marescq, 1899), 1230.

110 Alexandre Lacassagne, *Les médecins experts et les erreurs judiciaires* (Lyon: Storck, 1897), 8–9.

111 AN BB/18/6220 51 BL 26; Maurice Lailler and Henri Vonoven, *Les erreurs judiciaires et leurs causes* (Paris: Pédone, 1897), 404–18; Lacassagne, *Les médecins experts et les erreurs judicaires*, 5–6.

112 *Gazette des hôpitaux civils et militaires (La lancette française)* 69, no. 129 (November 10, 1896): 1265–66; Sandra Menenteau, "'L'édifice de l'expertise restera [...] comme bâti sur le sable': Enjeux et obstacles à la professionnalisation de la médecine légale dans la France du XIXe siècle," *Déviance et société* 41, no. 3 (2017): 343–69.

113 Jean Cruppi, "A propos de l'affaire Bianchini: L'expertise médico-légale," *Le Figaro*, series 3, no. 63 (March 10, 1899): 1; Laurence Dumoulin, "Les points aveugles de la législation au cœur des polémiques," in *Experts et expertise judiciaire: France, XIXe et XXe siècles*, ed. Frédéric Chauvaud and Laurence Dumoulin (Rennes: Presses universitaires de Rennes, 2003), 69–73; Société de médecine légale de France, "La réforme des expertises médico-légales," *Bulletin de la Société de la médecine légale de France* 16, part 1 (Clermont: Daix, 1899): 20–40.

114 Desmaze, *Histoire de la médecine légale en France*, 29–30.

Chapter 2

1 In 1836 the British chemist James Marsh published a paper describing his construction of a glass apparatus capable of detecting and measuring minute quantities of arsenic.

2 AN BB/18/1831; *Procès de Madame Lafarge* (Paris: Pagnerre, 1840); Armand Fouquier, *Causes célèbres de tous les peuples* (Paris: Lebrun, 1858), 1:1–32; François-Vincent Raspail, *Accusation d'empoisonnement par l'arsenic. Mémoire à consulter, à l'appui du pourvoi en Cassation de Dame Marie Cappelle* (Paris: Gazette des hôpitaux, 1840); *Gazette des tribunaux*, September 16, 1840; *Gazette des tribunaux*, September 17, 1840; *Gazette des tribunaux*, September 19, 1840.

3 On uncertainty, poisoning, and nineteenth-century forensic expertise, see José Ramón Bertomeu-Sánchez, "Managing Uncertainty in the Academy and the Courtroom: Normal Arsenic and Nineteenth-Century Toxicology," *Isis* 104, no. 2 (2013): 197–225; José Ramón Bertomeu-Sánchez, "Arsenic in France: The Cultures of Poison During the First Half of the Nineteenth Century," in *Compound Histories: Materials, Governance and Production, 1760–1840*, ed. Lissa L. Roberts and Simon Werrett (Leiden: Brill, 2018), 131–58; Mark R. Essig, "Science and Sensation: Poison Murder and Forensic Medicine in Nineteenth-Century America" (PhD diss., Cornell University, 2000); and Ian Burney, *Poison, Detection, and the Victorian Imagination* (Manchester: Manchester University Press, 2006).

4 N. Leclerc, *Essai médico-légal sur l'empoisonnement et sur les moyens que l'on doit employer pour le constater* (Paris: Levrault, year XI [1803]), 5–6.

5 Leclerc, *Essai médico-légal sur l'empoisonnement*, 28; A. E. Tartra, *Traité de l'empoisonnement par l'acide nitrique* (Paris: Méquignon, 1802), 202; Paul-Augustin-Olivier Mahon, *Médecine légale et police médicale* (Paris: Bertrand, 1807), 2:258.

6 Leclerc, *Essai médico-légal sur l'empoisonnement*, 10–11, 27, 48–49, quotation on pp. 48–49.

7 François Chaussier, *Consultations médico-légales sur une accusation d'empoisonnement par le sublimé corrosif* (Paris: Didot jeune, 1811), v, xii.

8 Fodéré, *Traité de médecine légale*, 4:185.

9 Tartra, *Traité de l'empoisonnement*, 1. On nineteenth-century toxicology textbooks, see Sacha Tomic, "Le rôle des manuels dans la disciplinarisation de la toxicologie en France au XIXe siècle," *Philosophia Scientiæ* 22, no. 1 (2018): 163–83.

10 Elie Calabre de Breuze, *Mémoire justificatif et consultation médico-légale, en faveur de Dominique François* ([Paris]: Didot jeune, 1814), 8–9.

11 Calabre de Breuze, *Mémoire justificatif*, 12–17.

12 *Journal général de médecine, de chirurgie et de pharmacie* 51 (Paris, 1814), 317–18; Jacques Poilroux, *Traité de médecine légale criminelle* (Paris: Levrault, 1834), x.

13 Dufour and Raige, *Réponse à un libelle diffamatoire de M. Calabre Debreuze* (n.p.: [1815]).

14 Jacques Raige-Delorme, *Considérations médico-légales sur l'empoisonnement par les substances corrosives* (Paris, 1819).

15 "Eloge de M. Orfila," *Gazette médicale de Paris* series 3, vol. 8 (1853): 795; Frédéric Chauvaud, "'Cet homme si multiple et si divers'": Orfila et la chimie du crime au XIXe siècle," *Sociétés & Représentations* 22, no. 2 (2006): 171–87; José Ramón Bertomeu-Sánchez, "Popularizing Controversial Science: A Popular Treatise on Poisons by Mateu Orfila (1818)," *Medical History* 53, no. 3 (2009): 358; José Ramón Bertomeu-Sánchez, "Mateu Orfila (1787–1853) and Nineteenth-Century Toxicology," in *It All Depends on the Dose Poisons and Medicines in European History*, ed. Ole Peter Grell, Andrew Cunningham, and Jon Arrizabalaga (New York: Routledge, 2018), 153.

16 Mathieu [Mateu] J.B. Orfila, *Traité des poisons tirés des règnes minéral, végétal et animal, ou, Toxicologie générale*, 2 vols. (Paris: Crochard, 1814–15).

17 Orfila, *Secours à donner aux personnes empoisonnées*; Hector Chaussier, "Epilogue," in *Contre-poisons, ou Moyens reconnus les plus efficaces dans les différens cas d'empoisonnement*, 2nd ed. (Paris, 1818), 1–2; also cited in Bertomeu-Sánchez, "Popularizing Controversial Science," 358.

18 Paul Elliot, "Vivisection and the Emergence of Experimental Physiology in Nineteenth-Century France," in *Vivisection in Historical Perspective*, ed. Nicholas Rupke (New York: Croom Helm, 1987), 48–77; Roger French, *Antivivisection and Medical Science in Victorian Society* (Princeton, NJ: Princeton University Press, 1975); Anita Guerrini, *Experimenting with*

Humans and Animals: From Galen to Animal Rights (Baltimore: Johns Hopkins University Press, 2003); Jean-Yves Bory, *La douleur des bêtes: La polémique sur la vivisection au XIXᵉ siècle en France* (Rennes: Presses universitaires de Rennes, 2013).

19 José Ramón Bertomeu-Sánchez, "Animal Experiments, Vital Forces and Courtrooms: Mateu Orfila, François Magendie and the Study of Poisons in Nineteenth-Century France," *Annals of Science* 69, no. 1 (2012): 1–26.

20 Orfila, *Traité des poisons*, 2:293–308, quotation on p. 293; Bertomeu-Sánchez, "Animal Experiments."

21 *Procès complet d'Edme-Samuel Castaing, docteur en médecine* (Paris: Pillet aîné, 1823).

22 *Journal des débats*, November 13, 1823.

23 *Journal des débats*, November 11–17, 1823; Linda Stratmann, *The Secret Poisoner: A Century of Murder* (New Haven: Yale University Press, 2006), 45.

24 *Journal des débats*, November 17, 1823; *Procès complet d'Edme-Samuel Castaing*, 122–23; *Causes criminelles célèbres du XIXe siècle* (Paris: Langlois fils, 1828), 4:76–77; *Le Sténographe Parisien: Affaire Castaing: Accusation d'empoisonnement* (Paris, 1823), 225.

25 Charles Dupressoir, *Drames judiciaires. Scènes correctionnelles. Causes célèbres de les peuples. Première série* (Paris: Libriarie ethnographique, 1849), 283.

26 AN BB/20/15/1.

27 M.-J.-B. Orfila, "Affaire d'empoisonnement porté devant la Cour d'assises du département de l'Aube, le 27 août 1824," *Gazette de santé*, March 5, 1825, vol. 52, no. 7 (1825): 49–53.

28 Orfila, "Affaire d'empoisonnement."

29 J.-B. Seurre-Bousquet, *Considérations générales sur l'empoisonnement par l'acide arsénieux* (Paris: Didot le jeune, 1829), 8–9.

30 Orfila made this case in the trial of Marie-Adélaïde Boursier and her lover Nicolas Kostolo for poisoning her husband. *Affaire de Marie-Adélaïde Bodin, veuve Boursier, et de Nicolas Kostolo* (Paris: Pillet aîné, 1823), 24; *Causes criminelles célèbres du XIXe siècle*, 3:114–15, 151–52.

31 *Gazette des tribunaux*, no. 1339, November 26, 1829; *Le messager des chambres*, November 27, 1829; Didier Veillon, "Un parricide par empoisonnement sous la Restauration: L'affaire Bouvier," in *Les vénéneuses: Figures d'empoisonneuses de l'Antiquité à nos jours*, ed. Lydie Bodiou and Myriam Soria (Rennes: Presses universitaires de Rennes, 2015), 71–84.

32 AN BB/24/2004; *Le messager des chambres*, no. 201, July 20, 1829; *Gazette des tribunaux*, no. 1231, July 21, 1829; *Gazette des tribunaux*, no. 1286, September 23, 1829.

33 AN BB/24/2003; *Gazette des tribunaux*, no. 1074, January 17, 1829.

34 AN BB/24/2004.

35 AN BB/20/63.

36 *Gazette médicale de Paris*, vol. 3, no. 35, May 22, 1832. On the cholera epidemics of 1832 and 1849 in Paris, see Catherine Jean Kudlick, *Cholera*

in Post-Revolutionary Paris: A Cultural History (Berkeley: University of California Press, 1996).

37 Karine Salomé, "Le massacre des 'empoisonneurs' à Paris au temps du choléra (1832)," *Revue historique* 673 (2015): 103–24.

38 *Archives parlementaires de 1789 à 1860: Recueil complet des débats législatifs & politiques des Chambres françaises* [AP] ed. Jérôme Mavidal et al., series 2, vol. 79 (Paris: Dupont, 1891): 239–40.

39 AN BB/24/2007.

40 Alphonse Chevallier and Jules Louis Charles Boys de Loury, *Essais sur les moyens à mettre en usage dans le but de rendre moins fréquent le crime d'empoisonnement* (Paris: Locquin, 1835).

41 AN BB/24/2007.

42 AN BB/20/93.

43 AN BB/20/97.

44 M.J.B. Orfila, *Mémoires sur plusieurs questions médico-légales* (Paris: Béchet jeune, 1839), 59; José Ramón Bertomeu-Sánchez, "Sense and Sensitivity: Mateu Orfila, the Marsh Test, and the Lafarge Affair," in *Chemistry, Medicine, and Crime: Mateu J.B. Orfila (1787–1853) and His Times*, ed. José Ramón Bertomeu-Sánchez and Augustí Nieto-Galan (Sagamore Beach, MA: Science History Publications, 2014), 215; *L'expérience: Journal de médecine et de chirurgie*, vol. 3, no, 92, April 4, 1839 (Paris, 1839), 224; C. James, "Empoisonnement de Soufflard," *L'expérience: Journal de médecine et de chirurgie*, vol. 3, no. 93, April 11, 1839 (Paris, 1839), 227–34.

45 *Gazette médicale de Paris*, 8, no. 32, August 8, 1840: 511–12; Orfila, *Traité de médecine légale*, 3rd ed. (Paris: Béchet jeune, 1836), 3:824; *Gazette des tribunaux*, December 2–3, 1839; *Gazette des tribunaux*, December 4, 1839.

46 François-Vincent Raspail, *Nouveau système de chimie organique, fondé sur des méthodes nouvelles d'observation* (Paris: Baillière, 1833), 381.

47 Raspail, *Accusation d'empoisonnement par l'arsenic*, 140–42, quotation on p. 140.

48 Raspail, *Nouveau système de chimie organique*, 381.

49 Francesco Rognetta and François-Vincent Raspail, *Nouvelle méthode de traitement de l'empoisonnement par l'arsenic* (Paris: Gardenbas, 1840), 81.

50 Raspail, *Accusation d'empoisonnement par l'arsenic*, 142–43.

51 Rognetta and Raspail, *Nouvelle méthode de traitement de l'empoisonnement*, 83.

52 Raspail, *Accusation d'empoisonnement par l'arsenic*, 161–62; Rognetta and Raspail, *Nouvelle méthode de traitement de l'empoisonnement*, 82; Bertomeu-Sánchez, "Arsenic in France," 133–37; James C. Whorton, *The Arsenic Century: How Victorian Britain Was Poisoned at Home, Work, and Play* (Oxford: Oxford University Press, 2011).

53 On the conflict between Raspail and Orfila, see José Ramón Bertomeu-Sánchez, "Orfila, Raspail et les cercles vicieux de l'expertise," in *Une*

imagination républicaine, François-Vincent Raspail (1794–1878), ed. Jonathan Barbier (Besançon: Presses universitaires de Franche-Comté, 2017), 39–62.

54 Estimates of the number of these experiments ranged from 3,000, according to Devergie, to 6,000, according to Metzger. Alphonse Devergie, *Médecine légale, théorique et pratique* (1852), 3:47; D. Metzger, *La vivisection, ses dangers, et ses crimes* (Paris: Siège social, 1906), 7.

55 "Expériences de M. Orfila, sur l'empoisonnement par l'arsenic et l'émétique," *La Phalange: Journal de la science sociale* 1, no. 33 (November 15, 1840): 576, 572.

56 Adolphe Bérigny, *Des médecins-légistes considérés dans leur rapport avec les cours de justice, à l'occasion de l'affaire Lafarge* (Paris: Baillière, 1840), 54.

57 Léonard Borie, *Catéchisme toxicologique ou essai sur l'empoisonnement* (Tulle: Drappeau, 1841), v–viii, 71, quotation on p. 71; Bertomeu-Sánchez, "Managing Uncertainty," 216.

58 Ambroise Tardieu, "Médecine légale théorique et pratique, par Alph. Devergie," *Annales d'hygiène publique et de médecine légale* series 1, vol. 27 (1842): 225–32, quotation on pp. 226–27; Bertomeu-Sánchez, "Mateu Orfila (1787–1853)," 165–66.

59 Cited and translated by Bertomeu-Sánchez, "Mateu Orfila (1787–1853)," 165.

60 Bertomeu-Sánchez, "Managing Uncertainty;" Ian A. Burney, "Bones of Contention: Mateu Orfila, Normal Arsenic and British Toxicology," in *Chemistry, Medicine, and Crime: Mateu J.B. Orfila (1787–1853) and His Times*, ed. José Ramón Bertomeu-Sánchez and Augustí Nieto-Galan (Sagamore Beach, MA: Science History Publications, 2014), 243–59; José Ramón Bertomeu-Sánchez, "From Forensic Toxicology to Biological Chemistry: Normal Arsenic and the Hazards of Sensitivity during the Nineteenth Century," *Endeavor* 40, no. 2 (2016): 82–92; Stratmann, *The Secret Poisoner*, 72–75; Flandin and Danger, *De l'arsenic, suivi d'une instruction propre à servir de guide aux experts dans les cas d'empoisonnement* (Paris: Bachelier, 1841); "Rapport sur plusieurs Mémoires concernant du procédé de Marsh, dans les recherches de médecine légale," *Comptes-rendus des séances de l'Académie des sciences de Paris* (Paris: Gauthier-Villars, 1841), 12:1076–109; Victor Regnault, *Rapport sur plusieurs mémoires concernant l'emploi du procédé de Marsh dans les recherches de médecine légale* ([Paris]: Bachelier, [1841]).

61 AN BB/20/110; Francesco Rognetta, "Procès de Dijon. Consultation médico-légale sur un cas de mort attribué à l'empoisonnement par l'arsenic," in *Nouvelle méthode de traitement de l'empoisonnement par l'arsenic, et documens médico-légaux sur cet empoisonnement* (Paris: Gardenbas, 1840).

62 AN BB/24/2013; *La Phalange: Journal de la science sociale* series 3, vol. 5, no. 75, June 24, 1842 (Paris, 1842), 1227.

63 *Gazette des tribunaux*, March 25, 1843, Bertomeu-Sánchez, "From Forensic Toxicology to Biological Chemistry," 88; Bertomeu-Sánchez, "Managing Uncertainty."

64 Mathieu Orfila, "Quelques réflexions critiques sur les moyens de conclure en médecine légale, et sur la prétendue localisation des poisons," *Annales d'hygiène publique et de médecine légale* series 1, vol. 31 (1844): 431; *L'ami de la Charte: Journal du Puy de Dôme, de la Haute-Loire et du Cantal*, December 9, 1843; Bertomeu-Sánchez, "From Forensic Toxicology to Biological Chemistry," 86.

65 Jules Barse, "Consultation médico-légale sur les rapports judiciaires de MM. Darles et Pipet, d'Yssengeaux, et de MM. Orfila, Chevallier, et Ollivier (d'Angers)," in Chevallier, Orfila, and Ollivier (d'Angers), "Triple accusation d'empoisonnement," *Annales d'hygiène publique et de médecine légale* series 1, vol. 28 (1842): 150–52, quotations on pp. 152, 150–51.

66 *Gazette des tribunaux*, June 11, 1842; De Beaumont, "Rapport sur un mémoire de M. de Cormenin relatif à l'empoisonnement par l'arsenic," *Séances et travaux de l'Académie des sciences morales et politiques* (Paris, 1842), 1:488–491, quotation on p. 488.

67 Jules Barse, *Manuel de la Cour d'assises dans les questions d'empoisonnement, à l'usage des magistrats, des avocats, des experts, des jurés et des témoins* (Paris: Labé, 1845), 152–53.

68 "Empoisonnement par l'arsenic administré à petites doses," *Annales d'hygiène publique et de médecine légale* series 1, vol. 37 (1847): 121–58; *Gazette des tribunaux*, June 30, 1847; *Gazette des tribunaux*, July 1, 1846; *Gazette des tribunaux*, July 2, 1846.

69 AN BB/24/2007.

70 "Une nouvelle Brinvilliers: Hélène Jégado (1851)," in *Causes célèbres de tous les peuples*, vol. 7, no. 320 (Paris: Lebrun, 1865–67); François-Vincent Raspail, *Revue complémentaire des sciences appliquées à la médecine et pharmacie, à l'agriculture, aux arts et à l'industrie*, vol. 4 (Paris, 1858), October 1, 1857, 65–76; *Condamnation à mort et exécution d'une servante coupable de quarante-trois empoisonnements* (Arras: Vve J. Degeorge, [1852]); *Acte d'accusation de la fille Hélène Jégado, auteur d'un nombre considérable d'empoisonnements. Mort de 47 personnes. Son jugement. Déposition des témoins. Sa condamnation à la peine de mort* ([Paris]: Chassaignon, [1851]).

71 Raspail, *Revue complémentaire des sciences*, October 1, 1857.

72 Raspail, *Revue complémentaire des sciences*, September 1, 1857, 37–41.

73 *La Belgique judiciaire*, vol. 9, nos. 44–52, June 1–29, 1851; *Procès du comte et de la comtesse de Bocarmé devant la cour* (Mons: Leroux, 1851), 32, 48.

74 *Gazette des tribunaux*, June 13, 1851.

75 Victor Pasquier, *De la priorité entre MM. Orfila et Stas, des moyens de déceler la nicotine dans les empoisonnements* (Brussels: Mortier, 1853).

76 J. Briand and Ernest Chaudé, *Manuel complet de médecine légale*, 8th ed. (Paris: Baillière, 1869), 417–18.

77 Séverin-Caussé and A. Chevallier fils, "Considérations générales sur l'empoisonnement par le phosphore, les pâtes phosphorées et les allumettes
chimiques," *Annales d'hygiène publique et de médecine légale* series 2,
vol. 3 (1855): 134–71; Ambroise Tardieu, "Etude hygiénique et médico-
légale sur la fabrication et l'emploi des allumettes chimiques: Rapport fait
au comité consultatif d'hygiène publique," *Annales d'hygiène publique et
de médecine légale* series 2, vol. 6 (1856): 5–54; Ambroise Tardieu, *Etude
médico-légale et clinique sur l'empoisonnement* (Paris: Baillière, 1867),
426–518; Albert Jabely, *De l'empoisonnement par le phosphore* (Paris:
Parent, 1864); Mialhe, "Rapport sur un cas d'empoisonnement par le
phosphore," *Annales d'hygiène publique et de médecine légale* series 2,
vol. 31 (1869): 134–8; Poggiale, "Empoisonnement par le phosphore, par
M. Réveil (Rapport de M. Poggiale)," *Bulletin de l'Académie de médecine*
(Paris: Baillière, 1858–59), 24:1230; Gallard, "Empoisonnement par le
phosphore," *L'Union médicale* 12, no. 130 (October 29, 1861): 203;
Alain Astier, "Les allumettes françaises ou la singulière histoire des empoisonnements par le phosphore blanc," *Revue d'histoire de la pharmacie* 316
(1997): 385–94.
78 A. Chevallier, "Sur la substitution du phosphore amorphe au phosphore
ordinaire et indications des moyens à mettre en pratique pour faire cesser
le danger d'empoisonnement et soustraire à la nécrose les ouvriers qui
fabriquent les allumettes chimiques," *Annales d'hygiène publique et de
médecine légale* series 2, vol. 3 (1855): 124–34; Séverin-Caussé and
Chevallier, "Considérations générales sur l'empoisonnement par le phosphore"; *Gazette médicale de Paris*, vol. 9, September 16, 1854: 575;
Anatole Hecquet, *Mémoire sur l'empoisonnement par les allumettes chimiques au phosphore blanc, nécessité d'en interdire l'usage et de les
remplacer par les allumettes chimiques au phosphore rouge ou amorphe*
(Abbeville: Briez, 1861).
79 Briand and Chaudé, *Manuel complet de médecine légale* (1869), 448.
80 T. Gallard, *De l'empoisonnement par la strychnine* (Paris: Baillière, 1865);
Henri-Paul de Meyrignac, *De l'empoisonnement par la strychnine* (Paris:
Rignoux, 1859); B. Danvin, *Empoisonnement par la strychnine. Rapport
médico-légal* (Paris: Martinet, 1861); Frédéric Duriau, *Etude clinique et
médico-légale sur l'empoisonnement par la strychnine* (Paris: Baillière,
1862); Ambroise Tardieu, P. Lorain, and Zacharie Roussin,
Empoisonnement par la strychnine, l'arsenic et les sels de cuivre (Paris:
Baillière, 1865); Ambroise Tardieu and Zacharie Roussin, *Etude médico-
légale et clinique sur l'empoisonnement* (Paris: Baillière, 1867), 916–1032;
Ambroise Tardieu, *Mémoire sur l'empoisonnement par la strychnine, con-
tenant la relation médico-légale complète de l'affaire Palmer* (Paris:
Baillière, 1857). Strychnine poisoning was relatively rare in France and
more common in Britain. On the most famous strychnine poisoner in
Britain, see Angus McLaren, *A Prescription for Murder: The Victorian
Serial Killings of Dr. Thomas Neill Cream* (Chicago: University of
Chicago Press, 1995).

81 Armand Fouquier, *Causes célèbres de tous les peuples* (Paris: Lebrun, 1858), 6:62.

82 Ambroise Tardieu and F. Zacharie Roussin, "Relation médico-légale de l'affaire Couty de la Pommerais. Empoisonnement par la digitaline," *Annales d'hygiène publique et de médecine légale* series 2, vol. 22 (1864): 80–141.

83 Armand Fouquier, *Causes célèbres de tous les peuples* (Paris: Lebrun, 1864), 6:1–240.

84 Alphonse Devergie, *L'expérimentation physiologique dans l'expertise médico-légale* (Paris: Baillière, 1866), 49, 57–60, quotation on p. 49.

85 Devergie, *L'expérimentation physiologique dans l'expertise médico-légale*, 58–60, quotation on p. 59.

86 *Gazette hebdomadaire de médecine et de chirurgie*, no. 42, October 18, 1867, quotations on pp. 667–68.

87 ADP D2U8/75; *Gazette hebdomadaire de médecine et de chirurgie*, no. 27, July 5, 1878; *Gazette des tribunaux*, June 30 1878.

88 Paul Brouardel and Louis-Désiré L'Hôte, "Relation médico-légale de l'affaire Pel: Accusation d'empoisonnement," *Annales d'hygiène publique et de médecine légale* series 3, vol. 15 (1886): 12–41, 106–32, quotation on p. 12; *Gazette des tribunaux*, August 13, 1885; *Gazette des tribunaux*, August 14, 1885; *Gazette des tribunaux*, August 15, 1885; ADP D1U8 78.

89 AN BB/18/6249 51 BL 695; *Gazette des tribunaux*, May 6–7, 1878; *Gazette des tribunaux*, May 9, 1878; *Gazette des tribunaux*, May 10, 1878; *Gazette des tribunaux*, May 11, 1878; Georges Bergeron, Emile Delens, and Désiré L'Hôte, "De l'empoisonnement arsenical par des doses médiocres et réitérées de poison: Relation médico-légale de l'affaire Danval," *Annales d'hygiène publique et de médecine légale* series 2, vol. 50 (1878): 72–144; *Le progrès médical: Journal de médecine, de chirurgie et de pharmacie* series 1, vol. 6, no. 20 (May 18, 1878): 380–83 and no. 22 (June 1, 1878): 418–20; "De quelques questions soulevées par l'affaire Danval (empoisonnement par l'arsenic)," *Gazette hebdomadaire de médecine et de chirurgie* 20 (May 17, 1878): 305–10; Archives de la Préfecture de police de Paris BA 1612.

90 Bruno Bertherat, "L'élection à la chaire de médecine légale à Paris en 1879. Acteurs, réseaux et enjeux dans le monde universitaire," *Revue historique* 4, no. 644 (2007): 843–45.

91 Bertomeu-Sánchez, "From Forensic Toxicology to Biological Chemistry;" Stratmann, *The Secret Poisoner*, 275; *Le Temps*, April 10, 1902; AN BB/18/6249 51 BL 695.

92 Emmanuelle Demartini, "La figure de l'empoisonneuse de Marie Lafarge à Violette Nozière," in *Figures d'empoisonneuses de l'Antiquité à nos jours*, ed. Lydie Boudiou, Frédéric Chauvaud, and Myriam Soria (Rennes: Presses universitaires de Rennes, 2015), 97–108.

93 Adolphe Magen, "Les poisons connus des anciens et l'empoisonnement au XIXe siècle," *Recueil des travaux de la société d'agriculture, sciences et arts d'Agen* (Agen: Noubel, [1848, misprinted as 1842]), 4:313; Henri

Legrand du Saulle, *Les hystériques: Etat physique et mental, actes insolites, délictueux et criminels*, 2nd ed. (Paris: Baillière, 1883), 470.

94 Fouquier, *Causes célèbres de tous les peuples* (1864), 6:238–39, quotations on p. 238.

95 Adolphe Chapuis, *Précis de toxicologie* (Paris: Baillière, 1882), 18.

96 Henri Roger, "Rapport général sur les prix décernés en 1874 à l'Académie de médecine," *L'Union médicale*, no. 56, May 13, 1875, quotation on p. 708.

97 Louis Hugounenq, *Traité des poisons* (Paris: Masson, 1891), 26–27; Georges Benoît, *De l'empoisonnement criminel en général* (Lyon: Storck, 1888), 2.

Chapter 3

1 Fodéré, *Traité de médecine légale*, 2:452.

2 André-Barthelemy Dehaussy Robécourt, *Dissertation sur une nouvelle exposition de la doctrine des maladies simulées* (Paris: Didot jeune, 1805), 16; J.-B. Létier, *Dissertation sur les maladies simulées et sur les moyens de les découvrir* (Paris, 1808), 30; Eugène Benoit, *Des maladies simulées et provoquées au bagne pénitencier de l'île Nau (Nouvelle-Calédonie)* (Nancy, 1881), 31.

3 They did note, however, the exception of intestinal worms. They also declared that any organism excreted from a woman's genitals, if not a human infant or fetus, did not constitute a birth. Dehaussy Robécourt, *Dissertation*, 35; Létier, *Dissertation sur les maladies simulées*, 29–31; H. M. E. Taufflieb, *Examen médico-légal des maladies simulées, dissimulées et imputées* (Strasbourg, 1835).

4 Edmond Boisseau, *Des maladies simulées et des moyens de les reconnaître: Leçons professées au Val-de-Grâce* (Paris: Baillière, 1870), 41.

5 Jean-Léo Tarneau, *Des maladies simulées des plus communes au point de vue du recrutement* (Montpellier, 1855), 5–6; A.-F. Burnot-Laboulay, *De la simulation confédérée au point de vue du recrutement* (Montpellier, 1844), 5–6; *Instruction pour service de guide aux officiers de santé dans l'appréciation des infirmités ou des maladies qui rendent impropre au service militaire... Extrait du journal militaire officiel*, 2nd ed. (Paris: J. Dumaine, 1865), 172–76.

6 Nonetheless, malingering has received relatively little scholarly attention. On malingering in France, see Matthew Ramsey, "Conscription, Malingerers, and Popular Medicine in Napoleonic France," *Proceedings of the Consortium on Revolutionary Europe* (1978), 7:188–99. On malingering in other historical contexts, see Stephen Watson, "Malingerers, the 'Weakminded' Criminal and the 'Moral Imbecile': How the English Prison Medical Officer Became an Expert in Mental Deficiency, 1880–1930," in *Legal Medicine in History*, ed. Michael Clark and Catherine Crawford (Cambridge: Cambridge University Press, 1994), 223–42; Roger Cooter, "Malingering in Modernity: Psychological Scripts and Adversarial

Encounters during the First World War," in *War, Medicine, and Modernity*, ed. Roger Cooter, Mark Harrison, and Steven Sturdy (Stroud: Sutton, 1998), 125–48; R. Gregory Lande, *Madness, Malingering, and Malfeasance: The Transformation of Psychiatry and the Law in the Civil War Era* (Washington, DC: Brassey's, 2003); R. Gregory Lande, *The Abraham Man: Madness, Malingering, and the Development of Medical Testimony* (New York: Algora, 2012); Lisa A. Long, *Rehabilitating Bodies: Health, History, and the American Civil War* (Philadelphia: University of Pennsylvania Press, 2004); Roger Cooter, "War and Modern Medicine," in *Companion Encyclopedia of the History of Medicine*, ed. W. F. Bynum and Roy Porter (New York: Routledge, 1993), 2:1536–73; Danuta Mendelson, "The Expert Deposes, but the Court Disposes: The Concept of Malingering and the Function of a Medical Expert Witness in the Forensic Process," *International Journal of Law and Psychiatry* 18, no. 4 (1995): 425–36.

7 Jean-Baptiste-Arnaud Murat, *Tableau synoptique d'une nosologie légale fondée sur le code social* (Paris: Méquignon l'aîné, 1803), 25–26.

8 Salomon-Louis Laurillard-Fallot, *De la simulation et de la dissimulation des maladies dans leurs rapports avec le service militaire* (Brussels: Tircher, 1836), 3.

9 Ramsey, "Conscription, Malingerers," 192–93; Pierre-François Percy and Charles Nicolas Laurent, "Simulation des maladies," in *Dictionnaire des sciences médicales*, eds. Adelon, Alard, Alibert, et al. (Paris: Panckoucke, 1819), 51:319–66; Salomon-Louis Laurillard-Fallot, *Mémorial de l'expert dans la visite sanitaire des hommes de guerre* (Brussels, 1837), 145.

10 Gabriel Tourdes, *Extrait du Dictionnaire encyclopédique des sciences médicales … article Simulation* (Paris: G. Masson, 1879), 718–19.

11 AN F/9/287; Percy and Laurent, "Simulation des maladies;" Ramsey, "Conscription, Malingerers," 192.

12 Ollivier (d'Angers), "Mémoire sur les maladies simulées," *Annales d'hygiène publique et de médecine légale*, series 1, vol. 25 (1841): 104; *Journal de médecine et de chirurgie pratiques* (Paris: Schneider & Langrand, 1841), 12:103.

13 AN F/9/286; Henri-Louis Bayard, *Manuel pratique de médecine légale* (Paris: Baillière, 1844), 294; Percy and Laurent, "Simulation des maladies," 332–33.

14 Baron Dominique Jean Larrey, *Mémoires de chirurgie militaire, et campagnes de D. J. Larrey* (Paris: Smith, 1817), 4:170–75.

15 Those who engaged in these and other criminal acts to help men evade conscription laws were subject to imprisonment or fines, but the application of these laws proved difficult. Joseph Briand, *Manuel complet de médecine légale* (Paris, 1821), 603–7; Laurillard-Fallot, *De la simulation et de la dissimulation des maladies*, 3; Ramsey, "Conscription, Malingerers," 193. On resistance to conscription, see Alan Forrest, *Conscripts and Deserters: The Army and French Society during the Revolution and Empire* (Oxford: Oxford University Press, 1989); and

Jennifer Heuer, "'No More Fears, No More Tears'?: Gender, Emotion, and the Aftermath of the Napoleonic Wars in France," *Gender and History* 28, no. 2 (2016): 437–59.

16 Joseph Huguet, *Recherches sur les maladies simulées et mutilations volontaires observées de 1859 à 1896* (Paris: H. Charles-Lavauzelle, 1896), 42.

17 Forrest, *Conscripts and Deserters*, 46–47.

18 Pierre-Jean Moricheau-Beaupré, *Mémoire sur le choix des hommes propres au service militaire de l'armée de terre, et sur leur visite devant les conseils de révision* (Paris: Anselin and Pochard, 1820), 46–47.

19 Percy and Laurent, "Simulation des maladies," 352; Emile-Auguste-Nicolas-Jules Bégin, "Réforme," in *Dictionnaire de médecine et de chirurgie pratiques*, eds. Gabriel Andral, Louis Jacques Bégin, Philippe Frédéric Blandin, et al. (Paris: Méquignon-Marvis, 1835), 14:174.

20 Laugier, "Simulées (maladies)," in *Nouveau dictionnaire de médecine et de chirurgie pratiques*, ed. Sigismond Jaccoud (Paris: Baillière, 1882), 33:204; Gustave-Adolphe Bürgkly, *De quelques maladies simulées, considérées sous le point de vue de la médecine légale militaire* (Montpellier, 1845), 31; Laurillard-Fallot, *Mémorial de l'expert*, 250–52; Victor Romuald Judas, *Essai sur les maladies simulées et les moyens de reconnaître la fraude* (Montpellier, 1827), 352, 358.

21 Percy and Laurent, "Simulation des maladies," 351; Orfila, *Leçons de médecine légale* (1823), 421–22; Joseph Briand and J.-X. Brosson, *Manuel complet de médecine légale*, 3rd ed. (Paris: Chaudé, 1836), 677–78; Laurillard-Fallot, *Mémorial de l'expert*, 286–87; Laurillard-Fallot, *De la simulation et de la dissimulation des maladies*, 97–98.

22 A.-F. Burnot-Laboulay, *De la simulation confédérée au point de vue du recrutement* (Montpellier, 1844), 28.

23 *Journal militaire*, no. 10, September 1828, in *Journal militaire, année 1828* (Paris: Anselin, 1828), 157.

24 Fodéré, *Traité de médecine légale*, 2:480.

25 Dehaussy Robécourt, *Dissertation*, 18; Léonard Borie, *Traité des maladies et des infirmités qui doivent dispenser du service militaire, lorsqu'elles ont résisté aux traitemens connus* (Paris: Jourdain, 1818), 169; J.-L. Daille, *Essai sur les maladies simulées* (Paris, 1818), 9–10, quotation on p. 9.

26 Percy and Laurent, "Simulation des maladies," 346.

27 Boisseau, *Des maladies simulées*, 271.

28 Paul-Augustin-Olivier Mahon, *Médecine légale et police médicale* (Paris: Buisson, 1801), 1:360–61.

29 Daille, *Essai sur les maladies simulées*, 9.

30 Laurillard-Fallot, *Mémorial de l'expert*, 229.

31 Percy and Laurent, "Simulation des maladies," 357.

32 See, e.g., Félix-Pierre-Auguste Gayet, *Des maladies simulées et dissimulées, considérées au point de vue du service militaire* (Montpellier, 1848), 14–15.

33 *Instruction pour servir de guide aux officiers de santé dans l'appréciation des infirmités ou maladies qui rendent impropre au service militaire, Paris 14 novembre 1845* (Paris, 1846), 30.

34 Charles-Chrétien-Henri Marc, "Matériaux pour l'histoire médico-légale de l'aliénation mentale," *Annales d'hygiène publique et de médecine légale*, series 1, vol. 2 (1829): 388.

35 Percy and Laurent, "Simulation des maladies," 344.

36 Devergie, *Médecine légale, théorique et pratique* (1840), 516–17; Bégin, "Réforme," 187–88; Gayet, *Des maladies simulées et dissimulées*, 22.

37 Fodéré, *Traité de médecine légale*, 2:481.

38 Percy and Laurent, "Simulation des maladies," 345.

39 A. E. Coche, *De l'opération médicale du recrutement, et des inspections générales* (Paris: Rouen, 1829), 218–19; Gayet, *Des maladies simulées et dissimulées*, 30–31; Jean-Jacques Fratini, *Essai médico-légal sur le recrutement de l'armée* (Montpellier, 1844), 30.

40 Gayet, *Des maladies simulées et dissimulées*, 31.

41 Devergie, *Médecine légale* (1840), 2:517; Bégin, "Réforme," 189.

42 Some medical men alleged that the majority of epilepsy patients in hospitals were faking the condition. Laurillard-Fallot, *De la simulation et de la dissimulation des maladies*, 23; Létier, *Dissertation sur les maladies simulées*, 21.

43 L. A. Hatterer, *Considérations médico-légales sur les maladies simulées et la manière de les reconnaître* (Strasbourg, 1826), 6–7; Coche, *De l'opération médicale du recrutement*, 297; Borié, *Traité des maladies et des infirmités*, 154; Létier, *Dissertation sur les maladies simulées*, 21; Gayet, *Des maladies simulées et dissimulées*, 30; Laurillard-Fallot, *De la simulation et de la dissimulation des maladies*, 25; François Fabre, *Bibliothèque du médecin-praticien, ou Résumé général de tous ouvrages de clinique médicale et chirurgicale* (Paris: Baillière, 1852), 15:485.

44 Hatterer, *Considérations médico-légales sur les maladies simulées*, 6–7.

45 Charles Sédillot, *Manuel complet de médecine légale, considérée dans ses rapports avec la législation actuelle* (Paris: Crochard, 1830), 87–88; Percy and Laurent, "Simulation des maladies," 337.

46 Prosper Sisteray, *Simulation de l'épilepsie aux points de vue de la pratique et de la médecine légale* (Paris: Parent, 1867), 40–41.

47 Gayet, *Des maladies simulées et dissimulées*, 14.

48 Thomas Dodman, *What Nostalgia Was: War, Empire, and the Time of a Deadly Emotion* (Chicago: University of Chicago Press, 2017).

49 Salle, *Traité de médecine légale*, 272; Daille, *Essai sur les maladies simulées*, 7; Percy and Laurent, "Simulation des maladies," 347.

50 Percy and Laurent, "Simulation des maladies," 363.

51 Percy and Laurent, "Simulation des maladies," 365–66.

52 Forrest, *Conscripts and Deserters*, 138–39.

53 Charles-Chrétien-Henri Marc, "Déception," in *Dictionnaire de médecine*, eds. Adelon, Alard, Alibert, et al. (Paris: Béchet jeune, 1823), 6:375.

54 Ollivier, "Mémoire sur les maladies simulées," 100.

55 Tourdes, *Extrait du Dictionnaire encyclopédique*, 690.

56 Ollivier, "Mémoire sur les maladies simulées," 114–26; *Journal de médecine et de chirurgie pratiques*, 12:104–6.

57 On poverty, private charity, and public welfare in nineteenth-century France, see Rachel Fuchs, *Gender and Poverty in Nineteenth-Century Europe* (Cambridge: Cambridge University Press, 2005), 196–238; Christine Adams, *Poverty, Charity, and Motherhood: Maternal Societies in Nineteenth-Century France* (Urbana: University of Illinois Press, 2010).

58 *Journal de médecine et de chirurgie pratiques*, 12:103.

59 Ollivier, "Mémoire sur les maladies simulées," 110–12.

60 Maurice Laugier, "Simulées (maladies)," 189–90; Henri Giraud, *Etude sur les blessures simulées dans l'industrie* (Lille: L. Quarré, 1895); Léonce Vienne, *Etude sur les blessures simulées dans les centres industriels* (Paris: Jouve, 1892); Huguet, *Recherches sur les maladies simulées*, 9.

61 Gabriel Tourdes and Edmond Metzquer, *Traité de médecine légale théorique et pratique* (Paris: Asselin and Houzeau, 1896), 897–98.

62 Benoit, *Des maladies simulées et provoquées*, 2–4.

63 Devergie, *Médecine légale, théorique et pratique* (1852), 1:637, 639.

64 *Archives d'anthropologie criminelle, de médecine légale et de psychologie normale et pathologique* (1889), 4:707.

65 AN BB/20/42.

66 Huguet, *Recherches sur les maladies simulées*, 154.

67 Dehaussy Robécourt, *Dissertation*, 30; Létier, *Dissertation sur les maladies simulées*, 29.

68 Jules-Théodore Brongniart, *Etude sur la gravelle urinaire simulée et ses rapports chez la femme avec l'hystérie* (Paris: Doin, 1884).

69 Taufflieb, *Examen médico-légal des maladies simulées*, 46.

70 Tourdes, *Extrait du Dictionnaire encyclopédique*, 690.

71 Laugier, "Simulées (maladies)," 204; Charles Schützenberger, *Etudes pathologiques et cliniques* (Paris: Masson, 1879), 570.

72 Laugier, "Simulées (maladies)," 204.

73 Létier, *Dissertation sur les maladies simulées*, 28; René-Claude Geoffroy de Villeneuve, "Ictère," in *Dictionnaire des sciences médicales*, ed. Adelon, Alard, Alibert, et al. (Paris: Panckoucke, 1818), 23:441; Laurillard-Fallot, *Mémorial de l'expert*, 242; Orfila, *Leçons de médecine légale* (1828), 2:30; Bürgkly, *De quelques maladies simulées*, 22; Fabre, *Bibliothèque du médecin praticien*, 15:487; A. Grissole, *Traité élémentaire et pratique de pathologie interne*, 8th ed. (Paris: Masson, 1862), 2:919; Henri Legrand du Saulle, *Traité de médecine légale, de jurisprudence médicale et de toxicologie*, 2nd ed. (Paris: Delahaye, 1886), 964; Laugier, "Simulées (maladies)," 225.

74 Laugier, "Simulées (maladies)," 216.

75 Percy and Laurent, "Simulation des maladies," 357–58, 348; Bürgkly, *De quelques maladies simulées*, 27.

76 Bürgkly, *De quelques maladies simulées*, 33.

77 Percy and Laurent, "Simulation des maladies," 339, 342; Laurillard-Fallot, *De la simulation et de la dissimulation des maladies*, 89–90; Fabre, *Bibliothèque du médecin-praticien*, 15:487.

78 Percy and Laurent, "Simulation des maladies," 328.

79 Laurillard-Fallot, *De la simulation et de la dissimulation des maladies*, 93–94.

80 Eugène Benoit, *Des maladies simulées et provoquées*, 31.

81 Boisseau, *Des maladies simulées*, 387; Tourdes, *Extrait du Dictionnaire encyclopédique*, 718.

82 *Journal de médecine et de chirurgie pratiques*, series 3, vol. 5 (Paris: 1879): 73–74.

83 Tourdes, *Extrait du Dictionnaire encyclopédique*, 716–17.

84 Fabre, *Bibliothèque du médecin-praticien*, 15:487; Laurillard-Fallot, *De la simulation et de la dissimulation des* maladies, 90; Devergie, *Médecine légale, théorique et pratique* (1852), 1:639; Sédillot, *Manuel complet de médecine légale*, 78; Tourdes, *Extrait du Dictionnaire encyclopédique*, 716.

85 Laurillard-Fallot, *Mémorial de l'expert*, 281; Létier, *Dissertation sur les maladies simulées*, 18; Bürgkly, *De quelques maladies simulées*, 22.

86 Jean-Baptiste Tyrbas de Chamberet, "Pissement," in *Dictionnaire des sciences médicales*, eds. Adelon, Alard, Alibert, et al. (Paris: Panckoucke, 1820), 42:505.

87 Boisseau, *Des maladies simulées*, 375; Laugier, "Simulées (maladies)," 227; Sédillot, *Manuel complet de médecine légale*, 78.

88 Laurillard-Fallot, *Mémorial de l'expert*, 281–82; Laugier, "Simulées (maladies)," 227; Devergie, *Médecine légale, théorique et pratique* (1840), 2:515.

89 Laugier, "Simulées (maladies)," 225; Devergie, *Médecine légale, théorique et pratique* (1852), 1:637, 639.

90 Coche, *De l'opération médicale du recrutement*, 306; Armand Laurent, *Etude médico-légale sur la simulation de la folie: Considérations cliniques et pratiques à l'usage des médecins experts, des magistrats et des jurisconsultes* (Paris: Victor Masson et fils, 1866), 374; Huguet, *Recherches sur les maladies simulées*, 46; Boisseau, *Des maladies simulées*, 173; Legrand du Saulle, *Traité de médecine légale* (1886), 951.

91 V. Parant, "Note sur la transformation de la folie simulée en folie véritable," *Annales médico-psychologiques*, series 7, vol. 1 (1885): 19–27.

92 Boisseau, *Des maladies simulées*, 173.

93 Marc, "Matériaux pour l'histoire médico-légale de l'aliénation mentale," 353.

94 Laurent, *Etude médico-légale sur la simulation de la folie*, 16–18.

95 Louis Victor Marcé, *Traité pratique des maladies mentales* (Paris: Baillière, 1862), 633; Paul Garnier, "La simulation de la folie et la loi sur la relégation," *Annales d'hygiène publique et de médecine légale*, series 3, vol. 19 (1888): 100–101; H. Dagonet, "L'expertise médico-légale en matière d'aliénation mentale," *Annales d'hygiène publique et de médecine légale*, series 3, vol. 31 (1894): 103–4.

96 Eugène Billod, *Des maladies mentales et nerveuses* (Paris: Masson, 1882), 2: 240; Auguste Corlieu, *Considérations médico-légales sur la mélancolie* (Paris: Courrier médical, 1870), 15.

97 Dagonet, "L'expertise médico-légale en matière d'aliénation mentale," 105.

98 Boisseau, *Des maladies simulées*, 271; Fodéré, *Traité de médecine légale*, 2:481.

99 Louis Fleury, *Cours d'hygiène, fait à la Faculté de médecine de Paris* (Paris: Asselin, 1863), 2:463.

100 Boisseau, *Des maladies simulées*, 44–45.

101 *Archives d'anthropologie criminelle, de médecine légale et de psychologie normale et pathologique* (1889), 4:706.

102 Prosper Gentilhomme, *Contribution à l'histoire de la simulation dans le service militaire* (Paris, 1884), 20.

103 Boisseau, *Des maladies simulées*, 44–45. On the colonial notion of "native mendacity" and forensics, see Mitra Sharafi, "The Imperial Serologist and Punitive Self-Harm: Bloodstains and Legal Pluralism in British India," in *Global Forensic Cultures: Making Fact and Justice in the Modern Era*, ed. Ian Burney and Christopher Hamlin (Baltimore: Johns Hopkins University Press, 2019), 60–85.

104 Tourdes and Metzquer, *Traité de médecine légale*, 899.

105 Tourdes, *Extrait du Dictionnaire encyclopédique*, 727.

106 François-Emmanuel Fodéré, *Les lois éclairées par les sciences physiques, ou Traité de médecine-légale et d'hygiène publique* (Paris: Croullebois, year 7), 1:153.

107 Gentilhomme, *Contribution à l'histoire de la simulation*, 71.

108 Percy and Laurent, "Simulation des maladies," 320.

109 Percy and Laurent, "Simulation des maladies," 361.

110 Percy and Laurent, "Simulation des maladies," 322.

111 Marc, "Déception," 6:375.

112 Taufflieb, *Examen médico-légal des maladies simulées*, 31.

113 Bégin, "Réforme," 195.

114 Marc, "Matériaux pour l'histoire médico-légale de l'aliénation mentale," 391–92.

115 Henry Connor, "The use of anaesthesia to diagnose malingering in the 19th century," *Journal of Royal Society of Medicine* 99, no. 9 (2006): 444; *Nouvelle encyclographie des sciences médicales* (Brussels: Grégoir, 1847), 4:175; Sosthène Dieu, *Traité de matière médicale et de thérapeutique* (Paris: Masson, 1853), 4:298; *Gazette médicale de Paris* (October 9, 1847), 2:209.

116 Henri-Louis Bayard, "Appréciation médico-légale de l'action de l'éther et du chloroforme," *Annales d'hygiène publique et de médecine légale*, series 1, vol. 42 (1849): 201–14; Connor, "The use of anaesthesia," 445.

117 *Bulletin général de thérapeutique médicale et chirurgicale* 41 (1851): 46.

118 Bénédict-Augustin Morel, "De l'éthérisation dans la folie au point de vue de diagnostic et de la médecine légale," *Archives générales de médecine*, February 1854; *Bulletin général de thérapeutique médicale, chirurgicale, obstétricale et pharmaceutique* 41 (1851): 46; Dieu, *Traité de matière médicale*, 4:298–301.

119 Gabriel Tourdes, "De l'anesthésie provoquée considérée sous le rapport médico-légal," *Gazette hebdomadaire de médecine et de chirurgie* (May 25, 1866 and June 4, 1866); Gabriel Tourdes, "Anesthésie (méd. légale)," in *Dictionnaire encyclopédique des sciences médicales* (Paris: Masson, 1866), 4:515–16. Tourdes did not object to the use of anesthesia if a suspected malingerer was being anesthetized for another reason or if it might serve his interests in some way.

120 Tourdes, "Anesthésie," 516; Ernest Martino, *Applications médico-légales de l'anesthésie* (Strasbourg, 1868), 17–18.

121 Boisseau, *Des maladies simulées*, 61, 66, 310.

122 Corlieu, *Considérations médico-légales sur la mélancolie*, 15.

123 Frantz Gromier, *Essai sur l'imbécillité et la folie simulée par l'imbécile* (Paris: Parent, 1872), 26.

124 L. Bécar, *De l'illégitimité du recours à la chloroformisation à propos des simulations morbides* (Brussels: A. Manceaux, 1887), 3, 5.

125 Xavier-Paul Aubert, *Médecine légale militaire: Surdité simulée* (Bordeaux, 1899), 41; Emile Duponchel, *Traité de médecine légale militaire* (Paris: Doin, 1890), 506–7, 622; Auguste Lutaud, *Manuel de médecine légale*, 5th ed. (Paris: Steinheil, 1892), 288.

126 Fratini, *Essai médico-légal sur le recrutement*, 30–31, quotation on p. 30.

127 Adelphe Espagne, *De l'incontinence d'urine, spécialement chez l'homme, dans ses rapports avec l'intégrité des fonctions sexuelles, de sa simulation, de sa curabilité par la ligature du prépuce* (Montpellier: Boehm, 1870).

128 Aubert, *Médecine légale militaire*, 41; Duponchel, *Traité de médecine légale militaire*, 612.

129 Huguet, *Recherches sur les maladies simulées*, 268.

130 César Zuber, *Des maladies simulées dans l'armée moderne* (Paris: Berger-Levrault, 1882), 3–4. He also maintained that faking conditions was rarer, but soldiers were increasingly exaggerating the severity of their illnesses.

131 For one exception, see Duponchel, *Traité de médecine légale militaire*, 621.

132 Zuber, *Des maladies simulées*, 3–4. He also maintained that faking conditions was rarer, but soldiers were increasingly exaggerating the severity of their illnesses.

133 Gentilhomme, *Contribution à l'histoire de la simulation*; Boisseau, *Des maladies simulées*, 41.

134 Tourdes, *Extrait du Dictionnaire encyclopédique*, 701; Louis-Ernest Catrin, "Le somnambulisme naturel: Observation de somnambulisme simulé," in *Mémoires et comptes-rendus de la Société des sciences médicales de Lyon* (Lyon: Mégret, 1890), 29:224–34, quotation on pp. 227–28.

135 Tourdes, *Extrait du Dictionnaire encyclopédique*, 701.

136 Zuber, *Des maladies simulées*, 4–5; Duponchel, *Traité de médecine légale militaire*, 621.

137 *Archives d'anthropologie criminelle* (1889), 4:705.

138 Percy and Laurent most clearly articulated this earlier view, which Laurillard-Fallot cited as the first general rule for doctors when considering malingering. Percy and Laurent, "Simulation des maladies," 321; Laurillard-Fallot, *De la simulation et de la dissimulation des maladies*, 13.

139 Duponchel, *Traité de médecine légale militaire*, 621; *Annales d'hygiène publique et de médecine légale*, series 6, no. 23 (1890): 561, quotation by Charles Burlureaux on p. 561.

140 Tourdes and Metzquer, *Traité de médecine légale*, 900.

141 Aubert, *Médecine légale militaire*, 17.

142 Aubert, *Médecine légale militaire*, 40.

143 Duponchel, *Traité de médecine légale militaire*, 621–22; *Archives d'anthropologie criminelle* (1889), 4:705.

144 Tourdes and Metzquer, *Traité de médecine légale*, 902.

145 Tourdes and Metzquer, *Traité de médecine légale*, 899; *Archives d'anthropologie criminelle*, 4:705.

146 Boisseau, *Des maladies simulées*, 238.

Chapter 4

1 AN BB/24/2007; *Gazette des tribunaux*, November 12, 1834; *Gazette des tribunaux*, November 13, 1834.

2 Articles 300 and 302 of the Penal Code of 1810 defined the crime as "the murder of a newborn child" and declared the death penalty for all convicted of the crime. On infanticide in modern France, see Rachel G. Fuchs, *Poor and Pregnant in Paris: Strategies for Survival in the Nineteenth Century* (New Brunswick, NJ: Rutgers University Press, 1992), 200–18; Tillier, *Des criminelles au village*; Silvia Chiletti, "Grossesses ignorées au prisme de l'infanticide: Savoirs médicaux et décisions de justice au XIXe siècle," *Revue d'histoire du XIXe siècle* 50 (2015): 165–79; Karen E. Huber, "Sex and Its Consequences: Abortion, Infanticide, and Women's Reproductive Decision-Making in France, 1901–1940" (PhD diss., Ohio State University, 2007); Karen Huber, "The Problem of Proof: Denunciations, Confessions, and Medical Evidence in Reproductive Crimes, 1900–1940," *Proceedings of the Western Society for French History* 34 (2006): 217–32; James Donovan, "Infanticide and the Juries in France, 1825–1913," *Journal of Family History* 16, no. 2 (1991): 157–76; Dominique Vallaud, "Le crime d'infanticide et l'indulgence des cours d'assises en France au XIXème siècle," *Information (International Social Science Council)* 21, no. 3 (1982): 475–98; Brigitte Bechtold, "Infanticide in 19th century France: A Quantitative Interpretation," *Review of Radical Political Economics* 33, no. 2 (2001): 165–87.

3 On the history of abortion in modern France, see Jean-Yves Le Naour and Catherine Valenti, *Histoire de l'avortement: XIXe–XXe siècle* (Paris: Seuil, 2003).

4 Fodéré, *Traité de médecine légale*, 1:420.

5 Stephanie Brown, "The Princess of Monaco's Hair: The Revolutionary Tribunal and the Pregnancy Plea," *Journal of Family History* 23, no. 2 (1998): 136–58; James Oldham, "On 'Pleading the Belly:' A Concise History of the Jury of Matrons," *Criminal Justice History* 6 (1985): 1–64; Sara Butler, "More than Mothers: Juries of Matrons and Pleas of the Belly in Medieval England," *Law and History Review* 37, no. 2 (2019): 353–96.

6 On the female medical expert in Old Regime France, see McClive, "Blood and Expertise;" Hardwick, *Sex in an Old Regime City*, 157–62.

7 Jean-Claude Farcy, *Histoire de la justice en France: De 1789 à nos jours* (Paris: La Découverte, 2015), 26; François-Alphonse Aulard, *The French Revolution: A Political History*, volume 2, *The Democratic Republic, 1792–1795* (New York: Charles Scribner's Sons, 1910), 286.

8 On pregnancy declarations during the Revolution, see Emmanuelle Berthiaud, "Les femmes enceintes devant la justice révolutionnaire à Paris (1793–1810): L'évolution des enjeux et des représentations de la grossesse," in *La culture judiciaire: Discours, représentations et usages de la justice du Moyen Age à nos jours*, ed. L. Faggion, C. Regina, and B. Ribémont (Dijon: Editions universitaires de Dijon, 2014), 123–41; Max Billard, *Les femmes enceintes devant le tribunal révolutionnaire d'après des documents inédits* (Paris: Perrin, 1911); Brown, "Princess of Monaco's Hair."

9 AN W/431/968.

10 AN W/269; *Bulletin du tribunal révolutionnaire*, nos. 70–71 (Paris: Clément, 1793), 280–82.

11 AN W/293; Brown, "Princess of Monaco's Hair."

12 The law of 23 germinal, year III [April 12, 1795]. *Journal des débats et des décrets* 64, no. 929 (Paris: Imprimerie nationale [Baudouin], 1795), 314.

13 The decision of 8 germinal year 13. Philippe Antoine Merlin, "Grossesse," in *Répertoire universel et raisonné de jurisprudence*, 3rd ed. (Paris: Garnery, 1808), 5:599; Marc, "Grossesse," 19:499.

14 Tourdes and Metzquer, *Traité de médecine légale*, 233.

15 See, e.g., Gabriel Tourdes, "Grossesse – Médecine légale," in *Dictionnaire encyclopédique des sciences médicales*, ed. Amédée Dechambre (Paris: Masson, 1886), 11:314; Jean-Eugène Ribes, *De la perversion morale chez les femmes enceintes, considérée principalement au point de vue médico-légal* (Strasbourg: Simon, 1866); Emile Lucchini, *De la responsabilité de la femme pendant la grossesse, au point de vue médico-légal* (Montpellier: Firmin and Montane, 1899).

16 Salle, *Traité de médecine légale*, 171–73, 278; Briand, *Manuel complet de médecine légale*, 102.

17 Lutaud, *Manuel de médecine légale*, 74.

18 Gabriel Tourdes, *Exposition historique et appréciation des secours empruntés par la médecine légale à l'obstétricie* (Strasbourg: Levrault, 1838), 34.

19 On uncertainty, pregnancy, and the mysteries of reproduction in early modern Europe, see Katharine Park, *Secrets of Women: Gender,*

Generation, and the Origins of Human Dissection (New York: Zone Books, 2006); Cathy McClive, "The Hidden Truths of the Belly: The Uncertainties of Pregnancy in Early Modern Europe," *Social History of Medicine* 15, no. 2 (2002): 209–27; Cathy McClive, *Menstruation and Procreation in Early Modern France* (New York: Routledge, 2015); Laura Gowing, *Common Bodies: Women, Touch, and Power in Seventeenth-Century England* (New Haven: Yale University Press, 2003); Lisa Forman Cody, *Birthing the Nation: Sex, Science, and the Conception of Eighteenth-Century Britons* (Oxford: Oxford University Press, 2005); Mary Fissell, *Vernacular Bodies: The Politics of Reproduction in Early Modern England* (Oxford: Oxford University, 2004).

20 Cody, *Birthing the Nation*, 282.

21 E. J. Aubinais, *Existe-t-il des signes propres à faire reconnaitre la vraie grossesse?* (Paris: Didot le jeune, 1824); L. Boislambert, *Recherches sur les moyens de reconnaître la grossesse utérine* (Paris: Didot le jeune, 1823); Adolphe Toulmouche, *Etudes sur l'infanticide et la grossesse cachée ou simulée* (Paris: Baillière, 1862); Fabre, *Bibliothèque du médecin-praticien*, 5:378–79; Tourdes, *Exposition historique*, 43–45; Briand, *Manuel complet de médecine légale*, 50.

22 Briand, *Manuel complet de médecine légale*, 50.

23 Eusèbe de Salle, "Médecine légale," in *Encyclopédie des sciences médicales* (Paris: Encyclopédie, 1835), 171.

24 T. Tessier, *Essai de médecine légale sur la grossesse, et tout ce qui en dépend* (Montpellier: Coucourdan, 1802), RB 648711d, The Huntington Library, San Marino, CA, 12.

25 Nestor-Joseph Pellassy des Fayolles, *Nouvelle question de médecine légale: L'introduction d'un placenta et de son cordon dans les parties génitales de la femme est-elle possible hors le temps de l'accouchement? Et peut-elle, dans certains cas, faire supposer un accouchement réel?* (Paris, 1833).

26 Nestor-Joseph Pellassy des Fayolles, *Nouvelle question de médecine légale: l'introduction d'un placenta et de son cordon dans les parties génitales de la femme est-elle possible hors le temps de l'accouchement? Et peut-elle dans certains cas faire supposer un accouchement réel?* (Paris: J. Ruvier et E. Lebouvier, 1838), v, vii.

27 Alfred-Armand-Louis-Marie Velpeau, *Traité complet de l'art des accouchements, ou tocologie théorique et pratique*, 2nd ed. (Paris: Baillière, 1835), 2:558.

28 Henri Legrand du Saulle, *Traité de médecine légale et de jurisprudence médicale* (Paris: Delahaye, 1874), 248.

29 Ambroise Tardieu, "Nouvelles études médico-légales sur l'avortement," *Annales d'hygiène publique et de médecine légale* series 2, vol. 9 (1858): 195.

30 Tardieu, "Nouvelles études médico-légales sur l'avortement," 195–99; *Gazette des hôpitaux*, September 28, 1858; Legrand du Saulle, *Traité de médecine légale*, 248–52.

31 AN BB/20/268.

32 Briand, *Manuel complet de médecine légale*, 50.

33 AN/BB/20/218/2; also cited in Tillier, *Des criminelles au village*, 306.

34 AN/BB/20/163/1; Briand, *Manuel complet de médecine légale*, 50; Tillier, *Des criminelles du village*, 165; Chiletti, "Grossesses ignorées."

35 Annick Tillier, "L'infanticide: La mauvaise mère," in *Présumées coupables: Les grands procès faits aux femmes*, ed. Claude Gauvard (Paris: L'Iconoclaste, 2016), 150; AN BB/24/2003.

36 Aldophe Toulmouche, "Etudes sur l'infanticide et la grossesse cachée ou simulée," *Annales d'hygiène publique et de médecine légale* series 2, vol. 18 (1862): 407–408.

37 Fodéré, *Traité de médecine légale*, 4:469, 2:8–9.

38 *Gazette des tribunaux*, January 30, 1869.

39 Paul Reille, "Responsabilité des experts: Affaire Méloche," *Annales d'hygiène publique et de médecine légale* series 3, vol. 40 (1898): 41–70.

40 Ollivier (d'Angers), "Mémoire médico-légal sur l'infanticide," *Annales d'hygiène publique et de médecine légale* series 1, vol. 16 (1836): 328–29.

41 Huber, "The Problem of Proof," 222.

42 A. Lecieux, *Considérations médico-légales sur l'infanticide* (Paris: Didot jeune, 1811), 5–6.

43 Huber, "The Problem of Proof," 222; Fuchs, *Poor and Pregnant*, 204–205; ADP D2U8 21.

44 ADBR 2U 1/1331.

45 Fuchs, *Poor and Pregnant*, 205; Ambroise Tardieu, *Etude médico-légale sur l'infanticide* (Paris: Baillière, 1868), 11.

46 Donovan, *Juries and the Transformation of Criminal Justice*, 68; Vallaud, "Le crime d'infanticide," 479.

47 On "correctionalization" in modern France, see Donovan, *Juries and the Transformation of Criminal Justice*.

48 Richard Lalou, "L'infanticide devant les tribunaux français (1825–1910)," *Communications* 44 (1986): 193; Fuchs, *Poor and Pregnant*, 207. In an 1837 infanticide prosecution, jurors concluded that the accused mother was guilty of murder but not infanticide, since the identified age of the child was one week old and the birth had been officially registered. Tillier, *Des criminelles au village*, 25.

49 Tardieu, *Etude médico-légale sur l'infanticide*, 27–31, 37–39; Ollivier (d'Angers), "Deuxième mémoire sur l'infanticide," *Annales d'hygiène publique et de médecine légale* series 1, vol. 27 (1842): 329–59; Legrand du Saulle, *Traité de médecine légale*, 297–98; Joseph Capuron, *La médecine légale, relative à l'art des accouchemens* (Paris: Croullebois, 1821), 257–58.

50 Eugène Haracque, *Considérations médico-légales sur la viabilité du foetus* (Paris: Didot jeune, 1820), RB 649970, The Huntington Library, San Marino, CA; Charles Billard, *Dissertation médico-légale sur la viabilité, considérée dans ses rapports avec la pathologie des nouveau-nés* (Paris: Didot le jeune, 1828), RB 649816, The Huntington Library, San Marino, CA; François Chaussier, *Mémoire médico-légal sur la viabilité de l'enfant*

naissant (Paris: Compère jeune, 1826); Henri-Marcel Kühnholz, *Des caractères et des conditions de la viabilité* (Montpellier, 1835).

51 Joseph Briand and Ernest Chaudé, *Manuel complet de médecine légale*, 5th ed. (Paris: Bernard Neuhaus, 1852), 177–79.

52 Emmanuel-Joseph Olivaud, *De l'infanticide et des moyens que l'on emploie pour le constater* (Paris: Gabon, 1802), 20.

53 Charles-Chrétien-Henri Marc, "Docimasie pulmonaire," in *Dictionnaire des sciences médicales*, ed. Adelon, Alard, Alibert, et al. (Paris: Panckoucke, 1810), 10:62–100; Orfila, *Leçons de médecine légale* (1828), 1:352–72; J. B. E. Edouard Crouzet, *Dissertation sur l'infanticide* (Paris: Didot le jeune, 1830), 14–20; Alphonse Devergie, "Docimasie," in *Encyclographie des sciences médicales* (Brussels: Etablissement Encyclographique, 1835), 10:225–43; *Encyclopédie des sciences médicales ou traité général, méthodique et complet des diverses branches de l'art de guérir – Deuxième division, Médecine légale – Jurisprudence Médicale* (Paris: Encyclopédie, 1835), 2:149–58.

54 Archives départementales du Nord 2U 1/252.

55 Tourdes, *Exposition historique*, 78.

56 Tardieu, *Etude médico-légale sur l'infanticide*, 62–63.

57 Mathieu [Mateu] J. B. Orfila and Octave Lesueur, *Traité des exhumations juridiques* (Paris: Béchet jeune, 1831); Devergie, *Médecine légale, théorique et pratique* (1840), 1:140–281, especially 278–79.

58 Louis François Etienne Bergeret, "Infanticide, momification naturelle du cadavre," *Annales d'hygiène publique et de médecine légale* series 2, vol. 4 (1855): 442–52.

59 Paul Brouardel, "De la détermination de l'époque de la naissance et de la mort d'un nouveau-né, faite à l'aide de la présence des acares et des chenilles d'aglosses dans un cadavre momifié," *Annales d'hygiène publique et de médecine légale* series 3, vol. 2 (1879): 153–58; Paul Brouardel, *Sur un cas de modification d'un cadavre: Applications médico-légales* (Paris: Masson, 1886); Georges P. Yovanovitch, *Entomologie appliquée à la médecine légale* (Paris: Ollier-Henry, 1888); J. P. Mégnin, *La faune des cadavres: Application de l'entomologie à la médecine légale* (Paris: Masson, Gauthier-Villars et Fils, 1894).

60 Ambroise Tardieu, "Mémoire sur la mort par suffocation," *Annales d'hygiène publique et de médecne légale* series 2, vol. 4 (1855): 371–441; Tardieu, *Etude médico-légale sur l'infanticide*, 99, 102–103, 105–109. On debates about Tardieu's views on subpleural ecchymoses, see Bruno Bertherat, "Cleaning out the Mortuary and the Medicolegal Text: Ambroise Tardieu's Modernizing Enterprise," in *Global Forensic Cultures: Making Fact and Justice in the Modern Era*, ed. Ian Burney and Christopher Hamlin (Baltimore: Johns Hopkins University Press, 2019), 264–67.

61 Fodéré, *Traité de médecine légale*, 4:498–99.

62 Tardieu, *Etude médico-légale sur l'infanticide*, 176–79.

63 Henri Chartier, *Examen médico-légal et autopsie des enfants nouveau-nés* (Lyon: Storck, 1890), 33; Paul Brouardel, *La mort et la mort subite* (Paris: Baillière, 1895), 100.

64 Joseph Briand and Ernest Chaudé, *Manuel complet de médecine légale*, 6th ed. (Paris: Baillière, 1858), 231.

65 Pierre Vavasseur, *Nouveau manuel complet des aspirants au doctorat en médecine . . . quatrième examen* (Paris: Crochard, 1834), 38–41; François Jean Matthyssens, *Précis élémentaire de médecine légale extrait des meilleurs ouvrages* (Anvers: Heirstraeten, 1837), 1:148–53.

66 Fodéré, *Traité de médecine légale*, 4:509; Matthyssens, *Précis élémentaire de médecine légale*, 1:148–50; J. B. Monfalcon, "Infanticide," in *Dictionnaire des sciences médicales*, eds. Adelon, Alard, Alibert, et al. (Paris: Panckoucke, 1818), 24:412–17.

67 Olivaud, *De l'infanticide*, 47–49; Vavasseur, *Nouveau manuel*, 39–40; Briand and Chaudé, *Manuel complet de médecine légale* (1858), 226; Joseph Balesi, *De l'arrêt spontané de la circulation fœto-placentaire : L'infanticide par omissions de la ligature du cordon est-il possible?* (Paris: Parent, 1880), 46; Velpeau, *Traité complet de l'art des accouchements*, 2:499–501.

68 Archives départementales de l'Hérault 2U 2/555; Archives départementales des Yvelines 2U 619; Archives départementales du Nord 2U 1/252; AN BB/20/128; AN BB/20/266; Orfila, *Leçons de médecine légale* (1828), 1:473–76; Charles-Claude Brillaud-Laujardière, *De l'infanticide: Etude médico-légale* (Paris: A. Durand, 1865), 200.

69 Brillaud-Laujardière, *De l'infanticide*, 200–202.

70 Fodéré, *Traité de médecine légale*, 4:500.

71 Briand and Chaudé, *Manuel complet de médecine légale* (1858), 243; Joseph Briand and J.-X. Brosson, *Manuel complet de médecine légale*, 2nd ed. (Brussels, 1830), 124; Télèphe P. Desmartis, *Médecine légale: Appréciation critique d'un rapport médico-légal ayant pour titre: Mémoire consultatif à l'occasion d'un fait d'infanticide; examen d'une cause de mort alléguée fréquemment dans les affaires de cette nature* (Paris: H. Plon, 1859), 8.

72 *Quelques idées sur l'infanticide* (Montpellier: imp. de l'Avignon, 1823), 10–11.

73 Archives départementales du Rhône 2U 1/252.

74 AN BB/20/110.

75 AN BB/20/120.

76 AN BB/20/133.

77 AN BB/20/172/2.

78 AN BB/20/133.

79 AN BB/20/218/2.

80 Decaisne, Vandermissen, and Bellefroid, "Rapport médico-légal et observations sur un cas d'infanticide," *Annales d'hygiène publique et de médecine légale* series 1, vol. 25 (1841): 437.

81 ADBR 2U 1/1331.

82 ADBR 2U 1/1331.

83 AN BB/20/110.

84 AN BB/20/120.

85 Fuchs, *Poor and Pregnant*, 201.
86 Article 340 of the Napoleonic Civil Code of 1804 had banned paternity suits. Rachel G. Fuchs, "Magistrates and Mothers, Paternity and Property in Nineteenth-Century French Courts," *Crime, Histoire & Sociétés* 13, no. 2 (2009): 13–26; Fuchs, *Poor and Pregnant*; Rachel G. Fuchs, *Contested Paternity: Constructing Families in Modern France* (Baltimore: Johns Hopkins University Press, 2008); Donovan, *Juries and the Transformation of Criminal Justice*, 67; *Annales d'hygiène publique et de médecine légale* series 2, vol. 29 (1868): 464.
87 Vallaud, "Le crime d'infanticide," 488–90; Rachel Fuchs, *Abandoned Children: Foundlings and Child Welfare in Nineteenth-Century France* (Albany: State University of New York Press, 1984), especially 42–46; Adams, *Poverty, Charity, and Motherhood*, 238, fn. 132; "Circulaire relative au service des enfants trouvés et des aliénés," in *Législation charitable, ou Recueil des lois, arrêtés, décrets, ordonnances*, ed. Adolphe de Watteville, 2nd ed. (Paris: Cotillon, 1847), 92–93; Ministère de l'intérieur, *Travaux de la Commission des enfants trouvés instituée le 22 août 1849 par arrêté du Ministre de l'intérieur*, vol. 2, *Documents sur les enfants trouvés* (Paris: Imprimerie nationale, 1850), 416; Jean-Pierre Beaude, "Infanticide," in *Dictionnaire de médecine usuelle*, ed. Jean-Pierre Beaude (Paris: Didier, 1849), 20:284; André Théodore Brochard, *La vérité sur les enfants trouvés* (Paris: Plon, 1876); Charles Dubreuilh, "De la suppression des tours au double point de vue de la morale et de la société," in *Congrès médical de France 3e session tenue à Bordeaux du lundi 2 octobre au samedi 7 octobre 1865* (Paris: Baillière, 1866), 545–73; Chatagnier, *De l'infanticide dans ses rapports avec la loi, la morale, la médecine légale, et les mesures administratives* (Paris: Cosse, 1855), 247–48.
88 Hamel, *Des enfants trouvés, et du danger de la suppression des tours dans la ville de Paris* (Paris: Baillière, 1838), 12–13.
89 *Gazette des tribunaux*, March 29, 1840.
90 Donovan, *Juries and the Transformation of Criminal Justice*, 67.
91 Fuchs, *Poor and Pregnant*, 216, 18.
92 Briand and Chaudé, *Manuel complet de médecine légale* (1858), 183.
93 *Annales d'hygiène publique et de médecine légale*, series 2, vol. 29 (1868): 463; Brillaud-Laujardière, *De l'infanticide*, 34–36, quotation on p. 36; Olivaud, *De l'infanticide*, 61.
94 Tardieu, *Etude médico-légale sur l'infanticide*, 10; Chatagnier, *De l'infanticide*, 1; Charles François Jacquier, *Des preuves et de la recherche de la paternité naturelle: Etude sur l'article 340 du Code Napoléon* (Grenoble: Baratier frères et Dardelet, 1874), 50–56.
95 Lalou, "L'infanticide devant les tribunaux," 189; Fuchs, *Poor and Pregnant*, 203; Donovan, "Infanticide and the Juries in France," 166; Tillier, *Des criminelles au village*, 121.
96 Donovan, "Infanticide and the Juries in France," 162. Over 47 percent of those accused of infanticide were acquitted between 1825 and 1831, and 36 percent were acquitted between 1832 and 1863.

97 Lalou, "L'infanticide devant les tribunaux," 190; Vallaud, "Le crime d'infanticide," 480; Fuchs, *Poor and Pregnant*, 204.

98 AN BB/20/114–15.

99 ADBR 2U 1/1331.

100 Donovan, "Infanticide and Juries in France," table 1, 159; Bechtold, "Infanticide," 168; Fuchs, *Poor and Pregnant*, 205, 287; René Bouton, *L'infanticide, étude morale et juridique* (Paris: Société d'édition scientifique, 1897), 155.

101 Donovan, "Infanticide and Juries in France," 160–61.

102 Fuchs, *Poor and Pregnant*, 205; Donovan, "Infanticide and Juries in France," 161; Tardieu, *Etude médico-légale sur l'infanticide*, 11–12.

103 Tourdes, "Grossesse – Médecine légale," 309.

104 On cryptic pregnancies, see Chiletti, "Grossesses ignorées;" Devergie, *Médecine légale* (1840), 1:463–65; Tardieu, *Etude médico-légale sur l'infanticide*, 218–21; Paul Brouardel, *Infanticide* (Paris: Baillière, 1897), 151–53; and Fabrice Cahen and Silvia Chiletti, "Les ambivalences du diagnostic précoce de grossesse (xvie-xxe siècle)," *Clio. Femmes, Genre, Histoire* 48, no. 2 (2018): 223–41.

105 Lecieux, *Considérations médico-légales sur l'infanticide*, 51–53; A. Lecieux, Gabriel Laisné, Athanase Renard, and J. J. Germain Rieux, *Médecine légale, ou Considérations sur l'infanticide, sur la manière de procéder à l'ouverture des cadavres, spécialement dans les cas de visites judiciaires, sur les érosions et perforations spontanées de l'estomac et sur l'ecchymose, la sugillation, la contusion, la meurtrissure* (Paris: Baillière, 1819), 64–66; Brillaud-Laujardière, *De l'infanticide*, 204–7; Tardieu, *Etude médico-légale sur l'infanticide*, 138–48, 289; AN BB/20/120; Fuchs, *Poor and Pregnant*, 209.

106 Tourdes, *Exposition historique*, 56–57.

107 Négrier, "Recherches médico-légales sur la longueur et la résistance du cordon ombilical au terme de la gestation," *Annales d'hygiène publique et de médecine légale* series 1, vol. 25 (1841): 126–40; Gellusseau and Houdet's response to Négrier in *Annales d'hygiène publique et de médecine légale* series 1, vol. 26 (1841): 244–49.

108 On infant strangulation and the umbilical cord, see, e.g., H. M. E. Taufflieb, "De la strangulation des nouveau-nés par le cordon ombilical," *Annales d'hygiène publique et de médecine légale* series 1, vol. 14 (1835): 340–49; Joseph Briand and Ernest Chaudé, *Manuel complet de médecine légale*, 4th ed. (Paris: Bernard Neuhaus, 1846), 208, 239–40; J.-B.-Jules Delaye, *Note médico-légale sur un cas d'asphyxie déterminée par l'enroulement du cordon ombilical autour du cou d'un enfant nouveau-né qui avait complètement respiré* (Toulouse: Douladoure, 1863); AN BB/20/268; AN BB/20/93.

109 Fuchs, *Poor and Pregnant*, 209, 213; ADP D2U8 135; Nicolas Philibert Adelon, "Rapport médico-légal sur une accusation d'infanticide," *Annales d'hygiène publique et de médecine légale* series 2, vol. 4 (1855): 453–70.

110 ADP D2U8 247.
111 Fuchs, *Poor and Pregnant*, 211.
112 Brouardel, *Infanticide*, vii.
113 Brouardel, *Infanticide*, v.
114 Willemijn Ruberg, "Travelling Knowledge and Forensic Medicine: Infanticide, Body and Mind in the Netherlands, 1811–1911," *Medical History* 57, 3 (2013): 359–76; Hilary Marland, *Dangerous Motherhood: Insanity and Childbirth in Victorian Britain* (Basingstoke: Palgrave Macmillan, 2004); Hilary Marland, "Disappointment and Desolation: Women, Doctors and Interpretations of Puerperal Insanity in the Nineteenth Century," *History of Psychiatry* 14 (2003): 303–20; Nancy Theriot, "Diagnosing Unnatural Motherhood: Nineteenth-Century Physicians and 'Puerperal Insanity,'" *American Studies* 30, no. 2 (1989): 69–88; Francesca Arena, "La folie des mères," *Rives méditerranéennes* (2008): 143–54.
115 Vallaud, "Le crime d'infanticide," 484; Donovan, "Infanticide and the Juries in France," 169; Donovan, *Juries and the Transformation of Criminal Justice*, 131; Fuchs, *Poor and Pregnant*, 210.
116 AN BB/20/120.
117 Beaude, "Infanticide," 284.
118 Matthieu Weill, *Considérations générales sur la folie puerpérale* (Strasbourg: Vve Berger-Levrault, 1851), quotation on p. 48.
119 Stéphane Tarnier and Pierre Budin, *Traité de l'art des accouchements* (Paris: Steinheil, 1888), 2:166.
120 Louis Victor Marcé, "Etudes sur les causes de la folie puerpérale," *Annales médico-psychologiques*, series 3, vol. 3 (1857): 583; Louis Victor Marcé, *Traité de la folie des femmes enceintes, des nouvelles accouchées et des nourrices, et des considérations médico-légales qui se rattachent à ce sujet* (Paris: Baillière, 1858), RB 649110, Huntington Library, San Marino, CA; Ruberg, "Travelling Knowledge and Forensic Medicine."
121 Tardieu, *Etude médico-légale sur l'infanticide*, 228–40; Ambroise Tardieu, *Etude médico-légale sur la folie* (Paris: Baillière, 1872), 179.
122 Pierre Léon Jacques Martin, *Considérations sur la folie puerpérale* (Paris: A. Parent, 1872); Lucien-Ernest Reibel, *De la folie puerpérale* (Paris: A. Parent, 1876); Georges Rocher, *Etude sur la folie puerpérale* (Paris: A. Parent, 1877); Germain Cortyl, *Etude sur la folie puerpérale* (Paris: A. Parent, 1877); Guillaume Boudrie, *Etude sur les causes de la folie puerpérale* (Paris: A. Parent, 1878); Mariano Garcia-Rijo, *Contribution à l'étude de la folie puerpérale* (Paris: A. Parent, 1879); Jules Chabanon, *Etude sur la folie puerpérale* (Montpellier: J. Martel ainé, 1879).
123 *Gazette médicale de Paris* series 4, vol. 6, no. 11 (March 17, 1877): 129.
124 Chabanon, *Etude sur la folie puerpérale*, 38–40.
125 ADP D2U8 83.
126 Fuchs, *Poor and Pregnant*, 212.
127 Vibert, *Précis de médecine légale*, 447–48.

128 Benjamin Ball, *Leçons sur les maladies mentales* (Paris: Asselin, 1880–83), 586–87.
129 Fuchs, *Poor and Pregnant*, 211.
130 Donovan, *Juries and the Transformation of Criminal Justice*, 132.

Chapter 5

1 Part of this chapter appeared as "Child Sexual Abuse and Medical Expertise in Nineteenth-Century France," *French Historical Studies* 42, no. 3 (2019): 391–421. Copyright 2019, Society for French Historical Studies. All rights reserved. I thank Duke University Press for permission to reprint a revised version here.
   AN BB/24/2019 dossier 5355; Ambroise Tardieu, *Etude médico-légale sur les attentats aux moeurs*, 2nd ed. (Paris: Baillière, 1858), 109–112. Bixner had previously been imprisoned for *outrage public à la pudeur* (indecent exposure or gross indecency) from 1842 to 1845.
2 The French state passed these laws between 1874 and 1898. Rachel Fuchs, "Crimes against Children in Nineteenth-Century France: Child Abuse," *Law and Human Behavior* 6, nos. 3–4 (1982): 237–59; Fuchs, *Abandoned Children*; Fuchs, *Poor and Pregnant in Paris*; Sylvia Shafer, *Children in Moral Danger and the Problem of Government in Third Republic France* (Princeton, NJ: Princeton University Press, 1997).
3 On sexual assault in modern France, see Anne-Claude Ambroise-Rendu, *Histoire de la pédophilie* (Paris: Fayard, 2014); Georges Vigarello, *Histoire du viol: XVIe–XXe siècle* (Paris: Editions du Seuil, 1998); James Donovan, "Combatting the Sexual Abuse of Children in France, 1825–1913," *Criminal Justice History* 15 (1994): 59–93; Isabelle Le Boulanger, *Enfance bafouée: La société rurale bretonne face aux abus sexuels du XIXe siècle* (Rennes: Presses universitaires de Rennes, 2015); Fabienne Giuliani, *Les liaisons interdites: Histoire de l'inceste au XIXe siècle* (Paris: Publications de la Sorbonne, 2014); Frédéric Chauvaud, "La preuve par l'hymen: Le viol des femmes sous l'œil des médecins légistes (1810–1890)," in *Le corps en lambeaux: Violences sexuelles et sexuées faites aux femmes*, ed. Lydie Bodiou, Frédéric Chauvaud, Ludovic Gaussot, et al. (Rennes: Presses universitaires de Rennes, 2016), 63–80; Aude Fauvel, "Femmes violeuses et hommes bafoués: Sexe, crime et médecine dans la France du XIXe siècle," in *Crimes et délits: Quinzième Colloque des Invalides, 18 novembre 2011*, ed. J.-J. Lefrère and M. Pierssens (Tusson: Du Lérot, 2012), 91–116; Anne-Marie Sohn, "Les attentats à la pudeur sur les fillettes en France (1870–1939) et la sexualité quotidienne," *Mentalités* 3 (1989): 71–112.
4 Philippe Ariès, *Centuries of Childhood: A Social History of Family Life*, trans. Robert Baldick (New York: Alfred A. Knopf, 1962). For an overview of challenges to Ariès's work, see Colin Heywood, "Centuries of Childhood: An Anniversary – and an Epitaph?" *Journal of the History of Childhood and Youth* 3 (2010): 341–65.

5 Hugh Cunningham, *Children and Childhood in Western Society Since 1500* (New York: Longman, 2005); Colin Heywood, *A History of Childhood* (Cambridge: Polity Press, 2018); Colin Heywood, *Growing Up in France: From the Ancien Régime to the Third Republic* (Cambridge: Cambridge University Press, 2007); Cat Nilan, "Hapless Innocence and Precocious Perversity in the Courtroom Melodrama: Representations of the Child Criminal in a Paris Legal Journal, 1830–1848," *Journal of Family History* 22, no. 3 (1997): 251–85; Jennifer Popiel, *Rousseau's Daughters: Domesticity, Education, and Autonomy in Modern France* (Durham: University of New Hampshire Press, 2008).

6 Nilan, "Hapless Innocence." On precocity and the age of consent in Britain, see Victoria Bates, *Sexual Forensics in Victorian and Edwardian England: Age, Crime and Consent in the Courts* (Basingstoke: Palgrave Macmillan, 2016); and Victoria Bates, "Forensic Medicine and Female Victimhood in Victorian and Edwardian England," *Past and Present* 245, no. 1 (2019): 117–51.

7 Fodéré, *Les lois éclairées par les sciences physiques*, 2:12; Fodéré, *Traité de médecine légale*, 4:370–72.

8 Fodéré, *Traité de médecine légale*, 4:370, 327.

9 Fodéré, *Traité de médecine légale*, 4:358, 370–71, 327.

10 Fodéré, *Traité de médecine légale*, 4:360.

11 For example, the lawyer defending an Alsatian parish priest, who was accused in 1827 of indecent assault of eight children in his parish, successfully argued before jurors that the priest might have employed "moral violence" but not physical violence and that only the latter was the constitutive quality of the crime of indecent assault (Vigarello, *Histoire du viol*, 153).

12 Vigarello, *Histoire du viol*, 153–54; *Recueil général des lois*, 21:413–14.

13 *Journal du droit criminel* and *Gazette des tribunaux* cited in Vigarello, *Histoire du viol*, 154.

14 On moral violence, see Anne-Claude Ambroise-Rendu, "Attentats à la pudeur sur enfants : Le crime sans violence est-il un crime ? (1810–années 1930)," *Revue d'histoire moderne et contemporaine* 56, no. 4 (2009): 165–89; Vigarello, *Histoire du viol*.

15 Articles 331, 332, and 333 of the penal code pertained to sexual offenses against children. Adolphe Chauveau, *Code pénal progressif: Commentaire sur la loi modificative du Code pénal* (Paris, 1832), 290–97, 464; Donovan, "Combatting the Sexual Abuse of Children," 65–68.

16 AN BB/20/102.

17 AN BB/20/102.

18 AN BB/20/137.

19 Faustin Hélie, *Théorie du Code pénal: Appendice de la quatrième édition contenant le commentaire de la loi du 13 mai 1863 modificative du Code pénal* (Paris: Cosse et Marchal, 1863), 94–96; Jean-Servais-Guillaume Nypels, *Le droit pénal français progressif et comparé: Code pénal de*

1810 (Paris: Durand, 1864), 616; Jean Baptiste Duvergier, *Collection complète des lois, décrets, ordonnances, règlemens avis du Conseil d'état* (Paris: A. Guyot et Scribe, 1863), 63:459.

20 ADBR 2U 1/1330.

21 ADBR 2U 1/1330.

22 ADBR 2U 1/1330.

23 AN BB/20/248/1.

24 ADBR 2U 1/1117.

25 Donovan, "Combatting the Sexual Abuse of Children," 60–61; Paul Bernard, *Des attentats à la pudeur sur les petites filles* (Paris: O. Doin, 1886), 31; *Compte général de l'administration de la justice criminelle en France pendant l'année 1851* (Paris: Imprimerie Royal, 1852), ix.

26 AN BB/20/114-15.

27 Henri Legludic, *Notes et observations de médecine légale: Attentats aux moeurs* (Paris: G. Masson et Cie, 1896), 29; Adolphe Toulmouche, "Des attentats à la pudeur," *Annales d'hygiène publique et de médecine légale*, series 2, vol. 6 (1856): 100.

28 *Annales d'hygiène publique et de médecine légale*, series 1, vol. 37 (1847): 462.

29 Louis Pénard, *De l'intervention du médecin légiste dans les questions d'attentats aux moeurs* (Paris: Baillière, 1860).

30 Tardieu, *Etude médico-légale sur les attentats aux moeurs* (1858), 49. On Tardieu's treatment of child abuse, see Denis Darya Vassigh, "Les experts judiciaires face à la parole de l'enfant maltraité: Le cas des médecins légistes de la fin du XIXe siècle," *Revue d'histoire de l'enfance « irrégulière »* 2 (1999): 97–111; Jeffrey Moussaieff Masson, *The Assault on Truth: Freud's Suppression of the Seduction Theory* (New York: Pocket, 1998), 15–24.

31 Henry Coutagne, *Précis de médecine légale* (Lyon: A. Storck, 1896), 398, 403-4.

32 "There is *not a sign, not a single sign*, that makes it possible to establish a differential diagnosis on solid grounds between a vulvar inflammation due to a criminal act, and one resulting from some other cause." Alfred Fournier, "Simulations d'attentats vénériens sur de jeunes enfants," *Annales d'hygiène publique et de médecine légale*, series 3, vol. 4 (1880): 504.

33 Victoria Bates, "'So Far as I Can Define without a Microscopical Examination': Venereal Disease Diagnosis in English Courts, 1850–1914," *Social History of Medicine* 26, no. 1 (2013): 38–55.

34 Tardieu, *Etude médico-légale sur les attentats aux moeurs* (1858), 50.

35 Tardieu noted that it "was not impossible" for a penis to have had entered her vagina, given the state of her hymen and the "deformation" of her genitals, but his report focused on the signs of masturbation that contributed to the supposedly flawed conclusions of the original forensic report. Tardieu dismissed the finding of the original forensic report, which he lamented was the product of an examination conducted while the girl

had been menstruating. Ambroise Tardieu, *Etude médico-légale sur les attentats aux moeurs*, 4th ed. (Paris: Baillière, 1862), 117–19.

36 Pénard, *De l'intervention du médecin légiste*, 67.

37 Léon-Henri Thoinot, *Attentats aux moeurs et perversions du sens génital: Leçons professées à la Faculté de médecine* (Paris: O. Doin, 1898), 161–62.

38 On discourses on masturbation, see Michel Foucault, *History of Sexuality*, volume 1, *An Introduction*, trans. Robert Hurley (New York: Pantheon Books, 1978); Michel Foucault, *Abnormal: Lectures at the Collège de France, 1974–1975*, ed. Valerio Marchetti and Antonella Salomoni, trans. Graham Burchell (New York: Picador, 2003); Thomas Laqueur, *Solitary Sex: A Cultural History of Masturbation* (New York: Zone Books, 2003); Patrick Singy, "The History of Masturbation: An Essay Review," *Journal for the History of Medicine and Allied Sciences* 59 (2004): 112–21; Michael Stolberg, "An Unmanly Vice: Self-Pollution, Anxiety, and the Body in the Eighteenth Century," *Social History of Medicine* 13, no. 1 (2000): 1–21.

39 AN BB/20/248/1.

40 Ambroise Tardieu, *Etude médico-légale sur les attentats aux moeurs*, 6th ed. (Paris: Baillière, 1873), 257.

41 Alexandre Lacassagne, "Pédérastie," in *Dictionnaire encyclopédique des sciences médicales*, ed. André Archambault, et al., series 2 (Paris: Masson, 1886), 22:257; Alexandre Lacassagne, *Précis de médecine judiciaire* (Paris: Masson, 1886), 482.

42 Giuliani, *Les liaisons interdites*, 224–25.

43 Armand B. Paulier and Frédéric Hétet, *Traité élémentaire de médecine légale, de jurisprudence médicale, et de la toxicologie*, part I (Paris: Doin, 1881), 600.

44 Société médico-psychologique, "Médecine légale. Attentat aux mœurs. Condamnation, appel, expertise médicale et prononcé du jugement," *Annales médico-psychologiques* 1 (1843): 289–98.

45 Archives départementales du Rhône 2U 356.

46 Goldstein, *Console and Classify*.

47 Daniel Pick, *Faces of Degeneration: A European Disorder (c. 1848—1918)* (Cambridge: Cambridge University Press, 1989); Nye, *Crime, Madness and Politics*; Ian Dowbiggin, *Inheriting Madness: Professionalization and Psychiatric Knowledge in Nineteenth-Century France* (Berkeley: University of California Press, 1991); Bénédict-Augustin Morel, *Traité des dégénérescences physiques, intellectuelles et morales de l'espèce humaine* (Paris: Baillière, 1857).

48 On sexology and the notion of perversion in nineteenth-century France, see Foucault, *History of Sexuality*; Robert A. Nye, *Masculinity and Male Codes of Honor in Modern France* (New York: Oxford University Press, 1993); Sylvie Chaperon, *Les origines de la sexologie (1850–1900)* (Paris: Louis Audibert, 2007); Claude-Olivier Doron, "La formation du concept psychiatrique de perversion au XIXe siècle en France," *L'information psychiatrique* 88, no. 1 (2012): 39–49; Amandine Malivin, "Le

nécrophile, pervers insaisissable (France, XIXe siècle)," *Criminocorpus* (October 7, 2016); and Frédéric Chauvaud, "L'invention du perverti: Les hommes de l'art et le 'beau cas' dans la France du second XIXe siècle," in *Michel Foucault: Savoirs, domination et sujet*, ed. Jean-Claude Bourdin, Frédéric Chauvaud, et al. (Rennes: Presses universitaires de Rennes, 2008), 57–65.

49 Ambroise-Rendu, *Histoire de la pédophilie*, 93. The term *pédophilie* was not introduced into the French lexicon until 1931.

50 Nye, *Crime, Madness and Politics*, 97–131; Renneville, *Crime et folie*.

51 Foucault, *Abnormal*, 291–321.

52 Henry Bonnet and Jules Bulard, *Rapport médico-légal sur l'état mental de Charles-Joseph Jouy, inculpé d'attentat aux moeurs* (Nancy: Veuve Raybois, 1868).

53 Foucault, *History of Sexuality*, 31.

54 Foucault, *Abnormal*, 291–321. Foucault omitted forty-year-old Jouy's second sexual assault of eleven-year-old Sophie Adam from his account in the *History of Sexuality*.

55 Bulard and Bonnet, *Rapport médico-légal*, 4.

56 Louise Jackson has argued that the likelihood of conviction of sexual offenses against children was inversely proportional to the social rank of the defendant in Victorian England. Louise Jackson, *Child Sexual Abuse in Victorian England* (London: Routledge, 2000), 108.

57 Rates of conviction varied but peaked at over 80 percent from 1863–80. Donovan, "Combatting the Sexual Abuse of Children," 72.

58 Fewer than twenty women faced charges each year. Some years the percentage was around 2 percent, such as in 1844 when 9 out of 406 people accused of rape or indecent assault of a child were women. Thoinot, *Attentats aux moeurs*, 161; *Compte général de l'administration de la justice criminelle en France pendant l'année 1844* (Paris: Imprimerie Royal, 1846), 20.

59 Coutagne, *Précis de médecine légale*, 398.

60 Thoinot, *Attentats aux moeurs*, 19–20.

61 Tardieu, *Etude médico-légale sur les attentats*, 5th ed. (Paris: Baillière, 1865), 57–58.

62 Tardieu, *Etude médico-légale sur les attentats aux moeurs* (1958), 117.

63 Ambroise Tardieu, *Etude médico-légale sur les attentats aux moeurs*, 7th ed. (Paris: Baillière, 1878), 261–62.

64 Tardieu, *Etude médico-légale sur les attentats aux moeurs* (1878), 218–43. Tardieu maintained that the penis of an "active pederast" was either very thin or large and tapered and that "passive pederasts" had an infundibular, or funnel-shaped, anus and large buttocks.

65 Thoinot, *Attentats aux moeurs*, 160–61. Thoinot also observed that women's abuse of boys was infrequent but occurred more than one would believe.

66 Giuliani, *Les liaisons interdites*, 341; Ambroise-Rendu, *Histoire de la pédophilie*, 247.

67 Henry Coutagne, *Notes sur la sodomie* (Lyon: Henri Georg, 1880), 16–19.
68 Thoinot, *Attentats aux moeurs*, 162–63.
69 The German physician Albert Neisser isolated the gonococcus bacteria in 1879. Pierre-André Lop, "Attentats à la pudeur commis par des femmes sur des petits garçons," *Archives de l'anthropologie criminelle et des sciences pénales* 10 (1895): 37–42.
70 Brouardel, "De la réforme," 356.
71 Alexandre Lacassagne, *L'Affaire du Père Bérard* (Lyon: Storck, 1890).
72 On fin de siècle debates about the nature of children among doctors, pedagogues, and philosophers, see Katharine H. Norris, "Child Psychology, Republican Pedagogy, and the Debate over Heredity in Fin-de-Siècle France" (PhD diss., University of California, Berkeley, 2000); Katharine H. Norris, "Mentir à l'âge de l'innocence: Enfance, science et anxiété culturelle dans la France fin-de-siècle," *Sociétés & Représentations* 38, no. 2 (2014): 171–202.
73 Thoinot, *Attentats aux moeurs*, 226.
74 Legludic, *Attentats aux moeurs*, 88.
75 On sexual blackmail in the eighteenth and nineteenth centuries, see Angus McLaren, *Sexual Blackmail: A Modern History* (Cambridge, MA: Harvard University Press, 2002); Antony E. Simpson, "Blackmail Myth and the Prosecution of Rape and Its Attempt in Eighteenth-Century London: The Creation of a Legal Tradition," *The Journal of Criminal Law and Criminology* 77, no. 1 (1986): 101–50.
76 Bernard, *Attentats à la pudeur*, 125–26.
77 Bernard, *Attentats à la pudeur*, 99.
78 *Lyon médicale: Gazette médicale et journal de médecine réunis* (Lyon: J.P. Megret, 1888), 59: 622.
79 Tardieu, *Etude médico-légale sur les attentats aux moeurs* (1858), 118–20.
80 AN BB/20/227/1. The roofer Collenot's defense was unsuccessful, and he was sentenced to six years in prison.
81 See, e.g., Pénard, *De l'intervention du médecin légiste*, 97; Fournier, "Simulations d'attentats vénériens;" Bernard, *Attentats à la pudeur*, 98–99, 126; Lacassagne, *Précis de médecine judiciaire*, 496; Legludic, *Attentats aux mœurs*, 89.
82 Pénard, *De l'intervention du médecin légiste*, 97. On discourses on defloration in nineteenth-century France, see Pauline Mortas, *Une rose épineuse. La défloration au XIXe siècle en France* (Rennes: Presses universitaires de Rennes, 2017).
83 Fournier, "Simulations d'attentats vénériens," 509–10, 500.
84 On masculinity and male honor in nineteenth-century France, see Nye, *Masculinity and Male Codes of Honor.*
85 Fournier, "Simulations d'attentats vénériens," 511–12; Bernard, *Attentats à la pudeur*, 100; Thoinot, *Attentats aux moeurs*, 227–33; *Lyon médical* 59: 622.
86 Fournier, "Simulations d'attentats vénériens," 517.

87 Norris, "Mentir à l'âge de l'innocence;" Norris, "Child Psychology,
   Republican Pedagogy;" Claude Bourdin, "Les enfants menteurs,"
   Annales médico-psychologiques, series 6, vol. 9, no. 41 (1883): 53–67,
   374–86; Paul Brouardel, "Des causes d'erreur dans les expertises relatives
   aux attentats à la pudeur," *Annales d'hygiène publique et de médecine
   légale*, series 3, vol. 10 (1883): 60–71, 148–78; Vassigh, "Les experts
   judiciaires."

88 Auguste Motet, *Les faux témoignages des enfants devant la justice* (Paris:
   Baillière, 1887), 9; Charles Lasègue, "Les hystériques, leur perversité,
   leurs mensonges," *Annales médico-psychologiques*, series 6, vol. 6
   (1881): 111–18.

89 Lasègue, "Les hystériques, leur perversité, leurs mensonges," 114–15;
   Motet, *Les faux témoignages des enfants*, 8–9, quotation on p. 8.

90 Brouardel, "Causes d'erreur," 63.

91 On the fin de siècle preoccupation with these issues, see Norris, "Mentir à
   l'âge de l'innocence;" Norris, "Child Psychology, Republican Pedagogy."

92 Brouardel, "Causes d'erreur," 63.

93 Legludic, *Attentats aux moeurs*, 88. For similar claims, see, e.g., Louis
   Dufestel, *Des maladies simulées chez les enfants* (Paris, 1888), 11.

94 Société médico-psychologique, "Du mensonge chez les enfants,"*Annales
   médico-psychologiques*, series 6, vol. 9 (1883): 133–37, 141, 280–84,
   quotation by Eugène Dally on p. 131; Société médico-psychologique,
   "L'éducation est une génération psychique," *Annales médico-psychologiques*, series 6, vol. 9 (1883): 284–305.

95 Société médico-psychologique, "Du mensonge chez les enfants," 281.

96 Lacassagne, *Père Bérard*, 17.

97 Bourdin, "Les enfants menteurs," 378, 386, 384; Norris, "Child
   Psychology, Republican Pedagogy," 248.

98 Pénard, *De l'intervention du médecin légiste*, 40; François-Maurice
   Rassier, *De la valeur du témoignage des enfants en justice* (Lyon:
   Storck, 1892).

99 Paul Bézy, "Un cas de pseudo-coxalgie chez un enfant menteur," *Revue
   de l'hypnotisme* 7 (1893): 306.

100 Legludic, *Attentats aux moeurs*, 90.

101 Lacassagne, *Père Bérard*, 63–64; Legludic, *Attentats aux moeurs*, 88.

102 Albert Florence, "Du sperme et des taches de sperme en médecine légale,"
    Archives d'anthropologie criminelle 10 (1895): 417–34, 520–43; 11
    (1896): 37–46, 146–63, 249–63.

103 Legludic, *Attentats aux moeurs*, 14; Donovan, "Combatting the Sexual
    Abuse of Children," 60–61.

104 Philosopher Kate Manne coined the term "himpathy" to describe
    this phenomenon in the present day. Kate Manne, *Down Girl: The
    Logic of Misogyny* (Oxford: Oxford University Press, 2017); Kate
    Manne, *Entitled: How Male Privilege Hurts Women* (New York:
    Crown, 2020).

Conclusion and Epilogue

1 AN BB/24/2082; Alexandre Lacassagne, "Vacher l'éventreur," *Archives d'anthropologie criminelle, de criminologie et de psychologie normale* 13 (1898): 632–95; Edouard Toulouse, *Le rapport des médecins experts sur Vacher* (Clermont: Daix frères, 1898); *Le tueur de bergers* (Paris: S. Schwarz, [1898]).

2 Lacassagne, "Vacher l'éventreur," 636.

3 AN BB/20/133.

4 Matt K. Matsuda, "Doctor, Judge, Vagabond: Identity, Identification, and Other Memories of the State," *History and Memory* 6, no. 1 (1994): 73–94; Angus McLaren, *The Trials of Masculinity: Policing Sexual Boundaries, 1870–1930* (Chicago, IL: University of Chicago Press, 1997), 167; Alphonse Bertillon, *Identification anthropométrique: Instructions signalétiques* (Melun: Ministère de l'Intérieur, 1885); Alphonse Bertillon, *Notice sur le fonctionnement du service d'identification de la préfecture de police* (Paris: Masson, 1889).

5 Edmond Locard, *L'enquête criminelle et les méthodes scientifiques* (Paris: Flammarion, 1920).

6 Bron McKillop, "Forensic Science in Inquisitorial Systems of Criminal Justice," in *Expert Evidence and Scientific Proof in Criminal Trials*, ed. Paul Roberts (Farnham: Ashgate, 2014), 36–43.

7 Jentzen, *Death Investigation in America.*

8 The Supreme Court subsequently affirmed and elaborated upon the Daubert standard with the *General Electric Co. v. Joiner* (1997) and *Kumho Tire Co. v. Carmichael* (1999) decisions. Golan, *Laws of Men and Laws of Nature*, 245–64; Jill Lepore, "On Evidence: Proving Frye as a Matter of Law, Science, and History," *The Yale Law Journal* 124, no. 4 (2015): 882–1344; "Admitting Doubt: A New Standard for Scientific Evidence," *Harvard Law Review* 123, no. 8 (2010): 2021–42.

9 "Admitting Doubt," 2030; Jennifer L. Mnookin, "Idealizing Science and Demonizing Experts: An Intellectual History of Expert Evidence," *Villanova Law Review* 52, no. 4 (2007): 763–66; Harry T. Edwards and Jennifer Mnookin, "A Wake-Up Call on the Junk Science Infesting Our Courtrooms," *Washington Post*, September 20, 2016.

10 Brandon L. Garrett, *Autopsy of a Crime Lab: Exposing the Flaws in Forensics* (Berkeley: University of California Press, 2021). On the CSI effect and debates about this theory, see Kimberlianne Podlas, "The *CSI* Effect": Exposing the Media Myth," *Fordham Intellectual Property, Media and Entertainment Law Journal* 16 (2006): 429–65; Simon A. Cole and Rachel Dioso-Villa, "*CSI* and Its Effects: Media, Juries, and the Burden of Proof," *New England Law Review* 41 (2007): 435–70; Simon A. Cole and Rachel Dioso-Villa, "Should Judges Worry about the 'CSI Effect'?" *Court Review* 47 (2011): 20–31; and Jason Chin and Larysa Workewych, "The CSI Effect," in *Oxford Handbooks Online*, ed. Markus

Dubber (New York: Oxford University Press, 2016) https://doi.org/10
.1093/oxfordhb/9780199935352.013.28.

11 Innocence Project, DNA Exonerations in the United States, www
.innocenceproject.org/dna-exonerations-in-the-united-states/ (last visited
October 27, 2019).

12 Gil Eyal, *The Crisis of Expertise* (Medford, MA: Polity Press, 2019); Tom
Nichols, *The Death of Expertise: The Campaign Against Established
Knowledge and Why It Matters* (Oxford: Oxford University Press, 2017).

13 Ronald Brownstein, "Trump's War on Expertise Is Only Intensifying,"
The Atlantic, November 21, 2019; Masha Gessen, "President Trump
Wages War on Government and Expertise, and Our Institutions
Surrender," *The New Yorker,* September 13, 2019.

14 Wellcome Global Monitor 2018, "Chapter 5: Attitudes to vaccines,"
https://wellcome.ac.uk/reports/wellcome-global-monitor/2018/chapter-5-
attitudes-vaccines (last visited November 12, 2021).

15 Wellcome Global Monitor 2020, "Chapter 3: Trust in and perceived value
of science amid Covid-19," https://wellcome.org/reports/wellcome-global-
monitor-covid-19/2020/chapter-3-trust-in-perceived-value-of-science-
amid-covid-19 (last visited December 8, 2021).

Bibliography

Manuscript and Archival Sources

Archives de Paris (ADP): D1U8; D2U8, Cour d'assises, dossiers de procédure

Archives départementales de l'Hérault: 2U, Cour d'assises, dossiers de procédure

Archives départementales des Bouches-du-Rhône (ADBR): 2U 1, Cour d'assises, dossiers de procédure

Archives départementales des Yvelines: 2U, Cour d'assises, dossiers de procédure

Archives départementales du Nord: 2U 1, Cour d'assises, dossiers de procédure

Archives départementales du Rhône: 2U, Cour d'assises, dossiers de procédure

Archives de la Préfecture de police de Paris: BA, Cabinet du préfet de police, affaires générales; LA, Registres de la morgue

Archives nationales de France, Pierrefitte-sur-Seine (AN):

BB/18, Correspondance de la division criminelle du ministère de la Justice

BB/20, Comptes rendus d'assises

BB/24, Grâces des condamnés à mort

F/9, Affaires militaires

W, Tribunal révolutionnaire

Bibliothèque municipale de Lyon: Fonds Lacassagne

Printed Primary Sources

Acte d'accusation de la fille Hélène Jégado, auteur d'un nombre considérable d'empoisonnements. Mort de 47 personnes. Son jugement. Déposition des

témoins. Sa condamnation à la peine de mort. [Paris]: Chassaignon, [1851].

Adelon, Nicolas Philibert. "Rapport médico-légal sur une accusation d'infanticide." *Annales d'hygiène publique et de médecine légale*, series 2, vol. 4 (1855): 453–70.

Affaire de Marie-Adélaïde Bodin, veuve Boursier, et de Nicolas Kostolo. Paris: Pillet aîné, 1823.

L'ami de la Charte: Journal du Puy de Dôme, de la Haute-Loire et du Cantal. Clermont-Ferrand, 1820–48.

Amoëdo, Oscar. *L'art dentaire en médecine légale.* Paris: Masson, 1898.

Annales d'hygiène publique et de médecine légale. Paris: Baillière, 1829–1922.

Archives d'anthropologie criminelle, de médecine légale et de psychologie normale et pathologique. Lyon: A. Storck; Paris: G. Masson, 1893–1907.

Archives générales de médecine. Paris: Béchet jeune; Migneret; Asselin, 1823–1914.

Archives parlementaires de 1787 à 1860: Recueil complet des débats législatifs et politiques des Chambres françaises, edited by Jérome Mavidal, Emile Laurent, et al. 102 vols. Paris: Paul Dupont; Centre national de la recherche scientifique, 1862–.

Aubert, Xavier-Paul. *Médecine légale militaire: Surdité simulée.* Bordeaux, 1899.

Aubinais, E. J. *Existe-t-il des signes propres à faire reconnaitre la vraie grossesse?* Paris: Didot le jeune, 1824.

Balesi, Joseph. *De l'arrêt spontané de la circulation fœto-placentaire : L'infanticide par omissions de la ligature du cordon est-il possible?* Paris: Parent, 1880.

Ball, Benjamin. *Leçons sur les maladies mentales.* Paris: Asselin, 1880–83.

Barrangeard. *Extrait de divers mémoires publiés depuis très-longtemps par le docteur Barrangeard, sur le danger des inhumations précipitées et sur la nécessité de constater avec soin tous les décès sans aucune exception.* Lyon: Jaillet, 1863.

Barse, Jules. "Consultation médico-légale sur les rapports judiciaires de MM. Darles et Pipet, d'Yssengeaux, et de MM. Orfila, Chevallier, et Ollivier (d'Angers)." In Chevallier, Orfila, and Olliver (d'Angers), "Triple accusation d'empoisonnement." *Annales d'hygiène publique et de médecine légale*, series 1, vol. 28 (1842): 150–52.

Manuel de la Cour d'assises dans les questions d'empoisonnement, à l'usage des magistrats, des avocats, des experts, des jurés et des témoins. Paris: Labé, 1845.

Bayard, Henri-Louis. "Appréciation médico-légale de l'action de l'éther et du chloroforme." *Annales d'hygiène publique et de médecine légale*, series 1, vol. 42 (1849): 201–14.

Manuel pratique de médecine légale. Paris: Baillière, 1844.

Beaude, Jean-Pierre. "Infanticide." In *Dictionnaire de médecine usuelle*, edited by Jean-Pierre Beaude, vol. 20, 280–85. Paris: Didier, 1849.

Beaumont, Gustave de. "Rapport sur un mémoire de M. de Cormenin relatif à l'empoisonnement par l'arsenic." *Séances et travaux de l'Académie des sciences morales et politiques*, vol. 1, 488–91. Paris, 1842.

Bécar, L. *De l'illégitimité du recours à la chloroformisation à propos des simulations morbides*. Brussels: A. Manceaux, 1887.

Bégin, Emile-Auguste-Nicolas-Jules. "Réforme." In *Dictionnaire de médecine et de chirurgie pratiques*, edited by Gabriel Andral, Louis Jacques Bégin, Philippe Frédéric Blandin, et al., vol. 14, 159–207. Paris: Méquignon-Marvis, 1835.

La Belgique judiciaire. 41 vols. Brussels, 1843–83.

Benoit, Eugène. *Des maladies simulées et provoquées au bagne pénitencier de l'île Nau (Nouvelle-Calédonie)*. Nancy, 1881.

Benoît, Georges. *De l'empoisonnement criminel en général*. Lyon: Storck, 1888.

Bergeret, Louis François l. "Infanticide, momification naturelle du cadavre." *Annales d'hygiène publique et de médecine légale*, series 2, vol. 4 (1855): 442–52.

Bergeron, Georges. "Quelques explications relatives à l'affaire de la femme coupée en morceaux (affaire Billoir)." *Annales d'hygiène publique et de médecine légale*, series 2, vol. 49 (1878): 134–37.

Bergeron, Georges, Emile Delens, and Désiré L'Hôte. "De l'empoisonnement arsenical par des doses médiocres et réitérées de poison: Relation médico-légale de l'affaire Danval." *Annales d'hygiène publique et de médecine légale*, series 2, vol. 50 (1878): 72–144.

Bérigny, Adolphe. *Des médecins-légistes considérés dans leur rapport avec les cours de justice, à l'occasion de l'affaire Lafarge*. Paris: Baillière, 1840.

Bernard, Paul. *Des attentats à la pudeur sur les petites filles*. Paris: O. Doin, 1886.

Bertillon, Alphonse. *Identification anthropométrique: Instructions signalétiques*. Melun: Ministère de l'Intérieur, 1885.

Notice sur le fonctionnement du service d'identification de la préfecture de police. Paris: Masson, 1889.

Bertrand, Charles-Alexandre-Hippolyte-Amable. *Manuel médico-légal des poisons*. Paris: Croullebois, 1817.

Bézy, Paul. "Un cas de pseudo-coxalgie chez un enfant menteur." *Revue de l'hypnotisme* 7 (1893): 298–306.

Bichat, Marie-François-Xavier. *Recherches physiologiques sur la vie et la mort*. Paris: Brosson, year VIII [1799].

Billard, Charles. *Dissertation médico-légale sur la viabilité, considérée dans ses rapports avec la pathologie des nouveau-nés*. Paris: Didot le jeune, 1828. RB 649816, The Huntington Library, San Marino, CA.

Billod, Eugène. *Des maladies mentales et nerveuses*. Paris: Masson, 1882.

Boislambert, L. *Recherches sur les moyens de reconnaître la grossesse utérine*. Paris: Didot le jeune, 1823.

Boisseau, Edmond. *Des maladies simulées et des moyens de les reconnaître: Leçons professées au Val-de-Grâce.* Paris: Baillière, 1870.

Bonnet, Henry, and Jules Bulard. *Rapport médico-légal sur l'état mental de Charles-Joseph Jouy, inculpé d'attentat aux mœurs.* Nancy: Vve Raybois, 1868.

Borie, Léonard. *Catéchisme toxicologique ou essai sur l'empoisonnement.* Tulle: Drappeau, 1841.

Traité des maladies et des infirmités qui doivent dispenser du service militaire, lorsqu'elles ont résisté aux traitemens connus. Paris: Jourdain, 1818.

Bouchut, Eugène. *Traité des signes de la mort et des moyens de prévenir les enterrements prématurés.* Paris: Baillière, 1849.

Boudrie, Guillaume. *Etude sur les causes de la folie puerpérale.* Paris: A. Parent, 1878.

Bourdin, Claude Etienne. "Les enfants menteurs." *Annales médico-psychologiques,* series 6, vol. 9 (1883): 280–305, 374–86.

Bouton, René. *L'infanticide, étude morale et juridique.* Paris: Société d'édition scientifique, 1897.

Briand, Joseph. *Manuel complet de médecine légale.* Paris, 1821.

Briand, Joseph, and J.-X. Brosson. *Manuel complet de médecine légale,* 2nd ed. Brussels, 1830.

Manuel complet de médecine légale, 3rd ed. Paris: Chaudé, 1836.

Briand, Joseph, and Ernest Chaudé. *Manuel complet de médecine légale,* 4th ed. Paris: Bernard Neuhaus, 1846.

Manuel complet de médecine légale, 5th ed. Paris: Bernard Neuhaus, 1852.

Manuel complet de médecine légale, 6th ed. Paris: Baillière, 1858.

Manuel complet de médecine légale, 8th ed. Paris: Baillière, 1869.

Brillaud-Laujardière, Charles-Claude. *De l'infanticide: Etude médico-légale.* Paris: A. Durand, 1865.

Brochard, André Théodore. *La vérité sur les enfants trouvés.* Paris: Plon, 1876.

Brongniart, Jules-Théodore. *Etude sur la gravelle urinaire simulée et ses rapports chez la femme avec l'hystérie.* Paris: Doin, 1884.

Brouardel, Paul. "De la détermination de l'époque de la naissance et de la mort d'un nouveau-né, faite à l'aide de la présence des acares et des chenilles d'aglosses dans un cadavre momifié." *Annales d'hygiène publique et de médecine légale,* series 3, vol. 2 (1879): 153–58.

"De la réforme des expertises médico-légales." *Annales d'hygiène publique et de médecine légale,* series 3, vol. 11 (1884): 344–82, 442–60.

"Des causes d'erreur dans les expertises relatives aux attentats à la pudeur." *Annales d'hygiène publique et de médecine légale,* series 3, vol. 10 (1883): 60–71, 148–78.

Du service des autopsies médico-légales à la morgue. Paris: Asselin, 1878.

Etude médico-légale sur la combustion du corps humain. Paris: Baillière, 1878.

Infanticide. Paris: Baillière, 1897.

La mort et la mort subite. Paris: Baillière, 1895.

Sur un cas de modification d'un cadavre: Applications médico-légales. Paris: Masson, 1886.

Brouardel, Paul, and Louis-Désiré L'Hôte. "Relation médico-légale de l'affaire Pel: Accusation d'empoisonnement." *Annales d'hygiène publique et de médecine légale*, series 3, vol. 15 (1886): 12–41, 106–32.

Bulletin du tribunal révolutionnaire. 8 vols. Paris: Clément, 1793–95.

Bulletin général de thérapeutique médicale et chirurgicale. 189 vols. Paris, 1831–1939.

Bürgkly, Gustave-Adolphe. *De quelques maladies simulées, considérées sous le point de vue de la médecine légale militaire.* Montpellier, 1845.

Burnot-Laboulay, A.-F. *De la simulation confédérée au point de vue du recrutement.* Montpellier, 1844.

Le cadavre de la rue du Pré-Maudit: Arrestation de l'assassin. Paris: Aubert, 1880.

Calabre de Breuze, Elie. *Mémoire justificatif et consultation médico-légale, en faveur de Dominique François.* [Paris]: Didot jeune, 1814.

Cambrelin, François. "Les médecins sont-ils tenus d'obtempérer aux réquisitoires qui leur sont adressés par les officiers de police judiciaire quand il s'agit de la recherche des preuves d'un crime ou d'un délit?" *Annales d'hygiène publique et de médecine légale*, series 1, vol. 24 (1840): 407–20.

Capuron, Joseph. *La médecine légale, relative à l'art des accouchemens.* Paris: Croullebois, 1821.

Catrin, Louis-Ernest. "Le somnambulisme naturel: Observation de somnambulisme simulé." In *Mémoires et comptes-rendus de la Société des sciences médicales de Lyon*, vol. 29, 224–34. Lyon: Mégret, 1890.

Causes criminelles célèbres du XIXe siècle. 4 vols. Paris: Langlois fils, 1827–28.

Chabanon, Jules. *Etude sur la folie puerpérale.* Montpellier: J. Martel ainé, 1879.

Chaillé, Stanford Emerson. *Origin and Progress of Medical Jurisprudence, 1776–1876: A Centennial Address.* Philadelphia: Collins, 1876.

Chapuis, Adolphe. *Précis de toxicologie.* Paris: Baillière, 1882.

Chartier, Henri. *Examen médico-légal et autopsie des enfants nouveau-nés.* Lyon: Storck, 1890.

Chatagnier. *De l'infanticide dans ses rapports avec la loi, la morale, la médecine légale, et les mesures administratives.* Paris: Cosse, 1855.

Chaudé, Ernest. "Rapport sur les droits et les devoirs des médecins appelés en justice comme experts." *Annales d'hygiène publique et de médecine légale*, series 2, vol. 44 (1875): 373–401.

Chaussier, François. *Consultations médico-légales sur une accusation d'empoisonnement par le sublimé corrosif.* Paris: Didot jeune, 1811.

Mémoire médico-légal sur la viabilité de l'enfant naissant. Paris: Compère jeune, 1826.

Recueil de mémoires, consultations, et rapports sur divers objets de médecine légale. Paris: Barrois, 1824.

Chaussier, Hector. "Epilogue." In *Contre-poisons, ou Moyens reconnus les plus efficaces dans les différens cas d'empoisonnement,* 2nd ed., 1–2. Paris, 1818.

Chauveau, Adolphe. *Code pénal progressif: Commentaire sur la loi modificative du code pénal.* Paris, 1832.

Chevallier, Alphonse. "Sur la substitution du phosphore amorphe au phosphore ordinaire et indications des moyens à mettre en pratique pour faire cesser le danger d'empoisonnement et soustraire à la nécrose les ouvriers qui fabriquent les allumettes chimiques." *Annales d'hygiène publique et de médecine légale,* series 2, vol. 3 (1855): 124–34.

Chevallier, Alphonse, and Jules Louis Charles Boys de Loury. *Essais sur les moyens à mettre en usage dans le but de rendre moins fréquent le crime d'empoisonnement.* Paris: Locquin, 1835.

Chirac, D. *Considérations sur la combustion du corps humain.* Paris: Didot jeune, 1805.

"Circulaire relative au service des enfants trouvés et des aliénés." In *Législation charitable, ou Recueil des lois, arrêtés, décrets, ordonnances,* edited by Adolphe de Watteville, 2nd ed., 92–95, Paris: Cotillon, 1847.

Coche, A. E. *De l'opération médicale du recrutement, et des inspections générales.* Paris: Rouen, 1829.

Collongues, Léon. *Traité de dynamoscopie, ou Appréciation de la nature et de la gravité des maladies par l'auscultation des doigts.* Paris: Asselin, 1862.

Compte général de l'administration de la justice criminelle en France pendant l'année 1844. Paris: Imprimerie Royal, 1846.

Compte général de l'administration de la justice criminelle en France pendant l'année 1851. Paris: Imprimerie Royal, 1852.

Condamnation à mort et exécution d'une servante coupable de quarante-trois empoisonnements. Arras: Vve J. Degeorge, [1852].

Congrès scientifique de France, seconde session tenue à Poitiers, 1834, vol. 2. Poitiers: Saurin, 1835.

Corlieu, Auguste. *Considérations médico-légales sur la mélancolie.* Paris: Courrier médical, 1870.

Cortyl, Germain. *Etude sur la folie puerpérale.* Paris: A. Parent, 1877.

Coutagne, Henry. *Des réformes les plus urgentes des honoraires médico-légaux.* Lyon: Association typographique, 1890.

Notes sur la sodomie. Lyon: Henri Georg, 1880.

Précis de médecine légale. Lyon: A. Storck, 1896.

Crouzet, J. B. E. Edouard. *Dissertation sur l'infanticide. Paris: Didot le jeune,* 1830.

Cruppi, Jean. "A propos de l'affaire Bianchini: L'expertise médico-légale." *Le Figaro*, series 3, no. 63, March 10, 1899.

Dagonet, H. "L'expertise médico-légale en matière d'aliénation mentale." *Annales d'hygiène publique et de médecine légale*, series 3, vol. 31 (1894): 97–110.

Daille, J.-L. *Essai sur les maladies simulées*. Paris, 1818.

Dally, Eugène. "L'éducation est une génération psychique." *Annales médico-psychologiques*, series 6, vol. 9 (1883): 284–305.

Danvin, B. "De la valeur de l'acupuncture du cœur proposée par M. le docteur Plouviez comme moyen de distinguer la mort réelle de la mort apparente." *L'Union médicale*, no. 131, October 31, 1861.

"De quelques questions soulevées par l'affaire Danval (empoisonnement par l'arsenic)." *Gazette hebdomadaire de médecine et de chirurgie* 20 (May 17, 1878): 305–10.

Empoisonnement par la strychnine. Rapport médico-légal. Paris: Martinet, 1861.

Decaisne, Vandermissen, and Bellefroid. "Rapport médico-légal et observations sur un cas d'infanticide." *Annales d'hygiène publique et de médecine légale*, series 1, vol. 25 (1841): 428–42.

Dehaussy Robécourt, André-Barthelemy. *Dissertation sur une nouvelle exposition de la doctrine des maladies simulées*. Paris: Didot jeune, 1805.

Delaye, J.-B.-Jules. *Note médico-légale sur un cas d'asphyxie déterminée par l'enroulement du cordon ombilical autour du cou d'un enfant nouveau-né qui avait complètement respiré*. Toulouse: Douladoure, 1863.

Descoust, Paul, Adhémar Robert, and Jules Ogier. "Expériences sur la combustion des cadavres." *Annales d'hygiène publique et de médecine légale*, series 3, vol. 31 (1894): 533–53.

Desgranges, Jean-Baptiste. *Supplément au Mémoire sur les moyens de perfectionner l'établissement public formé à Lyon en faveur des personnes noyées, etc.* Lyon, 1790.

Desmartis, Télèphe P. *Médecine légale: Appréciation critique d'un rapport médico-légal ayant pour titre: Mémoire consultatif à l'occasion d'un fait d'infanticide; examen d'une cause de mort alléguée fréquemment dans les affaires de cette nature*. Paris: H. Plon, 1859.

Desmaze, Charles. *Histoire de la médecine légale en France: D'après les lois, registres et arrêts criminels*. Paris: Charpentier, 1880.

Devergie, Alphonse. "Des signes de la mort: Etude de leur cause, appréciation de leur valeur." *Annales d'hygiène publique et de médecine légale*, series 2, vol. 41 (1874): 380–405.

"Docimasie." In *Encyclographie des sciences médicales*, vol. 10, 225–43. Brussels: Etablissement Encyclographique, 1835.

L'expérimentation physiologique dans l'expertise médico-légale. Paris: Baillière, 1866.

"Inhumations précipitées: Rapport fait au nom du conseil de salubrité du département de la Seine." *Annales d'hygiène publique et de médecine légale,* series 2 vol. 27 (1867): 293–328.

Médecine légale, théorique et pratique. 2 vols. Brussels: Dumont, 1837.

Médecine légale, théorique et pratique, 2nd ed. 2 vols. Paris : Baillière, 1840.

Médecine légale, théorique et pratique, 3rd ed. 3 vols. Paris: Baillière, 1852.

"Mémoire sur la combustion humaine spontanée." *Annales d'hygiène publiqueet de médecine légale,* series 1, vol. 46 (1851): 383–432.

"La morgue de Paris." *Annales d'hygiène publique et de médecine légale,* series 2, vol. 49 (1878): 49–79.

"Mort." In *Dictionnaire de médecine et de chirurgie pratiques,* edited by Gabriel Andral, Louis Jacques Bégin, Philippe Frédéric Blandin, et al., vol. 11, 544. Paris: Méquignon-Marvis, 1834.

Dieu, Sosthène. *Traité de matière médicale et de thérapeutique.* Paris: Masson, 1853.

Drioux, Joseph. *Etude sur les expertises médico-légales et l'instruction criminelle d'après les projets du Code d'instruction criminelle et les législations étrangères.* Paris: Pichon, 1886.

Dubreuilh, Charles. "De la suppression des tours au double point de vue de la morale et de la société." In *Congrès médical de France. 3e session tenue à Bordeaux du lundi 2 octobre au samedi 7 octobre 1865,* 545–73. Paris: Baillière, 1866.

Dufestel, Louis. *Des maladies simulées chez les enfants.* Paris, 1888.

Dufour, Frédéric. *La constatation des décès en France au point de vue des inhumations prématurées et des morts criminelles.* Poitiers: Blais et Roy, 1899.

Dufour, and Raige. *Réponse à un libelle diffamatoire de M. Calabre Debreuze.* n.p.: [1815].

Dumur, Albert. *Des dents: Leur importance et signification dans les questions médico-légales.* Lyon: Pastel, 1882.

Duponchel, Emile. *Traité de médecine légale militaire.* Paris: Doin, 1890.

Dupressoir, Charles. *Drames judiciaires. Scènes correctionnelles. Causes célèbres de tous les peuples. Première série.* Paris: Librairie ethnographique, 1849.

Dupuytren, Guillaume. "Combustion humaine spontanée." In *Dictionnaire de médecine et de chirurgie pratiques,* edited by Gabriel Andral, Louis Jacques Bégin, Philippe Frédéric Blandin, et. al., vol. 5, 367–82. Paris: Méquignon-Marvis, 1830.

Duriau, Frédéric. *Etude clinique et médico-légale sur l'empoisonnement par la strychnine.* Paris: Baillière, 1862.

Duvergier, Jean-Baptiste. *Collection complète des lois, décrets, ordonnances, règlemens avis du Conseil d'état.* 158 vols. Paris, 1824–1949.

"Eloge de M. Orfila." *Gazette médicale de Paris,* series 3, vol. 8 (1853): 792–98.

"Empoisonnement par l'arsenic administré à petites doses." *Annales d'hygiène publique et de médecine légale*, series 1, vol. 37 (1847): 121–58.

Encyclopédie des sciences médicales ou traité général, méthodique et complet des diverses branches de l'art de guérir – Deuxième division, Médecine légale – Jurisprudence Médicale. Paris: Encyclopédie, 1835.

Espagne, Adelphe. *De l'incontinence d'urine, spécialement chez l'homme, dans ses rapports avec l'intégrité des fonctions sexuelles, de sa simulation, de sa curabilité par la ligature du prépuce*. Montpellier: Boehm, 1870.

L'expérience: Journal de médecine et de chirurgie. 14 vols. Paris, 1837–44.

"Expériences de M. Orfila, sur l'empoisonnement par l'arsenic et l'émétique." *La Phalange* 1, no. 33, November 15, 1840.

Fabre, François. *Bibliothèque du médecin-praticien, ou résumé général de tous les ouvrages de clinique médicale et chirurgicale*. Paris: Baillière, 1851.

Le Figaro. Paris, 1826–.

Flandin, and Danger. *De l'arsenic, suivi d'une instruction propre à servir de guide aux experts dans les cas d'empoisonnement*. Paris: Bachelier, 1841.

Fleury, Louis. *Cours d'hygiène, fait à la Faculté de médecine de Paris*. Paris: Asselin, 1863.

Florence, Albert. "Du sperme et des taches de sperme en médecine légale." *Archives d'anthropologie criminelle* 10 (1895): 417–34, 520–43; 11 (1896): 37–46, 146–63, 249–63.

Fodéré, François-Emmanuel. *Les lois éclairées par les sciences physiques, ou Traité de médecine-légale et d'hygiène publique*. Paris: Croullebois, year 7.

Traité de médecine légale et d'hygiène, publique ou de police de santé. 6 vols. Paris: Mame, 1813.

Fouquier, Armand. *Causes célèbres de tous les peuples*. 8 vols. Paris: Lebrun, 1858–67.

Fournier, Alfred. "Simulations d'attentats vénériens sur de jeunes enfants." *Annales d'hygiène publique et de médecine légale*, series 3, vol. 4 (1880): 498–519.

Fratini, Jean-Jacques. *Essai médico-légal sur le recrutement de l'armée*. Montpellier, 1844.

Gallard, T. *De l'empoisonnement par la strychnine*. Paris: Baillière, 1865.

"Empoisonnement par le phosphore." *L'Union médicale* 12, no. 130, October 29, 1861.

Gannal, Félix. *Mort réelle et mort apparente*. Paris: Coccoz, 1868.

Garcia-Rijo, Mariano. *Contribution à l'étude de la folie puerpérale*. Paris: A. Parent, 1879.

Garnier, Paul. "La simulation de la folie et la loi sur la relegation." *Annales d'hygiène publique et de médecine légale*, series 3, vol. 19 (1888): 97–119.

Gaubert, B. *Le péril des inhumations précipitées en France: Société des chambres mortuaires d'attente de la ville de Paris*. Paris: Chevalier-Maresq, 1895.

Gavrelle, N. A. *Recherches sur les combustions humaines spontanées.* Paris: Didot le jeune, 1827.

Gayet, Félix-Pierre-Auguste. *Des maladies simulées et dissimulées, considérées au point de vue du service militaire.* Montpellier, 1848.

Gazette des hôpitaux civils et militaires (La lancette française). Paris: Gazette des hôpitaux, 1828–1972.

Gazette des tribunaux: Journal de jurisprudence et des débats judiciaires. Paris: 1825–1955.

Gazette hebdomadaire de médecine et de chirurgie. Paris: Masson, 1854–1902.

Gazette médicale de Paris. Paris: 1830–1916.

Gentilhomme, Prosper. *Contribution à l'histoire de la simulation dans le service militaire.* Paris, 1884.

Geoffroy de Villeneuve, René-Claude. "Ictère." In *Dictionnaire des sciences médicales*, edited by Adelon, Alard, Alibert, et al. vol. 23, 386–461. Paris: Panckoucke, 1818.

Giraud, Henri. *Etude sur les blessures simulées dans l'industrie.* Lille: L. Quarré, 1895.

Grissole, A. *Traité élémentaire et pratique de pathologie interne*, 8th ed. Paris: Masson, 1862.

Gromier, Frantz. *Essai sur l'imbécillité et la folie simulée par l'imbécile.* Paris: Parent, 1872.

Guillot, Adolphe. *Paris qui souffre: La basse geôle du Grand-Châtelet et les morgues modernes.* Paris: Roquette, 1887.

Hamel. *Des enfants trouvés, et du danger de la suppression des tours dans la ville de Paris.* Paris: Baillière, 1838.

A Handbook for Visitors to Paris, 2nd ed. London: John Murray, 1866.

Haracque, Eugène. *Considérations médico-légales sur la viabilité du fœtus.* Paris: Didot jeune, 1820. RB 649970, The Huntington Library, San Marino, CA.

Hatterer, L. A. *Considérations médico-légales sur les maladies simulées et la manière de les reconnaître.* Strasbourg, 1826.

Hecquet, Anatole. *Mémoire sur l'empoisonnement par les allumettes chimiques au phosphore blanc, nécessité d'en interdire l'usage et de les remplacer par les allumettes chimiques au phosphore rouge ou amorphe.* Abbeville: Briez, 1861.

Hélie, Faustin. *Théorie du code pénal: Appendice contenant le commentaire de la loi du 13 mai 1863 modificative du code pénal.* Paris: Cosse et Marchal, 1863.

Horteloup, M. E. *Du droit de réquisition des médecins-experts par la justice.* Paris: Baillière, 1890.

Hugounenq, Louis. *Traité des poisons.* Paris: Masson, 1891.

Huguet, Joseph. *Recherches sur les maladies simulées et mutilations volontaires observées de 1859 à 1896.* Paris: H. Charles-Lavauzelle, 1896.

Instruction pour service de guide aux officiers de santé dans l'appréciation des infirmités ou des maladies qui rendent impropre au service militaire… Extrait du journal militaire officiel, 2nd ed. Paris: J. Dumaine, 1865.

Instruction pour servir de guide aux officiers de santé dans l'appréciation des infirmités ou maladies qui rendent impropre au service militaire, Paris 14 novembre 1845. Paris, 1846.

Jabely, Albert. *De l'empoisonnement par le phosphore*. Paris: Parent, 1864.

Jacquier, Charles François. *Des preuves et de la recherche de la paternité naturelle: Etude sur l'article 340 du Code Napoléon*. Grenoble: Baratier frères and Dardelet, 1874.

James, C. "Empoisonnement de Soufflard." *L'expérience: Journal de médecine et de chirurgie*, vol. 3, no. 93, April 11, 1839 (Paris, 1839), 227–34.

Josat, Jules-Antoine. *De la mort et de ses caractères: Nécessité d'une révision de la législation des décès pour prévenir les inhumations et les délaissements anticipés*. Paris: Baillière, 1854.

Journal de médecine et de chirurgie pratiques. 159 vols. Paris: Schneider et Langrand, 1830–1988.

Journal des débats et des décrets. Paris: Baudoin, 1789–1805.

Journal général de médecine, de chirurgie et de pharmacie. 97 vols. Paris: Croullebois, 1802–30.

Journal militaire, année 1828. Paris: Anselin, 1828.

Judas, Victor Romuald. *Essai sur les maladies simulées et les moyens de reconnaître la fraude*. Montpellier, 1827.

Julia de Fontenelle, Jean-Sébastien-Eugène. *Recherches médico-légales sur l'incertitude des signes de la mort: Les dangers des inhumations précipitées*. Paris: Rouvier, 1834.

Kühnholz, Henri-Marcel. *Des caractères et des conditions de la viabilité*. Montpellier, 1835.

Laborde, Jean-Baptiste-Vincent. "Application de la méthode des tractions rythmées de la langue." *Bulletin de l'Académie de médecine*, series 3, vol. 42, no. 33 (1899): 273–88.

Le traitement physiologique de la mort: Les tractions rythmées de la langue, moyen rationnel et puissant de ranimer la fonction respiratoire et la vie, détermination expérimentale du mode d'action, ou mécanisme du procédé. Paris: Alcan, 1894.

Lacassagne, Alexandre. *L'affaire du Père Bérard*. Lyon: Storck, 1890.

"De la mensuration des différentes parties du corps dans les cas de dépeçage criminel." *Archives d'anthropologie criminelle* 3 (1888): 158–63.

"Du dépeçage criminel." *Archives d'anthropologie criminelle* 3 (1888): 229–55.

Les médecins-experts devant les tribunaux et les honoraires des médecins d'après le décret du 21 novembre 1893. Lyon: Storck, 1894.

Les médecins experts et les erreurs judicaires. Lyon: Storck, 1897.

"Pédérastie." In *Dictionnaire encyclopédique des sciences médicales*, edited by André Archambault, series 2, vol. 22, 239–597. Paris: Masson, 1886.

Précis de médecine judiciaire. Paris, 1886.

"Vacher l'éventreur." *Archives d'anthropologie criminelle, de criminologie et de psychologie normale* 13 (1898): 632–95.

Lailler, Maurice, and Henri Vonoven. *Les erreurs judiciaires et leurs causes.* Paris: Pédone, 1897.

Lair, Aimé. *Essai sur les combustions humaines produites par un long abus des liqueurs spiritueuses.* Paris: Gabon, 1800.

Larrey, Baron Dominique Jean. *Mémoires de chirurgie militaire, et campagnes de D. J. Larrey.* Paris: Smith, 1817.

Lasègue, Charles. "Les hystériques, leur perversité, leurs mensonges." *Annales médico-psychologiques*, series 6, vol. 6 (1881): 111–18.

Lasègue, Charles, Paul Brouardel, and Auguste Alexandre Motet, "Affaire Menesclou." *Annales d'hygiène publique et de médecine légale*, series 3, no. 4 (1880): 440.

Laugier, Maurice. "Simulées (maladies)." In *Nouveau dictionnaire de médecine et de chirurgie pratiques*, edited by Sigismond Jaccoud, vol. 33, 186–246. Paris: Baillière, 1882.

Laurent, Armand. *Etude médico-légale sur la simulation de la folie: Considérations cliniques et pratiques à l'usage des médecins experts, des magistrats et des jurisconsultes.* Paris: Victor Masson et fils, 1866.

Laurillard-Fallot, Salomon-Louis. *De la simulation et de la dissimulation des maladies dans leurs rapports avec le service militaire.* Brussels: Tircher, 1836.

Mémorial de l'expert dans la visite sanitaire des hommes de guerre. Brussels, 1837.

Le Cat, Claude-Nicolas. *Mémoire posthume sur les incendies spontanés de l'économie animale.* Paris: Migneret, 1813.

Lecieux, A. *Considérations médico-légales sur l'infanticide.* Paris: Didot jeune, 1811.

Lecieux, A., Gabriel Laisné, Athanase Renard, and J.-J.-Germain Rieux. *Médecine légale, ou Considérations sur l'infanticide, sur la manière de procéder à l'ouverture des cadavres, spécialement dans les cas de visites judiciaires, sur les érosions et perforations spontanées de l'estomac et sur l'ecchymose, la sugillation, la contusion, la meurtrissure.* Paris: Baillière, 1819.

Leclerc. *Essai médico-légal sur l'empoisonnement et sur les moyens que l'on doit employer pour le constater.* Paris: Levrault, year XI [1803].

Lecourt, Ernest Alcide. *Etude médico-légale sur la combustion du corps humain.* Paris: Imprimerie générale de la presse, 1881.

Legludic, Henri. *Notes et observations de médecine légale: Attentats aux mœurs.* Paris: G. Masson et Cie, 1896.

Legrand du Saulle, Henri. *Les hystériques: Etat physique et mental, actes insolites, délictueux et criminels*, 2nd ed. Paris: Baillière, 1883.

Traité de médecine légale et de jurisprudence médicale. Paris: Delahaye, 1874.

Traité de médecine légale, de jurisprudence médicale et de toxicologie, 2nd ed. Paris: Delahaye, 1886.

Létier, J.-B. *Dissertation sur les maladies simulées et sur les moyens de les découvrir*. Paris, 1808.

La Liberté. Paris, 1865–1940.

Locard, Edmond. *L'enquête criminelle et les méthodes scientifiques*. Paris: Flammarion, 1920.

Lop, Pierre-André. "Attentats à la pudeur commis par des femmes sur des petits garçons." *Archives de l'anthropologie criminelle et des sciences pénales* 10 (1895): 37–42.

Lucchini, Emile. *De la responsabilité de la femme pendant la grossesse, au point de vue médico-légal*. Montpellier: Firmin and Montane, 1899.

Lutaud, Auguste. *Manuel de médecine légale*, 5th ed. Paris: Steinheil, 1892.

Lyon médical: Gazette médicale et journal de médecine réunis. 253 vols. Lyon, 1869–1985.

Magen, Adolphe. "Les poisons connus des anciens et l'empoisonnement au XIXe siècle." *Recueil des travaux de la société d'agriculture, sciences et arts d'Agen*. vol. 4, 295–318. Agen: Noubel, [1848, misprinted as 1842].

Mahon, Paul-Augustin-Olivier. *Médecine légale et police médicale*. Paris: Buisson, 1801.

Médecine légale et police médicale. 3 vols. Paris: Bertrand, 1807.

Maillard, Firmin. *Recherches historiques et critiques sur la morgue*. Paris: Delahays, 1860.

Marc, Charles-Chrétien-Henri. "Déception." In *Dictionnaire de médecine*, edited by Adelon, Alard, Alibert, et al., vol. 6, 370–83. Paris: Béchet jeune, 1823.

"Docimasie pulmonaire." In *Dictionnaire des sciences médicales*, edited by Adelon, Alard, Alibert, et al., vol. 10, 62–100. Paris: Panckoucke, 1810.

"Grossesse." In *Dictionnaire des sciences médicales*, edited by Adelon, Alard, Alibert, et al., vol. 19, 370–546. Paris: Panckoucke, 1817.

"Inhumations." In *Dictionnaire des sciences médicales*, vol. 8, 307–18. Brussels: Dewaet, 1829.

"Introduction." *Annales d'hygiène publique et de médecine légale*, series 1, vol. 1 (1829): ix–xxxix.

"Matériaux pour l'histoire médico-légale de l'aliénation mentale." *Annales d'hygiène publique et de médecine légale*, series 1, vol. 2 (1829): 353–405.

"Politique (médecine)." In *Dictionnaire de médecine*, vol. 17, 309–17. Paris, 1827.

Marcé, Louis Victor. "Etudes sur les causes de la folie puerpérale." *Annales médico-psychologiques*, series 3, vol. 3 (1857): 562–84.

Traité de la folie des femmes enceintes, des nouvelles accouchées et des nourrices, et des considérations médico-légales qui se rattachent à ce sujet. Paris: Baillière, 1858. RB 649110, Huntington Library, San Marino, CA.

Traité pratique des maladies mentales. Paris: Baillière, 1862.

Martin, Pierre Léon Jacques. *Considérations sur la folie puerpérale.* Paris: A. Parent, 1872.

Martino, Ernest. *Applications médico-légales de l'anesthésie.* Strasbourg, 1868.

Matthyssens, François Jean. *Précis élémentaire de médecine légale extrait des meilleurs ouvrages.* 2 vols. Anvers: Heirstraeten, 1837.

Maze. *"L'Egalité devant la mort," signes de la mort et moyens de prévenir les inhumations précipitées.* Paris: Noblet et fils, 1892.

Mégnin, J. P. *La faune des cadavres: Application de l'entomologie à la médecine légale.* Paris: Masson, Gauthier-Villars et Fils, 1894.

Merlin, Philippe Antoine. "Grossesse." In *Répertoire universel et raisonné de jurisprudence,* 3rd ed., vol. 5, 598–603. Paris: Garnery, 1808.

Le messager des chambres: Journal des villes et des campagnes. Paris, 1828–46.

Metzger, D. *La vivisection, ses dangers, et ses crimes.* Paris: Siège social, 1906.

Meyrignac, Henri-Paul de. *De l'empoisonnement par la strychnine.* Paris: Rignoux, 1859.

Mialhe. "Rapport sur un cas d'empoisonnement par le phosphore." *Annales d'hygiène publique et de médecine légale,* series 2, vol. 31 (1869): 134–38.

Ministère de l'intérieur. *Travaux de la Commission des enfants trouvés instituée le 22 août 1849 par arrêté du Ministre de l'intérieur,* vol. 2, *Documents sur les enfants trouvés.* Paris: Imprimerie nationale, 1850.

Monfalcon, J. B. "Infanticide." In *Dictionnaire des sciences médicales,* edited by Adelon, Alard, Alibert, et al., vol. 24, 412–17. Paris: Panckoucke, 1818.

"Inhumations." In *Dictionnaire des sciences médicales,* edited by Adelon, Alard, Alibert, et al., vol. 25, 171–72, 179–80, 187–88. Paris: Panckoucke, 1818.

Morel, Bénédict-Augustin. "De l'éthérisation dans la folie au point de vue de diagnostic et de la médecine légale." *Archives générales de médecine,* February 1854.

Traité des dégénérescences physiques, intellectuelles et morales de l'espèce humaine. Paris: Baillière, 1857.

Moricheau-Beaupré, Pierre-Jean. *Mémoire sur le choix des hommes propres au service militaire de l'armée de terre, et sur leur visite devant les conseils de révision.* Paris: Anselin and Pochard, 1820.

Motet, Auguste. *Les faux témoignages des enfants devant la justice.* Paris: Baillière, 1887.

Murat, Jean-Baptiste-Arnaud. *Tableau synoptique d'une nosologie légale fondée sur le code social.* Paris: Méquignon l'aîné, 1803.

Necker, Suzanne. *Des inhumations précipitées*. Paris: Impr. royale, 1790.

Négrier. "Recherches médico-légales sur la longueur et la résistance du cordon ombilical au terme de la gestation." *Annales d'hygiène publique et de médecine légale*, series 1, vol. 25 (1841): 126–40.

"Une nouvelle Brinvilliers: Hélène Jégado (1851)." In *Causes célèbres de tous les peuples*, vol. 7, no. 320, 1–32. Paris: Lebrun, 1865–67.

Nouvelle encyclographie des sciences médicales. Brussels: Grégoir, 1847.

Nypels, Jean-Servais-Guillaume. *Le droit pénal français progressif et comparé: Code pénal de 1810*. Paris: Durand, 1864.

Olivaud, Emmanuel-Joseph. *De l'infanticide et des moyens que l'on emploie pour le constater*. Paris: Gabon, 1802.

Ollivier (d'Angers). "Deuxième mémoire sur l'infanticide." *Annales d'hygiène publique et de médecine légale*, series 1, vol. 27 (1842): 329–59.

"Mémoire médico-légal sur l'infanticide." *Annales d'hygiène publique et de médecine légale*, series 1, vol. 16 (1836): 328–56.

"Mémoire sur les maladies simulées." *Annales d'hygiène publique et de médecine légale*, series 1, vol. 25 (1841): 100–26.

Orfila, Mathieu [Mateu] Joseph Bonaventure. "Affaire d'empoisonnement porté devant la Cour d'assises du département de l'Aube, le 27 août 1824." *Gazette de santé*, March 5, 1825, vol. 52, no. 7 (1825): 49–53.

"Cadavre." In *Dictionnaire de médecine*, edited by Adelon, Alard, Alibert, et al., vol. 4, 9–29. Paris: Béchet jeune, 1822.

Leçons de médecine légale. 2 vols. Paris: Béchet jeune, 1823.

Leçons de médecine légale, 2nd ed. 3 vols. Paris: Béchet jeune, 1828.

"Mémoire sur la suspension, lu à l'Académie royale de médecine, le 6 octobre 1840." *Mémoires de l'Académie royale de médecine*, 234–76. Paris: Baillière, 1841.

Mémoires sur plusieurs questions médico-légales. Paris: Béchet jeune, 1839.

"Quelques réflexions critiques sur les moyens de conclure en médecine légale, et sur la prétendue localisation des poisons." *Annales d'hygiène publique et de médecine légale*, series 1, vol. 31 (1844): 430–42.

Secours à donner aux personnes empoisonnées ou asphyxiées, suivis des moyens propres à reconnaître les poisons, et les vins frelatés, et à distinguer la mort réelle de la mort apparente. Paris: Feugueray, 1818.

Traité de médecine légale, 3rd ed. 4 vols. Paris: Béchet jeune, 1836.

Traité des poisons tirés des règnes minéral, végétal et animal, ou, Toxicologie générale. 2 vols. Paris: Crochard, 1814–15.

Orfila, Mathieu [Mateu] J. B., and Octave Lesueur. *Traité des exhumations juridiques*. Paris: Béchet jeune, 1831.

Paillard de Villeneuve, Adolphe-Victor. "Rapport." In *Dictionnaire de médecine usuelle à l'usage des gens du monde*, vol. 9, 722–23. Paris: Didier, 1849.

Parant, V. "Note sur la transformation de la folie simulée en folie véritable." *Annales médico-psychologiques*, series 7, vol. 1 (1885): 19–27.

Parrot, Jules. *De la mort apparente.* Paris: Delahaye, 1860.

Pasquier, Victor. *De la priorité entre MM. Orfila et Stas, des moyens de déceler la nicotine dans les empoisonnements.* Brussels: Mortier, 1853.

Paulier, Armand B., and Frédéric Hétet, *Traité élémentaire de médecine légale, de jurisprudence médicale, et de la toxicologie,* part 1. Paris: Doin, 1881.

Pellassy des Fayolles, Nestor-Joseph. *Nouvelle question de médecine légale: L'introduction d'un placenta et de son cordon dans les parties génitales de la femme est-elle possible hors le temps de l'accouchement? Et peut-elle, dans certains cas, faire supposer un accouchement réel?* Paris, 1833.

Nouvelle question de médecine légale: L'introduction d'un placenta et de son cordon dans les parties génitales de la femme est-elle possible hors le temps de l'accouchement? Et peut-elle dans certains cas faire supposer un accouchement réel? Paris: J. Ruvier et E. Lebouvier, 1838.

Pénard, Louis. *De l'intervention du médecin légiste dans les questions d'attentats aux moeurs.* Paris: Baillière, 1860.

Percy, Pierre-François, and Charles Nicolas Laurent. "Simulation des maladies." In *Dictionnaire des sciences médicales,* edited by Adelon, Alard, Alibert, et al., vol. 51, 319–66. Paris: Panckoucke, 1819.

Pereyra, Emile. *Quelques réflexions sur l'insuffisance du jury en matière de médecine légale.* Bordeaux: Faye, 1842.

La Phalange: Journal de la science sociale. 9 vols. Paris: La Phalange, 1836–49.

Poggiale. "Empoisonnement par le phosphore, par M. Réveil (Rapport de M. Poggiale)." *Bulletin de l'Académie de médecine* 24 (Paris: Baillière, 1858-59): 1229–49.

Poilroux, Jacques. *Traité de médecine légale criminelle.* Paris: Levrault, 1834.

La presse illustrée. Paris: 1867–84.

Procès complet d'Edme-Samuel Castaing, docteur en médecine. Paris: Pillet aîné, 1823.

Procès de Madame Lafarge. Paris: Pagnerre, 1840.

Procès du comte et de la comtesse de Bocarmé devant la cour. Mons: Leroux, 1851.

Le progrès médical: Journal de médecine, de chirurgie et de pharmacie. Paris: Librairie A. Duval. 1873–1982.

Quelques idées sur l'infanticide. Montpellier: imp. de l'Avignon, 1823.

Raige-Delorme, Jacques. *Considérations médico-légales sur l'empoisonnement par les substances corrosives.* Paris, 1819.

Rambosson, J. "Les inhumations précipitées et les moyens de les prévenir." *Le Correspondant* 80. Paris: Douniol, 1869.

"Rapport sur plusieurs Mémoires concernant du procédé de Marsh, dans les recherches de médecine légale." *Comptes-rendus des séances de l'Académie des sciences de Paris,* vol. 12, 1076–1109. Paris: Gauthier-Villars, 1841.

Raspail, François-Vincent. *Accusation d'empoisonnement par l'arsenic. Mémoire à consulter, à l'appui du pourvoi en Cassation de Dame Marie Cappelle.* Paris: Gazette des hôpitaux, 1840.

Nouveau système de chimie organique, fondé sur des méthodes nouvelles d'observation. Paris: Baillière, 1833.

Revue complémentaire des sciences appliquées à la médecine et pharmacie, à l'agriculture, aux arts et à l'industrie. 4 vols. Paris, 1858.

Rassier, François-Maurice. *De la valeur du témoignage des enfants en justice.* Lyon: Storck, 1892.

Ravoux, Louis. *Du dépeçage criminel au point de vue anthropologique et médico-judiciaire.* Lyon: Storck, 1888.

Recueil général des lois et des arrêts. 156 vols. Paris, 1791–1950.

Regnault, Victor. *Rapport sur plusieurs mémoires concernant l'emploi du procédé de Marsh dans les recherches de médecine légale.* [Paris]: Bachelier, [1841].

Reibel, Lucien-Ernest. *De la folie puerpérale.* Paris: A. Parent, 1876.

Reille, Paul. "Responsabilité des experts: Affaire Méloche." *Annales d'hygiène publique et de médecine légale,* series 3, vol. 40 (1898): 41–70.

Ribes, Jean-Eugène. *De la perversion morale chez les femmes enceintes, considérée principalement au point de vue médico-légal.* Strasbourg: Simon, 1866.

Rivière, H. F. *Lois usuelles, décrets, ordonnances, avis du conseil d'état, et législation coloniale,* 27th ed. Paris: Chevalier-Marescq, 1899.

Rochard, Jules Eugène. *Traité d'hygiène publique et privée.* Paris: Doin, 1897.

Rocher, Georges. *Etude sur la folie puerpérale.* Paris: A. Parent, 1877.

Roger, Henri. "Rapport général sur les prix décernés en 1874 à l'Académie de médecine." *L'Union médicale,* no. 56, May 13, 1875.

Rognetta, Francesco. "Procès de Dijon. Consultation médico-légale sur un cas de mort attribué à l'empoisonnement par l'arsenic." In *Nouvelle méthode de traitement de l'empoisonnement par l'arsenic, et documens médico-légaux sur cet empoisonnement,* 1-99. Paris: Gardenbas, 1840.

Rognetta, Francesco, and François-Vincent Raspail. *Nouvelle méthode de traitement de l'empoisonnement par l'arsenic.* Paris: Gardenbas, 1840.

Salle, Eusèbe de. "Médecine légale." In *Encyclopédie des sciences médicales ou traité général, méthodique et complet des diverses branches de l'art de guérir – Deuxième division, Médecine légale – Jurisprudence Médicale,* 1–291. Paris: Encyclopédie, 1835.

Traité de médecine légale et jurisprudence médicale, comprenant les lois, ordonnances, réglements et décisions diverses de l'autorité. Paris: Gautret, 1838.

Schützenberger, Charles. *Etudes pathologiques et cliniques.* Paris: Masson, 1879.

Sédillot, Charles. *Manuel complet de médecine légale, considérée dans ses rapports avec la législation actuelle.* Paris: Crochard, 1830.

Seurre-Bousquet, J.-B. *Considérations générales sur l'empoisonnement par l'acide arsénieux*. Paris: Didot le jeune, 1829.

Séverin-Caussé, and A. Chevallier fils. "Considérations générales sur l'empoisonnement par le phosphore, les pâtes phosphorées et les allumettes chimiques." *Annales d'hygiène publique et de médecine légale*, series 2, vol. 3 (1855): 134–71.

Sisteray, Prosper. *Simulation de l'épilepsie aux points de vue de la pratique et de la médecine légale*. Paris: Parent, 1867.

Société de médecine légale de France. "Organisation de la médecine légale en France." *Annales d'hygiène publique et de médecine légale*, series 3, vol. 11 (1884): 157–88.

"La réforme des expertises médico-légales." *Bulletin de la Société de la médecine légale de France* 16, part 1, 20–40. Clermont: Daix, 1899.

Société médico-psychologique. "Du mensonge chez les enfants." *Annales médico-psychologiques*, series 6, vol. 9 (1883): 133–37, 141, 280–84.

"L'éducation est une génération psychique." *Annales médico-psychologiques*, series 6, vol. 9 (1883): 284–305.

"Médecine légale. Attentat aux mœurs. Condamnation, appel, expertise médicale et prononcé du jugement." *Annales médico-psychologiques* 1 (1843): 289–98.

Le Sténographe Parisien: Affaire Castaing: Accusation d'empoisonnement. Paris, 1823.

"Sur les morts apparentes et sur les moyens de prévenir les enterrements prématurés." *Annales d'hygiène publique et de médecine légale*, series 1, vol. 40 (1848): 78–110.

Tacheron, C.-F. *De la vérification légale des décès dans la ville de Paris, et de la nécessité d'apporter dans ce service médical plus de surveillance*. Paris: Gobin, 1830.

Tarde, Gabriel. "Les actes du Congrès de Rome." *Archives d'anthropologie criminelle* 3 (1888): 66–80.

Tardieu, Ambroise. "Etude hygiénique et médico-légale sur la fabrication et l'emploi des allumettes chimiques: Rapport fait au comité consultatif d'hygiène publique." *Annales d'hygiène publique et de médecine légale*, series 2, vol. 6 (1856): 5–54.

Etude médico-légale et clinique sur l'empoisonnement. Paris: Baillière, 1867.

Etude médico-légale sur la folie. Paris: Baillière, 1872.

Etude médico-légale sur la pendaison, la strangulation, et la suffocation, 2nd ed. Paris: Baillière, 1879.

Etude médico-légale sur l'infanticide. Paris: Baillière, 1868.

Etude médico-légale sur les attentats aux moeurs, 2nd ed. Paris: Baillière, 1858.

Etude médico-légale sur les attentats aux moeurs, 4th ed. Paris: Baillière, 1862.

Etude médico-légale sur les attentats aux moeurs, 5th ed. Paris: Baillière, 1865.

Etude médico-légale sur les attentats aux moeurs, 6th ed. Paris: Baillière, 1873.

Etude médico-légale sur les attentats aux moeurs, 7th ed. Paris: Baillière, 1878.

"Médecine légale théorique et pratique, par Alph. Devergie." *Annales d'hygiène publique et de médecine légale,* series 1, vol. 27 (1842): 225–32.

"Mémoire sur la mort par suffocation." *Annales d'hygiène publique et de médecine légale,* series 2, vol. 4 (1855): 371–441.

Mémoire sur l'empoisonnement par la strychnine, contenant la relation médico-légale complète de l'affaire Palmer. Paris: Baillière, 1857.

"La morgue: Les morts violentes, crimes et suicides." *Paris Guide,* part 2, *La vie,* 1996–2005. Paris: Lacroix, 1867.

"Nouvelles études médico-légales sur l'avortement." *Annales d'hygiène publique et de médecine légale,* series 2, vol. 9 (1858): 156–99.

Tardieu, Ambroise, P. Lorain, and Zacharie Roussin. *Empoisonnement par la strychnine, l'arsenic et les sels de cuivre.* Paris: Baillière, 1865.

Tardieu, Ambroise, and X. Rota. *Relation médico-légale de l'assassinat de la comtesse de Goerliltz, accompagnée de notes et réflexions pour servir à l'histoire de la combustion humaine spontanée.* Paris: Baillière, 1851.

Tardieu, Ambroise, and Zacharie Roussin. *Etude médico-légale et clinique sur l'empoisonnement.* Paris: Baillière, 1867.

"Relation médico-légale de l'affaire Couty de la Pommerais. Empoisonnement par la digitaline." *Annales d'hygiène publique et de médecine légale,* series 2, vol. 22 (1864): 80–141.

Tarneau, Jean-Léo. *Des maladies simulées des plus communes au point de vue du recrutement.* Montpellier, 1855.

Tarnier, Stéphane, and Pierre Budin. *Traité de l'art des accouchements.* Paris: Steinheil, 1888.

Tartra, A. E. *Traité de l'empoisonnement par l'acide nitrique.* Paris: Méquignon, 1802.

Taufflieb, H. M. E. "De la strangulation des nouveau-nés par le cordon ombilical." *Annales d'hygiène publique et de médecine légale,* series 1, vol. 14 (1835): 340–49.

Examen médico-légal des maladies simulées, dissimulées et imputées. Strasbourg, 1835.

Le Temps. Paris, 1861–1942.

Tessier, T. *Essai de médecine légale sur la grossesse, et tout ce qui en dépend.* Montpellier: Coucourdan, 1802. RB 648711d, The Huntington Library, San Marino, CA.

Thoinot, Léon-Henri. *Attentats aux moeurs et perversions du sens génital: Leçons professées à la Faculté de médecine.* Paris: Doin, 1898.

Touchard, Prosper. *Aperçu général des précautions prises en France avant l'inhumation des citoyens morts.* Tours: Placé, 1833.

Toulmouche, Adolphe. "Des attentats à la pudeur." *Annales d'hygiène publique et de médecine légale,* series 2, vol. 6 (1856): 100–145.

"Etudes sur l'infanticide et la grossesse cachée ou simulée." *Annales d'hygiène publique et de médecine légale,* series 2, vol. 16 (1862): 264–400; vol. 18 (1862): 157–426.

Etudes sur l'infanticide et la grossesse cachée ou simulée. Paris: Baillière, 1862.

Toulouse, Edouard. *Le rapport des médecins experts sur Vacher.* Clermont: Daix frères, 1898.

Tourdes, Gabriel. "Anesthésie (méd. légale)." In *Dictionnaire encyclopédique des sciences médicales.* vol. 4, 499–517. Paris: Masson, 1866.

"Combustion humaine spontanée." In *Dictionnaire encyclopédique des sciences médicales,* vol. 19, 269–92. Paris: Asselin, 1876.

"De l'anesthésie provoquée considérée sous le rapport médico-légal." *Gazette hebdomadaire de médecine et de chirurgie,* May 25, 1866 and June 4, 1866.

Exposition historique et appréciation des secours empruntés par la médecine légale à l'obstétricie. Strasbourg: Levrault, 1838.

Extrait du Dictionnaire encyclopédique des sciences médicales...article Simulation. Paris: G. Masson, 1879.

"Grossesse – Médecine légale." In *Dictionnaire encyclopédique des sciences médicales,* edited by Amédée Dechambre, vol. 11, 245–326. Paris: Masson, 1886.

"Mort (médecine légale)." In *Dictionnaire encyclopédique des sciences médicales,* series 2, vol. 9, 579–714. Paris: Masson, 1875.

Tourdes, Gabriel, and Edmond Metzquer. *Traité de médecine légale théorique et pratique.* Paris: Asselin and Houzeau, 1896.

Le tueur de bergers. Paris: S. Schwarz, [1898].

Tyrbas de Chamberet, Jean-Baptiste. "Pissement." In *Dictionnaire des sciences médicales,* edited by Adelon, Alard, Alibert, et al., vol. 42, 496–505. Paris: Panckoucke, 1820.

L'Union médicale: Journal des intérêts scientifiques et pratiques moraux et professionnels du corps médical. Paris, 1847–96.

Vavasseur, Pierre. *Nouveau manuel complet des aspirants au doctorat en médecine ... quatrième examen.* Paris: Crochard, 1834.

Velpeau, Alfred-Armand-Louis-Marie. *Traité complet de l'art des accouchements, ou tocologie théorique et pratique,* 2nd ed. Paris: Baillière, 1835.

Vibert, Charles. *Précis de médecine légale.* Paris: Baillière, 1886.

"Respiration artificielle." In *Nouveau dictionnaire de médecine et de chirurgie pratiques,* vol. 31, 314–15. Paris: Lahure, 1882.

Vienne, Léonce. *Etude sur les blessures simulées dans les centres industriels.* Paris: Jouve, 1892.

Vincent, Maxime. "Applications de la photographie à la médecine légale." *Annales d'hygiène publique et de médecine légale*, series 2, vol. 33 (1870): 239–51.

Weill, Matthieu. *Considérations générales sur la folie puerpérale*. Strasbourg: Vve Berger-Levrault, 1851.

Yovanovitch, Georges P. *Entomologie appliquée à la médecine légale*. Paris: Ollier-Henry, 1888.

Zuber, César. *Des maladies simulées dans l'armée moderne*. Paris: Berger-Levrault, 1882.

Secondary Sources

Ackerknecht, Erwin. *Medicine at the Paris Hospital, 1794–1848*. Baltimore, MD: Johns Hopkins University Press, 1967.

Adams, Christine. *Poverty, Charity, and Motherhood: Maternal Societies in Nineteenth-Century France*. Urbana: University of Illinois Press, 2010.

"Admitting Doubt: A New Standard for Scientific Evidence." *Harvard Law Review* 123, no. 8 (2010): 2021–42.

Ambroise-Rendu, Anne-Claude. "Attentats à la pudeur sur enfants: Le crime sans violence est-il un crime? (1810-années 1930)." *Revue d'histoire moderne et contemporaine* 56, no. 4 (2009): 165–89.

Histoire de la pédophilie. Paris: Fayard, 2014.

Arena, Francesca. "La folie des mères." *Rives méditerranéennes* (2008): 143–54.

Ariès, Philippe. *Centuries of Childhood: A Social History of Family Life*, translated by Robert Baldick. New York: Alfred A. Knopf, 1962.

Asen, Daniel. *Death in Beijing: Murder and Forensic Science in Republican China*. Cambridge: Cambridge University Press, 2016.

Astier, Alain. "Les allumettes françaises ou la singulière histoire des empoisonnements par le phosphore blanc." *Revue d'histoire de la pharmacie* 316 (1997): 385–94.

Aulard, François-Alphonse. *The French Revolution: A Political History, vol. 2, The Democratic Republic, 1792–1795*. New York: Charles Scribner's Sons, 1910.

Bates, Victoria. "Forensic Medicine and Female Victimhood in Victorian and Edwardian England." *Past and Present* 245, no. 1 (2019): 117–51.

Sexual Forensics in Victorian and Edwardian England: Age, Crime and Consent in the Courts. Basingstoke: Palgrave Macmillan, 2016.

"'So Far as I Can Define without a Microscopical Examination': Venereal Disease Diagnosis in English Courts, 1850–1914." *Social History of Medicine* 26, no. 1 (2013): 38–55.

Bechtold, Brigitte. "Infanticide in 19th century France: A Quantitative Interpretation." *Review of Radical Political Economics* 33, no. 2 (2001): 165–87.

Bertherat, Bruno. "Cleaning out the Mortuary and the Medicolegal Text: Ambroise Tardieu's Modernizing Enterprise." In *Global Forensic Cultures: Making Fact and Justice in the Modern Era*, edited by Ian Burney and Christopher Hamlin, 257–278. Baltimore, MD: Johns Hopkins University Press, 2019.

"L'élection à la chaire de médecine légale à Paris en 1879." *Revue historique* 4, no. 644 (2007): 823–56.

"La morgue de Paris au XIXe siècle (1804–1907): Les origines de l'Institut médico-légal ou les métamorphoses de la machine." PhD diss., Paris I, 2002.

"La mort en vitrine à la morgue à Paris au XIXe siècle (1804–1907)." In *Les narrations de la mort*, edited by Régis Bertrand, Anne Carol, and Jean-Noël Pelen, 181–196. Aix-en-Provence: Presses universitaires de Provence, 2005.

"Les mots du médecin légiste, de la salle d'autopsie aux Assises: l'affaire Billoir (1876–1877)." *Revue d'histoire des sciences humaines* 22, no. 1 (2010): 117–44.

"Visiter les morts: La Morgue (Paris, XIXe siècle)." *Hypothèses* 19, no. 1 (2016): 377–90.

Berthiaud, Emmanuelle. "Les femmes enceintes devant la justice révolutionnaire à Paris (1793–1810): L'évolution des enjeux et des représentations de la grossesse." In *La culture judiciaire: Discours, représentations et usages de la justice du Moyen Age à nos jours*, edited by L. Faggion, C. Regina, and B. Ribémont, 123–41. Dijon: Editions universitaires de Dijon, 2014.

Bertomeu-Sánchez, José Ramón. "Animal Experiments, Vital Forces and Courtrooms: Mateu Orfila, François Magendie and the Study of Poisons in Nineteenth-Century France." *Annals of Science* 69, no. 1 (2012): 1–26.

"Arsenic in France: The Cultures of Poison During the First Half of the Nineteenth Century." In *Compound Histories: Materials, Governance and Production, 1760–1840*, edited by Lissa L. Roberts and Simon Werrett, 131–58. Leiden: Brill, 2018.

"From Forensic Toxicology to Biological Chemistry: Normal Arsenic and the Hazards of Sensitivity during the Nineteenth Century." *Endeavor* 40, no. 2 (2016): 82–92.

"Managing Uncertainty in the Academy and the Courtroom: Normal Arsenic and Nineteenth-Century Toxicology." *Isis* 104, no. 2 (2013): 197–225.

"Mateu Orfila (1787–1853) and Nineteenth-Century Toxicology." In *It All Depends on the Dose Poisons and Medicines in European History*, edited by Ole Peter Grell, Andrew Cunningham, and Jon Arrizabalaga, 150–72. New York: Routledge, 2018.

"Orfila, Raspail et les cercles vicieux de l'expertise." In *Une imagination républicaine, François-Vincent Raspail (1794–1878)*, edited by

Jonathan Barbier, 39–62. Besançon: Presses universitaires de Franche-Comté, 2017.

"Popularizing Controversial Science: A Popular Treatise on Poisons by Mateu Orfila (1818)." *Medical History* 53, no. 3 (2009): 351–78.

"Sense and Sensitivity: Mateu Orfila, the Marsh Test, and the Lafarge Affair." In *Chemistry, Medicine, and Crime: Mateu J.B. Orfila (1787–1853) and His Times*, edited by José Ramón Bertomeu-Sánchez and Augustí Nieto-Galan, 207–42. Sagamore Beach, MA: Science History Publications, 2014.

Bertomeu-Sánchez, José Ramón, and Augustí Nieto-Galan, eds. *Chemistry, Medicine, and Crime: Mateu J.B. Orfila (1787–1851) and His Times*. Sagamore Beach, MA: Science History Publications, 2006.

Billard, Max. *Les femmes enceintes devant le tribunal révolutionnaire d'après des documents inédits*. Paris: Perrin, 1911.

Bondeson, Jan. *Buried Alive: The Terrifying History of Our Most Primal Fear*. New York: W. W. Norton, 2001.

Bory, Jean-Yves. *La douleur des bêtes: La polémique sur la vivisection au XIXe siècle en France*. Rennes: Presses universitaires de Rennes, 2013.

Brandli, Fabrice, and Michel Porret. *Les corps meurtris: Investigations judiciaires et expertises médico-légales au XVIIIe siècle*. Rennes: Presses universitaires de Rennes, 2014.

Brown, Stephanie. "The Princess of Monaco's Hair: The Revolutionary Tribunal and the Pregnancy Plea." *Journal of Family History* 23, no. 2 (1998): 136–58.

Brownstein, Ronald. "Trump's War on Expertise Is Only Intensifying." *The Atlantic*, November 21, 2019.

Burney, Ian A. *Bodies of Evidence: Medicine and the Politics of the English Inquest, 1830–1826*. Baltimore, MD: Johns Hopkins University Press, 2000.

"Bones of Contention: Mateu Orfila, Normal Arsenic and British Toxicology." In *Chemistry, Medicine, and Crime: Mateu J.B. Orfila (1787–1853) and His Times*, edited by José Ramón Bertomeu-Sánchez and Augustí Nieto-Galan, 243–59. Sagamore Beach, MA: Science History Publications, 2014.

Poison, Detection, and the Victorian Imagination. Manchester: Manchester University Press, 2006.

Burney, Ian, and Christopher Hamlin, eds. *Global Forensic Cultures: Making Fact and Justice in the Modern Era*. Baltimore, MD: Johns Hopkins University Press, 2019.

Butler, Sara. "More than Mothers: Juries of Matrons and Pleas of the Belly in Medieval England." *Law and History Review* 37, no. 2 (2019): 353–96.

Cahen, Fabrice, and Silvia Chiletti. "Les ambivalences du diagnostic précoce de grossesse (xvie–xxe siècle)." *Clio. Femmes, Genre, Histoire* 48, no. 2 (2018): 223–41.

Campion-Vincent, Véronique. "L'œil révélateur." *Cahiers internationaux de sociologie* 104 (1998): 55–75.

Carol, Anne. "Une histoire médicale des critères de la mort." *Communications* 97, no. 2 (2015): 45–55.

"Le 'médecin des morts' à Paris au XIXe siècle." *Annales de démographie historique* 127, no. 1 (2014): 153–79.

Les médecins et la mort, XIXe–XXe siècle. Paris: Aubier, 2004.

Chaperon, Sylvie. *Les origines de la sexologie (1850–1900)*. Paris: Louis Audibert, 2007.

Chappuis, Loraine, Frédéric Chauvaud, Marc Ortolani, and Michel Porret. *Faire parler les corps: François-Emmanuel Fodéré à la genèse de la médecine légale moderne*. Rennes: Presses universitaires de Rennes, 2021.

Chauvaud, Frédéric. "'Cet homme si multiple et si divers': Orfila et la chimie du crime au XIXe siècle." *Sociétés & Représentations* 22, no. 2 (2006): 171–87.

"Le déplacement des figures." In *Experts et expertise judiciaire: France, XIXe et XXe siècles*, edited by Frédéric Chauvaud and Laurence Dumoulin. Rennes: Presses universitaires de Rennes, 2003. http://books.openedition.org/pur/8459.

"L'essor des spécialités." In *Experts et expertise judiciaire: France, XIXe et XXe siècles*, edited by Frédéric Chauvaud and Laurence Dumoulin. Rennes: Presses universitaires de Rennes, 2003. http://books.openedition.org/pur/8459.

Les experts du crime: La médecine légale en France au XIXe siècle. Paris: Aubier, 2000.

"L'invention du perverti: Les hommes de l'art et le 'beau cas' dans la France du second XIXe siècle." In *Michel Foucault: Savoirs, domination et sujet*, edited by Jean-Claude Bourdin, Frédéric Chauvaud, Vincent Estellon, Bertrand Geay, and Jean-Michel Passerault, 57–65. Rennes: Presses universitaires de Rennes, 2008.

"La preuve par l'hymen: Le viol des femmes sous l'œil des médecins légistes (1810–1890)." In *Le corps en lambeaux: Violences sexuelles et sexuées faites aux femmes*, edited by Lydie Bodiou, Frédéric Chauvaud, Ludovic Gaussot, et al., 63–80. Rennes: Presses universitaires de Rennes, 2016.

Chauvaud, Frédéric, and Laurence Dumoulin, eds. *Experts et expertise judiciaire: France, XIXe et XXe siècles*. Rennes: Presses universitaires de Rennes, 2003.

Chiletti, Silvia. "Grossesses ignorées au prisme de l'infanticide. Savoirs médicaux et décisions de justice au XIXe siècle." *Revue d'histoire du XIXe siècle* 50, no. 1 (2015): 165–79.

Chin, Jason, and Larysa Workewych. "The CSI Effect." In *Oxford Handbooks Online*, edited by Markus Dubber. New York: Oxford University Press, 2016. https://doi.org/10.1093/oxfordhb/9780199935352.013.28.

Cody, Lisa Forman. *Birthing the Nation: Sex, Science, and the Conception of Eighteenth-Century Britons*. Oxford: Oxford University Press, 2005.

Cole, Simon A., and Rachel Dioso-Villa. "*CSI* and Its Effects: Media, Juries, and the Burden of Proof." *New England Law Review* 41 (2007): 435–70.

"Should Judges Worry about the 'CSI Effect'?" *Court Review* 47 (2011): 20–31.

Connor, Henry. "The use of anaesthesia to diagnose malingering in the 19th century." *Journal of Royal Society of Medicine* 99, no. 9 (2006): 444–47.

Cooter, Roger. "Malingering in Modernity: Psychological Scripts and Adversarial Encounters during the First World War." In *War, Medicine, and Modernity*, edited by Roger Cooter, Mark Harrison, and Steven Sturdy, 125–48. Stroud: Sutton, 1998.

"War and Modern Medicine." In *Companion Encyclopedia of the History of Medicine*, edited by W. F. Bynum and Roy Porter, vol. 2, 1536–73. New York: Routledge, 1993.

Coquillard, Isabelle. "Des médecins jurés au Châtelet de Paris aux médecins légistes: Genèse d'une professionnalisation (1692–1801)." *Histoire des sciences médicales* 46, no. 2 (2012): 133–44.

Cragin, Thomas. *Murder in Parisian Streets: Manufacturing Crime and Justice in the Popular Press, 1830–1900*. Lewisburg, PA: Bucknell University Press, 2006.

Cunningham, Hugh. *Children and Childhood in Western Society since 1500*. New York: Longman, 1995.

Darmon, Pierre. *Médecins et assassins à la Belle Epoque: La médicalisation du crime*. Paris: Seuil, 1989.

Demartini, Emmanuelle. "La figure de l'empoisonneuse de Marie Lafarge à Violette Nozière." In *Figures d'empoisonneuses de l'Antiquité à nos jours*, edited by Lydie Boudiou, Frédéric Chauvaud, and Myriam Soria, 97–108. Rennes: Presses universitaires de Rennes, 2015.

Dodman, Thomas. *What Nostalgia Was: War, Empire, and the Time of a Deadly Emotion*. Chicago, IL: University of Chicago Press, 2017.

Donovan, James. "Combatting the Sexual Abuse of Children in France, 1825–1913." *Criminal Justice History* 15 (1994): 59–93.

"Infanticide and the Juries in France, 1825–1913." *Journal of Family History* 16, no. 2 (1991): 157–76.

Juries and the Transformation of Criminal Justice in France in the Nineteenth and Twentieth Centuries. Chapel Hill: University of North Carolina Press, 2010.

Doron, Claude-Olivier. "La formation du concept psychiatrique de perversion au XIXe siècle en France." *L'information psychiatrique* 88, no. 1 (2012): 39–49.

Dowbiggin, Ian. *Inheriting Madness: Professionalization and Psychiatric Knowledge in Nineteenth-Century France*. Berkeley: University of California Press, 1991.

Dumoulin, Laurence. "Du quasi vide juridique à la reprise en main." In *Experts et expertise judiciaire: France, XIXe et XXe siècles*, edited by Frédéric Chauvaud and Laurence Dumoulin. Rennes: Presses universitaires de Rennes, 2003. http://books.openedition.org/pur/8459.

"Les points aveugles de la législation au cœur des polémiques." In *Experts et expertise judiciaire: France, XIXe et XXe siècles*, edited by Frédéric Chauvaud and Laurence Dumoulin. Rennes: Presses universitaires de Rennes, 2003. http://books.openedition.org/pur/8459.

Edwards, Harry T., and Jennifer Mnookin. "A Wake-Up Call on the Junk Science Infesting Our Courtrooms." *Washington Post*, September 20, 2016.

Elliot, Paul. "Vivisection and the Emergence of Experimental Physiology in Nineteenth-Century France." In *Vivisection in Historical Perspective*, edited by Nicholas Rupke, 48–77. New York: Croom Helm, 1987.

Essig, Mark R. "Science and Sensation: Poison Murder and Forensic Medicine in Nineteenth-Century America." PhD diss., Cornell University, 2000.

Eyal, Gil. *The Crisis of Expertise*. Medford, MA: Polity Press, 2019.

Fahmy, Khaled. *In Quest of Justice: Islamic Law and Forensic Medicine in Modern Egypt*. Berkeley: University of California Press, 2018.

Farcy, Jean-Claude. *Histoire de la justice en France: De 1789 à nos jours*. Paris: La Découverte, 2015.

Fauvel, Aude. "Femmes violeuses et hommes bafoués: Sexe, crime et médecine dans la France du XIXe siècle." In *Crimes et délits: Quinzième Colloque des Invalides, 18 novembre 2011*, edited by J.-J. Lefrère and M. Pierssens, 91–116. Tusson: Du Lérot, 2012.

Fissell, Mary. *Vernacular Bodies: The Politics of Reproduction in Early Modern England*. Oxford: Oxford University, 2004.

Forrest, Alan. *Conscripts and Deserters: The Army and French Society during the Revolution and Empire*. Oxford: Oxford University Press, 1989.

Foucault, Michel. *Abnormal: Lectures at the Collège de France, 1974–1975*, edited by Valerio Marchetti and Antonella Salomoni, translated by Graham Burchell. New York: Picador, 2003.

The Birth of the Clinic: An Archeology of Medical Perception. New York: Vintage Books, 1975.

History of Sexuality, vol. 1, An Introduction, translated by Robert Hurley. New York: Pantheon Books, 1978.

French, Roger. *Antivivisection and Medical Science in Victorian Society*. Princeton, NJ: Princeton University Press, 1975.

Freundschuh, Aaron. *The Courtesan and the Gigolo: The Murders in the Rue Montaigne and the Dark Side of Empire in Nineteenth-Century Paris*. Palo Alto: Stanford University Press, 2017.

Fuchs, Rachel G. *Abandoned Children: Foundlings and Child Welfare in Nineteenth-Century France*. Albany: State University of New York Press, 1984.

Contested Paternity: Constructing Families in Modern France. Baltimore, MD: Johns Hopkins University Press, 2008.

"Crimes against Children in Nineteenth-Century France: Child Abuse." *Law and Human Behavior* 6, nos. 3–4 (1982): 237–59.

Gender and Poverty in Nineteenth-Century Europe. Cambridge: Cambridge University Press, 2005.

"Magistrates and Mothers, Paternity and Property in Nineteenth-Century French Courts." *Crime, Histoire & Sociétés* 13, no. 2 (2009): 13–26.

Poor and Pregnant in Paris: Strategies for Survival in the Nineteenth Century. New Brunswick, NJ: Rutgers University Press, 1992.

Garrett, Brandon L. *Autopsy of a Crime Lab: Exposing the Flaws in Forensics*. Berkeley: University of California Press, 2021.

Gessen, Masha. "President Trump Wages War on Government and Expertise, and Our Institutions Surrender." *The New Yorker*, September 13, 2019.

Giuliani, Fabienne. *Les liaisons interdites: Histoire de l'inceste au XIXe siècle*. Paris: Publications de la Sorbonne, 2014.

Golan, Tal. *Laws of Men and Laws of Nature: The History of Scientific Expert Testimony in England and America*. Cambridge, MA: Harvard University Press, 2007.

"Revisiting the History of Scientific Expert Testimony." *Brooklyn Law Review* 73, no. 3 (2008): 879–1033.

Goldstein, Jan. *Console and Classify: The French Psychiatric Profession in the Nineteenth Century*. New York: Cambridge University Press, 1987.

Gowing, Laura. *Common Bodies: Women, Touch, and Power in Seventeenth-Century England*. New Haven, CT: Yale University Press, 2003.

Guerrini, Anita. *Experimenting with Humans and Animals: From Galen to Animal Rights*. Baltimore, MD: John Hopkins University Press, 2003.

Guignard, Laurence. *Juger la folie: La folie criminelle devant les Assises au XIXe siècle*. Paris: Presses universitaires de France, 2010.

Hardwick, Julie. *Sex in an Old Regime City: Young Workers and Intimacy in France, 1660–1789*. New York: Oxford University Press, 2020.

Harris, Ruth. *Murders and Madness: Medicine, Law, and Society in the Fin de Siècle*. Oxford: Clarendon Press, 1989.

Heilbron, J. L. "The Affair of the Countess Görlitz." *Proceedings of the American Philosophical Society* 138, no. 2 (1994): 284–316.

Heuer, Jennifer. "'No More Fears, No More Tears'?: Gender, Emotion, and the Aftermath of the Napoleonic Wars in France." *Gender and History* 28, no. 2 (2016): 437–59.

Heywood, Colin. "Centuries of Childhood: An Anniversary – and an Epitaph?" *Journal of the History of Childhood and Youth* 3, no. 3 (2010): 341–65.

Growing Up in France: From the Ancien Régime to the Third Republic. Cambridge: Cambridge University Press, 2007.

A History of Childhood. Cambridge: Polity Press, 2018.

Huber, Karen. "The Problem of Proof: Denunciations, Confessions, and Medical Evidence in Reproductive Crimes, 1900–1940." *Proceedings of the Western Society for French History* 34 (2006): 217–32.

"Sex and Its Consequences: Abortion, Infanticide, and Women's Reproductive Decision-Making in France, 1901–1940." PhD diss., Ohio State University, 2007.

Innocence Project. "DNA Exonerations in the United States." www.innocenceproject.org/dna-exonerations-in-the-united-states/ (last visited October 27, 2019).

Jackson, Louise. *Child Sexual Abuse in Victorian England*. London: Routledge, 2000.

Jentzen, Jeffrey. *Death Investigation in America: Coroners, Medical Examiners, and the Pursuit of Medical Certainty*. Cambridge, MA: Harvard University Press, 2009.

Kalifa, Dominique. *Les Bas-fonds: Histoire d'un imaginaire*. Paris: Seuil, 2013.

Crime et culture au XIXe siècle. Paris: Perrin, 2005.

L'Encre et le sang: Récits de crimes et société à la Belle Epoque. Paris: Fayard, 1995.

Kudlick, Catherine Jean. *Cholera in Post-Revolutionary Paris: A Cultural History*. Berkeley: University of California Press, 1996.

Lalou, Richard. "L'infanticide devant les tribunaux français (1825–1910)." *Communications* 44 (1986): 175–200.

Lande, R. Gregory. *The Abraham Man: Madness, Malingering, and the Development of Medical Testimony*. New York: Algora, 2012.

Madness, Malingering, and Malfeasance: The Transformation of Psychiatry and the Law in the Civil War Era. Washington, DC: Brassey's, 2003.

Laqueur, Thomas. *Solitary Sex: A Cultural History of Masturbation*. New York: Zone Books, 2003.

Le Boulanger, Isabelle. *Enfance bafouée: La société rurale bretonne face aux abus sexuels du XIXe siècle*. Rennes: Presses universitaires de Rennes, 2015.

Le Naour, Jean-Yves, and Catherine Valenti. *Histoire de l'avortement: XIXe–XXe siècle*. Paris: Seuil, 2003.

Lepore, Jill. "On Evidence: Proving Frye as a Matter of Law, Science, and History." *The Yale Law Journal* 124, no. 4 (2015): 882–1344.

Long, Lisa A. *Rehabilitating Bodies: Health, History, and the American Civil War*. Philadelphia: University of Pennsylvania Press, 2004.

Magraw, Roger. *France, 1800–1914: A Social History*. London: Routledge, 2002.

Malivin, Amandine. "Le nécrophile, pervers insaisissable (France, XIXe siècle)." *Criminocorpus*, 2016. https://journals.openedition.org/criminocorpus/3381.

Manne, Kate. *Down Girl: The Logic of Misogyny*. Oxford: Oxford University Press, 2017.

Entitled: How Male Privilege Hurts Women. New York: Crown, 2020.

Marland, Hilary. *Dangerous Motherhood: Insanity and Childbirth in Victorian Britain*. Basingstoke: Palgrave Macmillan, 2004.

"Disappointment and Desolation: Women, Doctors and Interpretations of Puerperal Insanity in the Nineteenth Century." *History of Psychiatry* 14 (2003): 303–20.

Mason, Laura. "The 'Bosom of Proof': Criminal Justice and the Renewal of Oral Culture during the French Revolution." *Journal of Modern History* 76, no. 1 (2004): 29–61.

Masson, Jeffrey Moussaieff. *The Assault on Truth: Freud's Suppression of the Seduction Theory*. New York: Pocket, 1998.

Matsuda, Matt K. "Doctor, Judge, Vagabond: Identity, Identification, and Other Memories of the State." *History and Memory* 6, no. 1 (1994): 73–94.

McClive, Cathy. "Blood and Expertise: The Trials of the Female Medical Expert in the Ancien-Régime Courtroom." *Bulletin of the History of Medicine* 82, no. 1 (2008): 86–108.

"The Hidden Truths of the Belly: The Uncertainties of Pregnancy in Early Modern Europe." *Social History of Medicine* 15, no. 2 (2002): 209–27.

Menstruation and Procreation in Early Modern France. New York: Routledge, 2015.

"'Witnessing of the Hands' and Eyes: Surgeons as Medico-Legal Experts in the Claudine Rouge Affair, Lyon, 1767." *Journal for Eighteenth-Century Studies* 35 no. 4 (2012): 489–503.

McKillop, Bron. "Forensic Science in Inquisitorial Systems of Criminal Justice." In *Expert Evidence and Scientific Proof in Criminal Trials*, edited by Paul Roberts, 36–43. Farnham: Ashgate, 2014.

McLaren, Angus. *A Prescription for Murder: The Victorian Serial Killings of Dr. Thomas Neill Cream*. Chicago, IL: University of Chicago Press, 1995.

Sexual Blackmail: A Modern History. Cambridge, MA: Harvard University Press, 2002.

The Trials of Masculinity: Policing Sexual Boundaries, 1870–1930. Chicago, IL: University of Chicago Press, 1997.

Mendelson, Danuta. "The Expert Deposes, but the Court Disposes: The Concept of Malingering and the Function of a Medical Expert Witness in the Forensic Process." *International Journal of Law and Psychiatry* 18, no. 4 (1995): 425–36.

Menenteau, Sandra. "L'art d'improviser: La pratique des autopsies médico-légales au XIXe siècle." *Histoire des sciences médicales* 2 (2012): 151–62.

L'autopsie judiciaire: Histoire d'une pratique ordinaire au XIXe siècle. Rennes: Presses universitaires de Rennes, 2013.

"Dans les coulisses de l'autopsie judiciaire: Cadres, contraintes et conditions de l'expertise cadavérique dans la France du XIXe siècle." PhD diss., Université de Poitiers, 2009.

"'L'édifice de l'expertise restera [...] comme bâti sur le sable': Enjeux et obstacles à la professionnalisation de la médecine légale dans la France du XIXe siècle." *Déviance et société* 41, no. 3 (2017): 343–69.

Mnookin, Jennifer L. "Idealizing Science and Demonizing Experts: An Intellectual History of Expert Evidence." *Villanova Law Review* 52, no. 4 (2007): 763–99.

Mohr, James Crail. *Doctors and the Law: Medical Jurisprudence in Nineteenth-Century America.* New York: Oxford University Press, 1993.

Mortas, Pauline. *Une rose épineuse. La défloration au XIXe siècle en France.* Rennes: Presses universitaires de Rennes, 2017.

Murat, Laure. *The Man Who Thought He Was Napoleon: Toward a Political History of Madness*, translated by Deike Dusinberre. Chicago, IL: University of Chicago Press, 2014.

Nichols, Tom. *The Death of Expertise: The Campaign Against Established Knowledge and Why It Matters.* Oxford: Oxford University Press, 2017.

Nilan, Cat. "Hapless Innocence and Precocious Perversity in the Courtroom Melodrama: Representations of the Child Criminal in a Paris Legal Journal, 1830–1848." *Journal of Family History* 22, no. 3 (1997): 251–85.

Norris, Katharine H. "Child Psychology, Republican Pedagogy, and the Debate over Heredity in Fin-de-Siècle France." PhD diss., University of California, Berkeley, 2000.

"Mentir à l'âge de l'innocence: Enfance, science et anxiété culturelle dans la France fin-de-siècle." *Sociétés et représentations* 38, no. 2 (2014): 171–202.

Nye, Robert A. *Crime, Madness, and Politics in Modern France: The Medical Concept of National Decline.* Princeton, NJ: Princeton University Press, 1984.

Masculinity and Male Codes of Honor in Modern France. New York: Oxford University Press, 1993.

Oldham, James. "On 'Pleading the Belly:' A Concise History of the Jury of Matrons." *Criminal Justice History* 6 (1985): 1–64.

Park, Katharine. *Secrets of Women: Gender, Generation, and the Origins of Human Dissection.* New York: Zone Books, 2006.

Pernick, Martin. "Back from the Grave: Recurring Controversies over Defining and Diagnosing Death in History." In *Death: Beyond Whole-Brain Criteria*, edited by Richard M. Zaner, 17–74. Dordrecht: Kluwer Academic Publishers, 1988.

Pick, Daniel. *Faces of Degeneration: A European Disorder (c. 1848-1918).* Cambridge: Cambridge University Press, 1989.

Podlas, Kimberlianne. "The *CSI* Effect": Exposing the Media Myth." *Fordham Intellectual Property, Media and Entertainment Law Journal* 16 (2006): 429–65.

Popiel, Jennifer. *Rousseau's Daughters: Domesticity, Education, and Autonomy in Modern France.* Durham: University of New Hampshire Press, 2008.

Porret, Michel. *Sur la scène du crime. Pratique pénale, enquête et expertises judiciaires à Genève (XVIIIe–XIXe siècles).* Montreal: Presses de l'Université de Montréal, 2008.

Porret, Michel, and Fabrice Brandli. *Les corps meurtris: Investigations judiciaires et expertises médico-légales au XVIIIe siècle.* Rennes: Presses universitaires de Rennes, 2014.

Quinlan, Sean M. "Apparent Death in Eighteenth-Century France and England." *French History* 9, no. 2 (1995): 27–47.

Rabier, Christelle. "Defining a Profession: Surgery, Professional Conflicts and Legal Powers in Paris and London, 1760–1790." In *Fields of Expertise: A Comparative History of Expert Procedures in Paris and London, 1600 to Present,* edited by Christelle Rabier, 85–114. Newcastle: Cambridge Scholars Publishing, 2007.

Ramsey, Matthew. "Conscription, Malingerers, and Popular Medicine in Napoleonic France." *Proceedings of the Consortium on Revolutionary Europe.* vol. 7, 188–99. Tallahassee, FL: Institute on Napoleon and the French Revolution, 1978.

Renneville, Marc. *Crime et folie: Deux siècles d'enquêtes médicales et judiciaires.* Paris: Fayard, 2003.

Roberts, Meghan K. "Spontaneous Human Combustion and Claude-Nicolas Le Cat's Hunt for Fame." *Journal of Modern History* 93, no. 4 (2021): 749–82.

Ruberg, Willemijn. "Travelling Knowledge and Forensic Medicine: Infanticide, Body and Mind in the Netherlands, 1811–1911." *Medical History* 57, 3 (2013): 359–76.

Sage-Pranchère, Nathalie. "La mort apparente du nouveau-né dans la littérature médicale (France, 1760–1900)." *Annales de démographie historique* 1 (2012): 127–48.

Salomé, Karine. "Le massacre des 'empoisonneurs' à Paris au temps du choléra (1832)." *Revue historique* 673 (2015): 103–24.

Sawyer, Stephen. "A Question of Life and Death: Administrating Bodies and Administrative Bodies in Nineteenth-Century Paris." In *Fields of Expertise: A Comparative History of Expert Procedures in Paris and London, 1600 to Present,* edited by Christelle Rabier, 291–315. Newcastle: Cambridge Scholars Publishing, 2007.

Schwartz, Vanessa. *Spectacular Realities: Early Mass Culture in Fin-de-Siècle Paris.* Berkeley: University of California Press, 1999.

Serdeczny, Anton. *Du tabac pour le mort: Une histoire de la réanimation.* Paris: Champ Vallon, 2018.

Shafer, Sylvia. *Children in Moral Danger and the Problem of Government in Third Republic France.* Princeton, NJ: Princeton University Press, 1997.

Sharafi, Mitra. "The Imperial Serologist and Punitive Self-Harm: Bloodstains and Legal Pluralism in British India." In *Global Forensic Cultures: Making Fact and Justice in the Modern Era,* edited by Ian Burney and

Christopher Hamlin, 60–85. Baltimore, MD: Johns Hopkins University Press, 2019.

Simpson, Antony E. "Blackmail Myth and the Prosecution of Rape and Its Attempt in Eighteenth-Century London: The Creation of a Legal Tradition." *Journal of Criminal Law and Criminology* 77, no. 1 (1986): 101–50.

Singy, Patrick. "The History of Masturbation: An Essay Review." *Journal for the History of Medicine and Allied Sciences* 59, no. 1 (2004): 112–21.

Sohn, Anne-Marie. "Les attentats à la pudeur sur les fillettes en France (1870–1939) et la sexualité quotidienne." *Mentalités* 3 (1989): 71–112.

Stolberg, Michael. "An Unmanly Vice: Self-Pollution, Anxiety, and the Body in the Eighteenth Century." *Social History of Medicine* 13, no. 1 (2000): 1–21.

Stratmann, Linda. *The Secret Poisoner: A Century of Murder*. New Haven, CT: Yale University Press, 2006.

Theriot, Nancy. "Diagnosing Unnatural Motherhood: Nineteenth-Century Physicians and 'Puerperal Insanity.'" *American Studies* 30, no. 2 (1989): 69–88.

Tillier, Annick. *Des criminelles au village: Femmes infanticides en Bretagne (1825–1865)*. Rennes: Presses universitaires de Rennes, 2001.

"L'infanticide: La mauvaise mère." In *Présumées coupables: Les grands procès faits aux femmes*, edited by Claude Gauvard, 148–89. Paris: L'Iconoclaste, 2016.

Tomic, Sacha. "Le rôle des manuels dans la disciplinarisation de la toxicologie en France au XIXe siècle." *Philosophia Scientiæ* 22, no. 1 (2018): 163–83.

Trépardoux, Francis. "Les secours aux noyés dans la ville de Paris, 1772–1831: Composition des boîtes de secours en ustensiles et médicaments." *Revue d'histoire de la pharmacie* 84, no. 312 (1996): 370–73.

Vallaud, Dominique. "Le crime d'infanticide et l'indulgence des cours d'assises en France au XIXème siècle." *Information (International Social Science Council)* 21, no. 3 (1982): 475–98.

Vassigh, Denis Darya. "Les experts judiciaires face à la parole de l'enfant maltraité: Le cas des médecins légistes de la fin du XIXe siècle." *Revue d'histoire de l'enfance « irrégulière »* 2 (1999): 97–111.

Veillon, Didier. "Un parricide par empoisonnement sous la Restauration: L'affaire Bouvier." In *Les vénéneuses: Figures d'empoisonneuses de l'Antiquité à nos jours*, edited by Lydie Bodiou and Myriam Soria, 71–84. Rennes: Presses universitaires de Rennes, 2015.

Vigarello, Georges. *Histoire du viol: XVIe–XXe siècle*. Paris: Editions du Seuil, 1998.

Watson, Katherine. *Forensic Medicine in Western Society: A History*. New York: Routledge, 2010.

Medicine and Justice: Medico-Legal Practice in England and Wales, 1700–1914. Abingdon: Routledge, 2020.

Watson, Stephen. "Malingerers, the 'Weakminded' Criminal and the 'Moral Imbecile': How the English Prison Medical Officer Became an Expert in Mental Deficiency, 1880–1930." In *Legal Medicine in History*, edited by Michael Clark and Catherine Crawford, 223–42. Cambridge: Cambridge University Press, 1994.

Wellcome Global Monitor 2018. "Chapter 5: Attitudes to vaccines." https://wellcome.ac.uk/reports/wellcome-global-monitor/2018/chapter-5-attitudes-vaccines (last visited November 12, 2021).

2020. "Chapter 3: Trust in and perceived value of science amid Covid-19." https://wellcome.org/reports/wellcome-global-monitor-covid-19/2020/chapter-3-trust-in-perceived-value-of-science-amid-covid-19 (last visited December 8, 2021).

Whorton, James C. *The Arsenic Century: How Victorian Britain Was Poisoned at Home, Work, and Play*. Oxford: Oxford University Press, 2011.

INDEX

CPSIA information can be obtained
at www.ICGtesting.com
Printed in the USA
LVHW100310200922
728806LV00003B/118

9 781009 198332